LOOK AT ME

THE LONG-AWAITED MEMOIR OF
COCO ROPER

Look at Me
Copyright © Nicole "CoCo" Roper, 2024.

No part of this publication may be reproduced, stored in a retrieval system, or transmitted in any form or by any means, electronic, mechanical, photocopying, recording, scanning, or otherwise, without the prior written permission of the author, except by reviewers, who may quote brief passages in a review.

To request permissions, contact the publisher at
jennifer@entouragemedia.ca.

Cover Art: Daniel Vargas (IG:@la_chaquetica)

ISBN (English Paperback): 978-1-7381171-2-3
ISBN (Spanish Paperback): 978-1-7381171-4-7
ISBN (English e-Book): 978-1-7381171-3-0
ISBN (Spanish e-Book): 978-1-7381171-5-0

First Paperback Edition: May 2024

Printed in the USA
1 2 3 4 5 6 7 8 9 10

ENTOURAGE

Published by Entourage Media
www.entouragemedia.ca

For Ellie,
May you always remember your strength, resilience, and how dearly you are loved.
Don't ever let anyone dim your light.

CONTENTS

PROLOGUE xi

INTRODUCTION xvii

FAIRYTALES AND NIGHTMARES 1
    Extravagantly Rich 5
    Weekends 9
    Can't You See Me? 19

A NEW LIFE 23
    Shopping Spree 26
    Bulletproof 29
    Pura Vida Life 30
    Sex by Choice 36
    It's Always Something 41
    Blue Kamikazes 44
    Fights & Fuckups 47

GOODBYE GARY 51
    Racing 58
    Family 63
    Remembering 66
    Christmas 71
    Aspen 73

DOCTORS 77
    I Know What You Need 82
    Bad for My Health 84
    Suicide Watch 91
    Twelve Steps 93
    Tijuana 102
    Fixed 104

SWEET HOME ALABAMA 107
    New Normal 109
    Por Arriba 111
    Pumpkin Spice & Match.Com 114

  Birthday Fight 117
  The J Charm 121
  Texas Chic 124
  Fucking Crazy 128
  Great on Paper 134

FAMILY 137
  Don't Make Me Go 138
  This Is Happening 141
  Last Chance 142
  Unfit 145
  Listen to Me 147
  How Dare You 156
  This Is New 161
  This Is Bad 163

I CAN TAKE IT 165
  The Last Pour 166
  Forgiven 172
  Goodbye Hair 173

VIRAL 177
  Trying 178
  Don't Stop 180
  At Your Mercy 181
  Let's Do This 196

NO FILTER 199
  Ramona Is a Bitch 200
  #CoCoStrong 203
  Working for My Dream 206
  The Spring Surgery 208
  Heartbreak 209
  I Need You 213
  Together at Last 216

A STORY WORTH TELLING 221

FROM THE #COCOSTRONG COMMUNITY 223

LETTERS 231
ACKNOWLEDGMENTS 241
RESOURCES 245

This book contains graphic depictions of substance abuse and addiction, eating disorders, sexual assault, child abuse, domestic violence, self-harm, and suicide.

In order to maintain their anonymity in some instances, the author has changed the names of individuals and places, may have changed some identifying characteristics and details such as physical properties, occupations and places of residence. This memoir is a truthful recollection of actual events in the author's life.

PROLOGUE

I click *Join* to log into that night's Zoom session with my new publisher. It is our fourth meeting that week since the deadline is approaching fast, and we still have an obscene amount of work to do. We usually meet in the evenings because it's when I feel the most awake and in the least amount of pain. I don't know if that is due to knowing I can finally rest without guilt—the chores and errands have been done, and Ellie has been tucked into bed—or if it's because I usually save my most powerful pain medications until the end of the day after Ellie is asleep.

For months, I have been having nightmares that I would be gone before my book is finished. Even during the day, it feels as if I am being suffocated with the dread of Ellie being left with nothing—no memory of her mom, no memory of how much I love her. When she grows up, will she remember our love and how special it was? Will she remember dancing with me to our favorite songs in our cutest outfits? This book, our moments together, and the principles I have tried to instill in Ellie are the only real legacies I can give her. So, I'm going to make it good.

I plate the three *arepas* I just made for myself, grab my laptop, and head for my bedroom. I can hear Jenn logging in and turning on her sound as I close the door to my sanctuary and sink into my desk with the first meal I've had all day. I know my body won't get much value out of the snack before delivering it promptly into Ramona (my ileostomy bag), but I don't care. It's delicious.

My bedroom is my safe space—at least now it is. It's where my dog, Bruno, jumps onto the bed and lays his head on my legs when I cry. It's where Ellie and I cuddle, pray, watch movies, and just enjoy being in our own mother-daughter bubble. And it's away from my husband, J.

"Hey, girl," I smile at the screen, exhaling for the first time in hours. "Sorry, J was in the living room, so I had to move."

"Ah, okay. No problem." Jenn nods, looking like she is biting her tongue. I know how she feels about J's tendency to get annoyed simply by the sound of his wife's voice.

J couldn't care less about my book, my story, or my general existence in his world—at least, that's what he does his best to make me think. He probably views the book as just a bunch of lies and drama. His perception of reality is so opposite to mine.

"He's not going to want to hear what we're talking about today, anyway," Jenn says and begins to share her screen with me. The screen is set to the outline of *Look at Me* and focused on the ending.

Jenn is my ghostwriter, editor, publisher, and rescuer of my life's story. She stepped up after I called her sobbing and desperate for someone to help me finish what my previous writer essentially put on the back burner—my book, my life's work.

Our task for tonight's Zoom meeting was a big one: finish telling my story—my true story—so that others might finally see the real me, my heart, hopes, lessons, and life. What I hope is that by sharing the good and the bad, the wins and the losses, the moments of hope, the humiliating failures, and ultimately, the breakthroughs that have made me who I am today, others will also feel seen and heard. They will know they are not the only ones who feel like a mess, broken, or unforgivable.

If I can just get my story out there, I can give others hope. I can make a difference, an impact that matters.

I can't begin to guess why my book was put on hold for months, even though the previous writer knew my health was deteriorating. All I can assume is that she didn't care or didn't understand the essence of time (or rather, the essence of the time *left*), despite my diagnosis and the large amount of money that she kept. So, when I called Jenn, I was in real trouble: I had no book, my health was deteriorating, and I was out about twenty thousand dollars.

I stare at the outline and try to come up with something to say about the last few chapters. "The other writer said she was feeling stuck," I explain, trying to find the right words. "She said she didn't know how my story ends. Like, there's no conclusion, no purpose … no happy ending to the story."

I don't know if I'm remembering her exact words, but I do remember how I felt when she said them. Secretly, I hoped she was just making excuses for missing deadlines. If it wasn't that, then am I living a life without purpose? Is all the work I've done and the people I've reached not a story worth writing? Worth finishing?

I look down at my lap and admit my worst fears out loud: "Maybe she was right."

Jenn shakes her head emphatically. "No. Absolutely not."

Tears sting my eyes.

"Not only is there a wonderful, heartfelt direction and conclusion for your story, but it's going to be a page-turner."

I think of all the mistakes I've made, the hurt I've caused, all the pain I've suffered, and how my story might just remain unwritten, played out in silence in the oncology ward of a Texas hospital with an angry husband at my side, a sobbing daughter, my sister, and possibly my mother.

"I just don't see it." I shake my head and feel the shame and guilt of a life filled with mistakes I can't take back.

"CoCo, your story is one of the most incredible ones I've ever heard," Jenn continues. "You will melt people's hearts, get them angry, make them cry, shock them, surprise them, and in the end, have them dancing and celebrating right alongside you, with your book in their hands."

By now, she is beaming.

I look at her doubtfully. All I can think about is the fact that everyone in my life is against me writing this book. More accurately, everyone in my life is scared of what will come when I publish this book—my mother, who doesn't want our complicated past shared with the world; my sister, who worries about me blowing up our entire family with what I put on these pages; and even (likely) my biological father, who once put a hit out on my family to keep us from talking about our past—the world is against me telling this story and yet I feel the suffocating pressure to do exactly that. Tell it all.

So, I guess the question is: *Am* I blowing up my life by writing this? Is telling my truth the wrong thing to do? And if so, how is that even fair? I'm human. This is what happened to me. These are my crosses to bear.

"CoCo," Jenn interrupted. "This is going to be big. Like *really* big …"

I knew it was true. My community has been dying to get their hands on my book ever since I even just hinted that it was coming. But I'm terrified, so I don't reply to Jenn. I just listen and hold my breath.

"The last time you went live on Instagram, over a thousand people logged on just to watch you make dinner with Ellie," she reminds me. Your online community is waiting, wanting, and asking you for *your* story, the true story, *your* book."

I have to admit that with my growing social media community, I finally have found a place where I feel heard, companionship, empathy, and where I feel seen, for the first time ever. No mask. No filter. Just me. CoCo.

I take a long, deep breath and say, "Okay. Let's do this."

Jenn and I spend the rest of the night outlining the last few chapters of *Look at Me* and I can feel my hopes rising. After a couple of hours, I have to stand and lean over my desk chair to take the edge off the pain. My cannabis vape helps a little bit, but sitting doesn't.

Finally, I give up and crawl into bed, taking my laptop with me and propping it up on the bedside table, and continue the meeting as I lay against my mountain of pillows.

We talk about the story and its path from Costa Rica to the United

States, from being a child who was sexually abused to raising a child of my own, and the many milestones, traumas, and revelations that have come in between. We talk about what this book is going to be, and what it will mean to readers.

With loneliness and rejection being a common thread to my narrative, I have made the conscious decision to share the good and the bad, the wonder and the abuse, the fairytale homes and the loneliness within them, the exciting relationships and the ones that end in tragedy.

It's *all* in here: innocence, loneliness, betrayal, guilt, addiction, stealing, a high-profile trial, money, fame, love, lust, hate, self-destruction, meaning, purpose, community, impact, and ultimately, my legacy.

You wouldn't think that a "terminal" cancer diagnosis could save someone, but I'm about to show you that it can, and it has. At twenty-nine years old, I have already lived many different lives. Surprisingly it is this life—the one infiltrated by cancer, surgeries, mobility aids, and the fight of my life—that saved me.

So yes. Tonight's task is a big one.

And it's made even more critical by the fact that we are making up for a *lot* of lost time.

INTRODUCTION

I may be only twenty-nine years old, but I've lived many different lives. In most of them, I was either near or *in* the spotlight. Newspapers, gossip magazines, and TV shows often followed us. We (especially my mother) were always dressed to the nines, and most of what we touched turned to either drama or gold—*or both*.

From the outside looking in, our lives have always looked like a rich, high-fashion, beautiful mess to most of our fans and followers. *And they're not wrong*. But there's a reason for the "mess." My mom (Lynda Diaz), my sister (Linda Diaz), and I have been fighting our own massive, cruel demons for a very long time.

And demons are not pretty.

You're about to get an intimate look into the darkness of my past, the mistakes I've made, the blessings I've received, and how I conquered my demons. I hope you are inspired to find your light, no matter how far down into the abyss your life might have led you.

First and most importantly, I've written *Look at Me* for my sweet, beautiful, resilient five-year-old daughter, Ellie. It's not exactly "PG" so there are parts in this story she may never get to read (at least not until she's eighteen!), but this book is *Ellie's legacy fund*. Long after I'm gone, I hope people will still be reading and sharing my story. And every time they do, Ellie will have a little bit more of me as well as some additional financial freedom in her life so that she can achieve all of her biggest dreams.

Ellie is my own little miracle. She knows how to change my

ileostomy bag, brings me fluids for my I.V., and hugs me when I'm crying out in pain. She even joins me for Instagram Lives and loves my online community as much as I do. Yes, she struggles against her own anger and outbursts (because her world is always close to crashing down around her at any moment), but let's be clear: Ellie has earned every bit of goodness and love that will come her way as a result of who she is.

The Ellie fund will be hers, without catches or conditions. I want her to experience the joy of making her own decisions without them being tied to or punished with money (or lack thereof).

As I write this, Ellie is curled up on my bed, covered in blankets, with her favorite movie playing on her iPad. I know she is watching me out of the corner of her eye (she is always watching, always checking on me), and I am at a loss for words to describe how much I love her.

I want to give Ellie everything in life, especially the things I never had. I want to always be by her side to cherish her. I want to pick out her outfits and help style her hair. I want her to have all the love, acceptance, pride, stability, and support she could ever need. Most of all, I want her to know that her mom is a safe place in all ways. I want to give her the guidance I so desperately needed and wished for when I was her age. She deserves ALL of this and more.

* * *

MY REQUEST OF YOU: As you read, please give every person in my life, with the exception of Carlos, some grace. Demons make you do awful things, and there isn't a single person in this book who wasn't fighting their own when they said or did the things you're about to read about, including me. Cut them some slack. Look beyond the headline. Pray for them so they may have some of the peace within their own hearts that I now have within mine. And for my family, friends, and community; I ask that you read this all the way through before reacting. I may not deserve your grace or forgiveness, but I admit that in my heart, having it is my deepest wish.

CHAPTER ONE

FAIRYTALES AND NIGHTMARES

The first four and a half years of my life are a blur. I wish I could say I have memories of those impactful times and how they have directly contributed to who I am today. That way, it would be easier to put the things my mom has told me into some sort of context, but there's nothing there—no happy memories of my parents' marriage, much less a happy home. Whenever I get frustrated or furious with my mother, I try to envision where she came from, what she went through, and what her story is. Because we all have one.

When my mother met Carlos, their connection was instant. They met in a Costa Rican beauty pageant. My mother was representing Puerto Rico. They got married after a whirlwind romance giving my mom the perfect opportunity to escape the Puerto Rican life that she desperately wanted to leave behind. Blinded by the desire to start her own fairy-tale life, she agreed to move to Costa Rica.

At just nineteen years old, she soon found herself pregnant, bringing her modeling career to a halt. That's when Carlos's true colors began to appear. His adoration for my mom was soon replaced by belittlement, arguments, and abuse. In fact, belittlement seemed to be his toxic relationship trait of choice, something she was already familiar with.

Being from Puerto Rico, my mother had a thick accent which was much different from those in Costa Rica. Carlos thought it made her look like she was an outsider, and he didn't like it. He would tell her to keep her mouth shut when others were around. She embarrassed him.

At first, she argued to defend herself, but it would be met with swearing, snide comments, or flash anger and a smack across the face.

This cruelty soon evolved.

For example, when Carlos's brothers would come over for a visit, he would ask my mother to make Chicharrónes rice and beans, a traditional dish everyone loved. It was his favorite meal and she made it perfectly. The house would soon be filled with delicious aromas from the ingredients and spices of his favorite dish as she cooked.

Once dinner was ready, Carlos would order my mother to go to her bedroom so that he and his brothers could enjoy their meal without her.

Mom would disappear into her room as instructed, stomach grumbling, and stay there until it was time for coffee, dessert, and cleanup.

No, thank you. No love. No family time with his brothers. And no dinner.

Lynda became well acquainted with Carlos's anger and knew better than to argue. Fighting back would bring instant anger and repercussions.

She also became acquainted with his infidelity. As the kids grew up, he began giving her sleeping medication so that she'd go to sleep early, allowing him the freedom to go out while she slept.

Some nights, she would manage to stay awake to see him return home. She would pretend she didn't notice he was permeated by the scent of booze and other women. She'd soon find herself cleaning lipstick off of his clothes the next morning.

She learned to keep her thoughts, anger, and depression to herself for her own sake and that of the kids.

But on one occasion, she couldn't help herself. He had ordered her to come to him, whistling at her like he would call a dog.

"I'm not a dog, Carlos!" she exclaimed out of frustration.

"Bitch, shut up!" he spat at her, his rage immediately triggered by her audacity to defend herself. "You are what I say you are, and you will do as you're told."

She wished he would see her as a person again, as a woman he loved and the mother of his children. "But Carlos—"

"No!" He cut her off. Before she could get out another word, he wrapped one of his large, strong hands around her tiny wrist, and squeezed. Hard. The pain was excruciating. Then he began to twist. She screamed out in agony as the pain drove her down to her knees. He continued squeezing and twisting while lowering his hand until he had her down on the floor in the position of a dog.

He glared down at her with disgust and shouted, "You are nothing without me!"

He liked to remind her how dependent on him she was. He put the roof over her head and food in the pantry. "Without me, you have nothing. You are nothing. You're worth nothing."

As she wondered how long before her bones broke in his grip, my mother was filled with fury hotter than she'd ever felt before. Her fairytale story had turned into a nightmare. To this day, she says she remembers that moment as if it were yesterday. While down on her knees, with a man in control of who she was, where she lived, and even where she was allowed to eat, she made a decision. In that moment, her mind was crystal clear. She made a silent promise to Carlos: "Motherfucker, you are going to see who I will become." She became laser fucking focused on getting away from him, regaining her power, and becoming successful while standing on her own two feet.

She knew she would do whatever it took to never be this vulnerable again.

Her accent wasn't good enough for her husband. Her appearance wasn't good enough for him. Her performance as a wife and a mother was not good enough. And she felt as if the more he sensed that she wanted out and away from him, the more he used shame and fear to control her.

Whether it was inevitable or simply fate, Mom was rediscovered while running errands in town one day. Someone in the media and television recognized her from her modeling days and welcomed her back into the work she had always longed to pursue. Soon, she was being connected to more influential people in the media and booking auditions.

Once she was free of Carlos, her modeling career picked up where it had left off before she started having babies. But this time, her popularity was even better than before. She landed a job as a host on Channel 7, called 7 Stars, which became Costa Rica's most popular entertainment television show. She was a star in every meaning of the word. Everyone wanted to be near her, talk to her, interview her, photograph her. She was back - better and stronger than before. But that was the Lynda that the world saw.

At home, Linda, my mother, and I would eat noodle soup for a full week at times, splurging on something more only on paydays. Working in television in a third-world country didn't pay much at the time because the understanding was that it would set up the host for other opportunities, such as brand deals, to contribute to the household budget. The child support received from Carlos barely covered our school tuition.

Although my mom spent a lot of time working, it wasn't all bad. When it was just the three of us, she would throw "A quien le importa" by Thalia on the stereo, and we would each grab kitchen utensils as our microphones. We'd sing at the top of our lungs, jumping on the couches and dancing through the apartment. The lyrics essentially meant, "Who cares what I say, how I say it? This is who I am, and I'll never change!" It became the Diaz anthem.

After Carlos, my mother was clear on what she wanted. And she wanted *more*.

Her first attempt at her fairytale had exploded in her face, but now she was even more determined to achieve it.

She had no intention of returning to the humble Puerto Rican home of her childhood, and the male chauvinistic culture that her alcoholic father had created. In her home, women didn't have a voice. They served the men. The cost of fighting against this hierarchy was not something her sister, her mother—even her brother—could afford to risk.

It was her time, and I think she knew that. She deserved more. Not just for us, but for herself too and to reclaim the years lost to an unhappy, abusive marriage.

EXTRAVAGANTLY RICH

When she met Gary, everything changed for all of us. He was thirty years older than my mom, so everyone automatically assumed my mom married him for his money (and he for her youth and beauty). But if it wasn't real at the beginning, it eventually grew to be real. Say what you want, but my mom fell hard for Gary, and he for her.

Gary was caring, smart, generous, powerful, and safe. Most importantly, he was head over heels in love with my mother.

He was also undeniably, incredibly, *extravagantly* rich. Before him, we would have been considered by most to be "well off" when living with my biological father. But with Gary, wealth took on a whole new meaning. We could barely comprehend how much money he had. It came from being a high-profile sports gambler in Costa Rica. His pockets were always filled with cash. His left pocket would bulge with a roll of hundreds in American dollars and his right pocket with a roll of thousands in colones (Costa Rican currency).

We adored Gary. He was so sweet and loving that I started calling him "Daddy" almost immediately. It was a title he accepted with honor and all the responsibilities that came along with it. And when we moved in with him, it was like moving into our very own fairy tale. We had a full staff to serve us and maintain the house, including maids, groundskeepers, armed bodyguards, and drivers. And it wasn't just the money. It was the 360-degree change our life had made. Almost overnight we had a new family, new reputation, new home, new friends, new everything. My mom was happier than I had ever seen her. We all were.

Within a year or so, we moved into an even bigger home in the same neighborhood, just a few blocks away.

Gary wanted to give my mother the home of her dreams, and money was no object. So, she chose every paint color, every decor detail. It soon became the home where everyone – all my friends from school, and the neighborhood kids - wanted to come and hang out. It was my first taste of popularity. The house had an indoor pool, a spa with a massage room, an adjoining gym, a sauna, massive grounds, a pond, and beautiful gardens. The ceilings were high, and there were windows everywhere (even though they all had window-guard bars on them). There are videos of television segments during which my mom was interviewed in the house, showing off its beauty and architecture—basically, like *Lifestyles of the Rich and Famous*, but Costa Rican style.

My sister and I had the biggest playroom you've ever seen. The walls were hand-painted golden-yellow with a mural depicting a circus, including images of hot air balloons, Ferris wheels, and elephants doing circus tricks (Gary loved elephants, they were his favorite animal). The room was filled with toys, craft centers, doll houses, and a dark wooden stage where we would both sing karaoke and put on plays for friends or whoever was taking care of us at the time. The stage had entrances on both ends with big gold-colored stage curtains that would be opened and closed marking the beginning and end of our performances.

You could see the great care and detail put into the space's design. Looking back, I am grateful for how much care my mom put into that space. I know this has stayed with me as I have found myself doing everything I can to create a fairytale bedroom for my own daughter, something that will be special and unforgettable, like what I had when I was her age.

Linda and I each had our own walk-in closets filled with cute dresses, purses, and high-fashion clothing and accessories. My mom had given me a new school "backpack," although it wasn't a backpack, it was a black Gucci tote with the classic red and green Gucci stripe - my first big statement of wealth and style to everyone at school, friends and teachers included. I remember being so proud, enjoying the feeling of seeing heads turning as I walked down the school corridors. I loved feeling seen for the first time. I remember wondering, *Is this what my new life was going to be like?*

Life wasn't just amazing at the house; it was also wonderful when we were traveling. One of the last trips I remember taking just us four—my mother, my sister, Gary, and me – was to Park City, Utah. My mother had more freedom to travel after leaving her job because, with Gary, she had all the money she could ever need.

I remember staying in a fancy Ritz-Carlton hotel, eating my first "authentic New York pizza" (even though we were in Utah!). I almost felt like I had a new mom. She wasn't the careful, perfect "Lynda Diaz" everyone saw on television. She was carefree and happy. She didn't mind getting messy. We hugged and sang and giggled over silly things. She was able to step out of the public icon persona and just be Mom. This was as much a part of my fairytale as the mansion and the money. I loved Gary for making her so happy.

We went racing down the big mountains on our plastic sleds, laughing and screaming at the top of our lungs. We went so fast that steering was almost impossible. One time, my mom and I almost ran into a tree at full speed, but my mother, just before we made impact, grabbed me and dove with me off to the side. She was so quick to act, saving us both from serious injury.

We flipped over and lay on the ground, half crying, half laughing until we could barely breathe.

We created lifelong memories on that trip—for all of us.

The Utah trip was one of the last family adventures we took together before Mom became pregnant with twins. They had been trying to have a baby for years, inevitably turning to in-vitro insemination treatments in Miami at one of the most expensive programs in the world.

Because of the treatments, trips back and forth to Miami with her and Gary became a regular occurrence.

Mom endured countless injections with Gary at her side. Part of the reason Mom stopped working was so that she could dedicate her time and energy to the in vitro treatments. Frankly, there was no need for generating additional income. She had already achieved her goals of becoming an iconic public figure and having more money than she could ever spend.

The stress of trying to get pregnant was wearing on Gary and Mom's relationship. I heard them arguing more and could feel the tension between them. When she finally did become pregnant, it was with twins, and they were thrilled.

Mom didn't make it to full term, but she still managed to give birth to two healthy babies, a boy and a girl—Tiffany and Gary.

Our family was growing and filling more of the space in our massive home.

An area of the house had already been converted into a massive, presidential-suite-sized nursery. Like our massive playroom, it was absolutely beautiful. One of the walls was painted with a mural of a park. They had an entire wall of closets, fully stocked with designer clothes and shoes.

I still remember their tiny little Gucci shoes. Tiffany's were cream and light brown slippers with a strap and light pink interior. Little Gary had Gucci loafers in nude and light brown colors to match. The twins were always dressed to a T every single day.

The twins each had nannies who were always nearby and ready to help. The nannies also traveled with us. I love Gary to death, but I don't think he has ever changed a diaper in his life! He didn't tend to the more tedious or messy parts of parenthood.

I adored the twins, but one of my worries was that I would lose some of my mother's love and attention, now that it had to be shared with more siblings. Unfortunately, that's exactly what happened. We soon spent more and more time with the maids and babysitters (keeping an eye on us came with their job descriptions) and less and less time with my mother and Gary. Linda and I were often left to find ways of entertaining ourselves.

Once everyone had finally gone to sleep, I would go to the kitchen pantry to find some snacks—usually sweet ones—and bring them back to my room, hiding them in my nightstand or beneath my bed. I didn't want anyone to see me snacking. One of the places I started finding companionship was in the pantry. I started binge-eating and hiding snacks in the nightstand of my room. My relationship with food changed.

WEEKENDS

Just because my mother was done with Carlos, didn't mean that we were. Every other weekend, for two days and one night, my sister and I went to Carlos's house for our court-mandated visits. Saturday, around 11 a.m., Carlos would roll up to the house in the latest BMW X6 or whatever brand-new car he had. Windows down, rooftop open, Carlos would have a big smile on his face and be singing along to his stereo. If we were lucky, the passenger side would be empty, which meant it was up for grabs.

The first one to scream "*Shotgun!*" at the top of our lungs and jump into the front row passenger side seat got to ride in that spot. We loved it because the rule at home was that the oldest got to sit in the car. That ruled me out most of the time.

I had that shotgun shit down pat. I *always* got to sit in the coveted front seat, unless my older brother, Andre, (Carlos had a son from another relationship who was just a few years older) wasn't already sitting there.

Sometimes Carlos would bring one of his girlfriends instead of his son. He tended to date women under the age of thirty who were models (or wannabe models). They were gorgeous, and their financial motives were obvious. Status and stability weren't easy to come by in Costa Rica, so who could blame them?

Some of Carlos's girlfriends looked so much like my sister that it was creepy.

After Linda and I piled into his car, there was a feeling of freedom because the rules changed. They were looser when we were with Carlos.

Carlos had a big house in the mountains. It didn't have modern finishes or anything, but if you factor in the four floors, beautiful architecture, huge square footage, and breathtaking views of Costa Rica countryside (including the volcano on certain days), it was a mansion by most people's standards.

During the weekend days, life with Carlos felt almost normal. Linda and Andre and I were close. We'd have a lot of fun together. Carlos had ATVs that we would each ride like lunatics, chasing each other around the property, hooting and hollering in delight, and aiming for mud puddles. We'd speed, spin our wheels, take tight turns, and eventually, end up back at the house, laughing and out of breath, covered in mud from head to toe. If the weather was right, we'd finish it off by jumping in the pool.

I'd hate to be the pool maintenance guy after that.

After we got cleaned up from our ATV adventures, we'd regroup around the pool. Carlos would barbecue, and we'd hang out, talk, tease each other, or goof off. Linda and I were a bit crazy, and Andre was too, which was why we made a good trio. We were close. Andre was our cooler older brother. He was popular, good-looking, funny, and the golden child in Carlos's eyes.

The girlfriends were there too, but I tried to avoid getting too close to them because I knew they had an expiration date. They may have been there with us, but they weren't one of us. Sometimes, they would be condescending when they spoke to me, but for the most part, they knew their place. So did I. And they didn't appreciate that too much. I'll give Carlos one thing; he didn't let them call the shots with his kids. In fact, he made sure they knew they didn't have authority over anyone or anything.

Andre treated Carlos's girlfriends the worst. He probably didn't like having to compete with them for Carlos's attention, or his money. When they were around, there was less money for Andre's expensive hobbies. Looking back, I realize Carlos was teaching us all where women rank in the world. He also taught us that if you were a man, you could potentially get away with just about anything. After cleaning up and getting ready for dinnertime, things began to shift. Even though I was only five by then, Carlos would sometimes give me big sips (sometimes gulps) of Johnnie Walker Black. I couldn't have been more than forty-five pounds at the time, so it made my head spin and my stomach burn as if it were on fire. It's a sensation I feel immediately to this day. Having seen adults around me drinking often, I thought everyone had the same sensation. My head and limbs would feel lighter. I felt carefree … happy … numb … "less." I liked it.

Once the sun disappeared behind the mountains, the air got thicker somehow. Everyone must have felt it, but no one said anything. Carlos changed. Daytime dad was far different from nighttime dad.

To start with, he would have drunk a lot by the evening. His loving smiles became a bit more like sneers. My brother would disappear into his room. Carlos would often put Linda to bed in our shared bedroom while I stayed up, watching television in Carlos's massive king-sized bed.

Once she was asleep, he began touching me.

* * *

The years of sexual abuse that I suffered at the hands of my own biological father is remembered in flashes and glimpses. I am sure that I have suppressed a lot of the worst of it. Even now, I still get slammed in the stomach with sharp memories of what took place.

First, it was his hands on me in places no one had touched like that before. Then it was him rubbing himself against me until something hot and sticky got on my pajamas or my skin. I didn't know what it was, just that it was gross.

That went on for some time.

Eventually, he didn't stop at touching and rubbing. The first time I felt his penis push all the way, I screamed so loud and so long that I lost my voice.

He put his hand on my mouth to shush me, but the sound came anyway as tears were streaming down my face.

"Be strong, Nicole. Shhhh," he whispered while he continued tearing and hurting me in ways no father should ever do his little girl.

But he didn't stop.

The blood and my horrified sobbing didn't stop him.

Nothing stopped him.

I had never felt pain like that before. It was like he was angry with me, but I never knew why.

After that first time, I had to wonder how the world didn't see that I was a completely different girl now. Couldn't they see the anguish in my eyes? There's no way that I could have hidden it in those early days of my abuse.

Once Carlos knew he could go all the way, he did. More often and more brutally. Even when I would cry out, because I was sobbing so hard, little to no sound made it out of my throat. But when it did get out, it was ear-piercing. I would release all the pain and confusion through my scream, but it was only a second before he clamped my mouth shut with his meaty, sweaty hands. *Even now, the thought of his heat and sweat nauseates me. I wanted to wipe, scratch, and wash his touch off of me.*

With me, he was aggressive and cruel. It was hard to breathe under the weight of him. I detested the feel of him on me, against me, inside me. One time I bit his hand as he muzzled me with it. That was one of the worst rape experiences I had at the hands of my father. He punished me for biting him.

Sometimes, if he was more drunk or angry than usual, he would take me down to the maid's room on the lowest floor. No one was down there. The maids didn't sleep down in the lower bedroom anymore because they had been given a newer one higher up in the house. Down there, I could (and did) scream my lungs out, but no one would ever hear me, especially not his girlfriends, who were sound asleep in their master suite,

I screamed. No one came. I screamed for help from staff, family, God, the universe, and anyone who might come to my rescue. I screamed as loud as I could until I lost my voice. I can't put into words how alone in the world that made me feel, how powerless. I was begging with all of my mind, spirit, and soul. But no one ever came.

I've always wondered if the maids did hear me but were too afraid to stop it.

It didn't matter how I pleaded with him to stop. He had no empathy—just a desire for release and anger at me. For what, I'll never know.

"Don't make so much noise! It upsets me. No one can hear you anyway, Nicole."

"But Papi—"

"Just do as I say, and it'll all be over." He taught me that the better I behaved, the sooner he would finish and leave me alone.

It was pitch black when he threatened me, but I swear I could see the sneer across his face.

In the maid's room, there was pretty much nothing in the way of furniture except for a single bed. That's all he needed anyway. There was no other purpose for the space other than to hurt me. I don't know if he took other young girls down there for the same reason.

"I'm sorry, Papi!" I would cry while trying to figure out what I had done so wrong to make him need to treat me this way. Sometimes I would ask, "Why me?" or "Why are we doing this?"

Sometimes he would just growl or grunt and continue. Sometimes he would just use his power as my father to excuse his behavior, saying something along the lines of: "How many times have I told you that I'm your father? *You* don't get to question *me*. *I* discipline *you*."

Other times, he would guilt-trip me instead. "I'm your father. I would never do anything to hurt you," he said as if what he was doing didn't hurt. It made me feel like I was going insane. He'd then tell me, "I do this because I love you."

It's embarrassing to admit but, at first, I didn't realize what he was doing was something we shouldn't be doing. I knew I didn't fucking like it. I knew it hurt. But at the same time, I didn't like getting beaten for misbehaving either, and lots of fathers did that to lots of daughters in Costa Rica.

It wasn't until he swore me to secrecy afterward that I understood he was breaking the rules. He wasn't supposed to be doing those things to me.

"If you *ever* speak of this to anyone, Nicole ..." he would say with the most serious, terrifying expression on his face, sometimes burying his face in his hands as if to weep. "If you tell anyone, something very bad might happen to me. I could go to jail, and you would never see me again."

Whether it makes sense or not, I didn't want something bad to happen to him. He played on that, asking: "If something happens to me, then how will you feel?"

The power he held over me, just with the threat that I would cause him harm, kept me quiet. I was five. I didn't know anything other than what my parents told me. And I couldn't imagine what would happen if he ended up in jail or in trouble because of me.

At the same time, he doted on my sister. She could do no wrong. I felt like a failure, dirty, bad. I felt worthless. I didn't know why he loved her and hurt me. Or was his treatment of me the way he showed love? Did it mean he loved me more? In my young mind and broken heart, nothing made sense. I believe that my abuse began a never-ending cycle of comparing myself to my sister. She was beautiful and sweet and seemed to never get in trouble. In comparison, my feeling of worthlessness and shame for my own behavior continued to grow.

As time went on, Carlos grew more daring with his abuse. And I grew quieter. He would fondle or have sex with me while my sister lay just a meter away, fast asleep. He always had a girlfriend, and because it was such a gigantic bed, whatever girlfriend he had at the time would sometimes be asleep on the other end of the bed.

Maybe his girlfriends knew the whole time? Maybe they were just pretending to be asleep. Carlos didn't have Gary-level money, but he was extremely wealthy compared to most other people in Costa Rica, and so being his girlfriend came with many financial perks that they might not have been willing to risk on my behalf. They sold their souls—and mine—for a set of boobs and a new car.

If they ever said anything to him or to me about the abuse, I can't remember it.

My psychiatrist says these memory blocks are a common self-protection coping mechanism for those who have experienced extremely traumatic events. It's survival instinct at its best. And it is the only way I was able to live with the shame and guilt, even though it eventually managed to do so anyway.

Some people live in a constant state of fight or flight mode, after suffering the trauma like I have. For me, it soon became fight mode. When the body lives in this constant state, it affects not just the mind, but every system of the body, including the immune system.

Are those memory gaps filled with information that would make my life make sense?

The morning after the abuse, the girlfriend of the week, my brother, my sister, and I would all sit at the breakfast table, jockeying for the position of most loved, portrayed by who was invited to sit closest to Carlos. The family all eat eggs together, including me, from my position farthest away from him. If I hadn't fought him the night before, if I had just let him do what he wanted without a word of protest, would it have earned me a spot near Carlos?

And I would say nothing. As if nothing happened.

My biological father sexually assaulted me from the time I was five until I was nine.

I was penetrated.

Tortured.

Punished.
Broken.
Aggressively.
Mercilessly.
Over and over. And over. And over.

* * *

After weekends with Carlos, I would return home, relieved to be away from him, yet filled with rage. I wanted to scream and yell and cry and rip things and punch things. I was mad at everything and everyone, but I never had the words at just five, six, seven, or eight years old to explain it. Whether it made sense or not, I was most angry with my mother.

Somehow it felt like my suffering was at her hands, even though it was Carlos who was traumatizing me. I am sure my mother didn't understand it. She must have thought I was just "acting up" again, being bad. The usual CoCo behavior she had come to expect.

"Hello, girls!" my mother would greet us when we arrived back home.

Her happy face and sing-song voice would make my blood boil. I knew Carlos wanted me to live with him. If my mother had just let me stay with him, maybe he would not have been so angry with me all the time. Maybe I wouldn't have had to be punished.

"I am lonely when you aren't here, Nicole," he told me, his voice dripping with false sadness that I was too young to recognize as an act. I felt guilty for his sadness, even though I had no control over where I lived.

"It hurts me to have you away from me all the time," he would say as if that was why he had to do those things to me.

Those words played in my head as I lashed out at Gary and my mother. She quickly became annoyed and frustrated, her smile disappearing within minutes of interacting with me.

At Carlos's house, I was broken, punished for fighting back and for not being there more. At home, I was punished for acting out. It became clear to me that no matter where I was, I was the bad girl. And no one was coming to my rescue.

* * *

Despite my behavior, Gary was more patient with me than my mother or my teachers. He supported my passion for learning, especially for reading and writing in English. I'd pull homework pages from my backpack filled with a thousand-page reading challenge.

Before Gary, no one had asked me about my homework before.

"What did you learn in school today?" he often asked with a big smile when he got home from work.

I'd excitedly show him a grade I'd achieved on a test or share a lesson I had learned in one of my classes.

If it was after dinner and my mother was occupied in another room, Gary would take a shower and then invite me up to his room. We would cuddle up together on his gigantic bed, ignoring his wall of televisions, and we would learn my words, practicing writing, reading, and pronunciation. As I worked my way through my thousand words, he would encourage me: "Wow! You're doing so well!"

Before Gary we didn't really speak English in our daily life, but now that we were going to American school and had an American dad, I wanted to not only triumph in my schoolwork, but I wanted to be fluent in English. I wanted to be able to fully communicate without being embarrassed by what I was saying. Despite my thick accent, I reminded myself not to let anyone's critique—or my own insecurities—get in the way.

Gary and I would read books together—books by Judy Bloom, books from the *Goosebumps* series, and favorites like *There's Something in the Attic*. When I loved a book, Gary would read it with me over and over, never showing a hint of annoyance at the repetition.

When we were getting close to the end of the book, I'd be hoping we could keep reading and not be too tired.

As if he sensed my worry, he'd ask, "Do you want to keep going?"

"Yes, please!!" I'd say and hug him.

He wasn't reading with me to check off some sort of parenting to-do list. He was doing it because he loved to see me learn and embrace language—and because he loved me.

Here was a man with hundreds of people working for him, but the one thing he always did was make time for me. He wasn't just there; he was truly present.

Gary is one of the reasons I write. He always encouraged my writing, telling me how good at it I was. Now, I find writing therapeutic and fulfilling. Gary is the only family member who didn't try to stop me from writing this book.

Because our life was so different once Gary came along, Carlos sometimes became irritable or jealous if we talked about our life at home. It was hard, at that age, to not be excited about a big new gift or extravagant shopping trip we'd just been taken on by Gary.

It was obvious my sister and I adored Gary and that we called him Daddy. Carlos could see that our life was drastically different—better—with him. And he didn't like that.

Carlos started making disparaging comments and grumbling under his breath when we'd mention our home life with Gary.

One day, I had been chattering away about Gary, not thinking anything about it, when I stepped on a nerve.

He pounded his fist down on the table in front of me.

"Gary does *not* love you, Nicole," he spat.

I stiffened in my chair, knowing I should stay quiet, but I couldn't help myself. "Yes, he does love me."

He sneered, "He only cares about your mother, and only because she's half his age."

I stared at my utensils and tried not to cry.

I could feel my face grow hot with anger. "He does love me, but when he shows it to me, he doesn't hurt me like you do!" The words were out before I could stop them.

He had been eating his breakfast and froze with food on his fork.

Oh no.

"He's your stepfather, not your father. Never forget that." He slammed his fist down on the table. "Gary's *never* going to love you enough to do the things that I do for you."

I kept quiet. I'd already pushed it too far. I cringed, envisioning the beating I was about to get. Or worse.

After a moment, Carlos shoved a big wad of eggs into his mouth. Talking with his mouth open, he focused his angry eyes on me and said, "If you ever question how much love I have for you, all you need to do is come back to live at my house. I'll make sure that you'll remember."

I was eight.

CAN'T YOU SEE ME?

Sexual abuse is a curse that feels irreversible. You are forced to grow up overnight, and you are faced with danger no adult or child should ever have to face. To keep it quiet, you are usually sworn to secrecy and warned against asking anyone for help. You are isolated and ashamed.

Like so many other sexual abuse survivors, I became "hypersexual." Sex was turned into a constant, agonizing need. I grew to need sexual relief any way that I could find it. It became a way of numbing my pain, of regaining some sense of control over my own body and sexuality.

I didn't know what to do about the adult needs my young body craved, so I began rubbing against anything I could find in an attempt to masturbate. I was in desperate need to numb the pain. I now know that many sexual assault and abuse survivors go through this.

What first broke me became a need and a form of release. Then when I filled the need, I would be filled with shame, leading me to crave more release. And around and around I go.

Research shows that when a child of preschool age is sexually abused, they tend to show signs in many ways. I know for a fact that I exhibited more than a few of them. Some signs include abrupt changes in behavior, not wanting to be alone, changes in the quality of schoolwork or grades, substance abuse, acting out, defiant behavior, self-mutilation (or careless behavior that results in self-harm), excessive play with their own private body parts, persistent sex play with friends or toys, frequent drawings that have sexual content, and unusual, persistent, or developmentally inappropriate questioning about human sexuality. I exhibited most if not all of the above list of obvious signs of sexual abuse.

Sometimes my sister or my maid would find me with my legs straddling the railing of the stairs, sweating, with legs crossed, with my eyes rolling back as I found the release that my body was now addicted to. It had become something in me I couldn't turn off, something that I knew I was doing, but I didn't know why. I couldn't connect the dots at that time.

To my horror, my sister walked in on me doing this, more than once. Her face went from confusion to amusement. "Nicole, stop doing that! You are so weird. What are you even doing?"

I didn't even know what to answer. What *was* I doing?

I hated that she looked like she was about to laugh. "It isn't funny, Linda. *Please* don't tell anyone."

One day when I was at home in my bedroom, my mother walked in on me rubbing myself on the railed footboard of my four-poster canopy bed. She didn't look surprised by what I was doing, just mad. She barked at me, "Nicole, I don't want to see you doing that anymore! What is *wrong* with you?"

I uncurled my legs from the rails and screamed, "Just leave me alone!"

For the rest of that night I wondered if my mother knew the truth, now that she'd caught me doing that. She must have wondered how or why I knew how or even wanted to do that, right? Would she save me? Would she force me to explain? Would she stop my abuse?

Sadly, none of the above happened. My attitude is what really upset my mom. To her, it was a sign of a bigger problem and a lack of respect toward her. That's what really got me in trouble. Once my mom left the room, I would lay my head on my pillow and cry my eyes out, filled with fury and confusion. *Why could I not stop this behavior?!* Why was no one else behaving the way I was?

I was caught trying to "satisfy myself" several times, to the point that it became a running joke around the house. I became a running joke around the house.

When I think of that time, I wonder if somewhere deep down, my mother realized something was happening to me. Even though I wasn't allowed to tell anyone what I was going through, I have always felt like I was wearing a neon sign on my back saying, "*Somebody help me!*"

But no one saw the sign. Why didn't anyone ever just stop to look at me—to ask questions that were *not* just, "What's wrong with you?!" If they had, they would have learned that something was horribly, hauntingly wrong.

How different would my life be now if someone I loved had sat me down and said, "Are you okay?" or "How can I help?" or "Are you safe?"

Instead, I was abused until the age of nine, when I got my period.

CHAPTER TWO

A NEW LIFE

Gary was the glue that held our family together during the week. I still screamed and yelled and argued, but when he was around, I found myself trying to hold it in, to be a better person. We all wanted to be better people when he was around.

But aside from shopping sprees and homework sessions, the fallout of my abuse and the effect of being surrounded by limitless money was starting to show up in new ways in my behavior.

I started paying for all their lunches every day and lending them whatever they needed if they asked. I started really seeing the power and safety that money could provide. With money, things just get easier, including making friends.

Before life with Gary and after my mother left Carlos, I didn't have many friends. The parents of the kids at my old school teased me about my mother because she was in the public eye. She was famous and single, and her modeling work often showed her in bathing suits and bikinis that left very little to the imagination. People didn't realize that her modeling work is what put food on our table. She was doing everything she could to support us and change our lives. Whether it was fair or not, that teasing meant I was isolated and added to my ever-growing anger.

But now, in my new life, I was a new CoCo, and everyone wanted to be around me.

To this day, when my sister and I reminisce, it's our time living with Gary that shines the brightest in our memories. When he was part of our family, we were all different—happier. They were some of the best years of our lives. A few nights ago, my publisher was on Zoom (via my computer), my online community was on my phone (I was live streaming while doing my makeup in a portable mirror propped up on my hospital bedside tray), and my sister was sitting at the foot of the bed. She was keeping me company in the hospital for the Christmas holidays.

"Remember how scary it was just to get a drink from the kitchen at night?" Linda asked me, referring to our collective fear of nighttime in Gary's house.

"Yasss!" I exclaimed. "If it was past bedtime, all the lights would be off, and the rooms and hallways were so big—"

"And dark! SO dark!" Linda's green eyes were big at the memory.

We were so young and little, and yet everything in that house was gigantic. In the daytime, it was beautiful. At night, it was ominous and scary. I remember the feeling of big dark spaces and things lurking in the shadows well. "It was almost as if something was hiding in the darkness, about to reach out and grab us!"

"So, we would *run*," Linda reminded me. "Run as fast as we fucking could. Like we were in a damn marathon."

"OMG yes! Run so fast with our drinks from the kitchen to our bedrooms, trying to get there before something could grab our feet!"

Because the house was a smart house (surely one of the first and most modern in Costa Rica, if not anywhere), everything was controlled through apps and control panels. At night, Gary would use the system remotely when he turned in, shutting off the lights, making sure the doors were locked, checking the cameras, and such.

The guards, the barred windows, the heavy-duty locks, and the smart home controls all worked together to make sure we were all safe. Wealthy families in Central America were often targets for kidnapping for ransom. It had unfortunately happened to some of my friends. Daddy made sure to have the best possible security so that didn't happen to us.

A NEW LIFE

I felt safe most of the time, but it was a fact that the more influence or wealth you had in Costa Rica, the more at risk you were.

Because the controller for the lights was in Gary's room with him, Linda and I had no way of turning them on outside our own rooms and bathrooms if we dared to leave them in the night. I'm not sure if we were truly scared or if we just loved scaring ourselves, considering how hard we laugh about it as adults.

We were wild when we were young and when we were together. Screaming our heads off while sprinting through the house wasn't that far out of the ordinary for us!

After countless nighttime drink runs, I began filling up my thermos with my new favorite drink—a cocktail of HiC and Bacardi. By the time I was in grade 6, I found myself looking forward to that moment, the first drink of the night. I'd been drinking here and there because of Carlos since I was very young. It became easier as time went on.

I would jump into my room and take a long sip from my thermos. Then another. Until I then dissolved happily into that numbing, soothing feeling that flooded over my body. I loved how it made me feel. I also loved who I was when I drank it. I loved feeling like I could talk to anyone.

I was desperate to be a different person and desperate to forget, flooded with unresolved turmoil stemming from moments I wished I could bury it all away, now that my abuse had ended.

I knew I was broken, but I was too young to fully pinpoint why. All I knew is that when I thought of Carlos or the sexual urges I had at such a young age, my stomach ached and my body ran hot with anger and frustration. To make matters worse, everyone around me—especially the people I loved—had gotten good at reminding me, "Something is wrong with you …" So, I believed them.

Alcohol became the easiest, most immediate solution within reach that even slightly lessened the pain and confusion of everyday life.

SHOPPING SPREE

Gary liked to spend his money and spoil us. Unlike many men, he loved to shop. One way he used to spoil us was with shopping spree challenges. The first time this happened, I thought we were just going on a regular shopping trip. We arrived at the Aventura Mall in Miami and were just about to set out in different directions to browse when Gary stopped us to say, "Let's see if you can really shop."

He had the biggest mischievous grin on his face!

"I'm giving you this …" He placed five thousand dollars in cash in my hands and then into Linda's. "*But* you have to spend every single dollar of it … if you don't …" he paused dramatically, "you will have to give it *all* back to me. Every last dollar."

I considered the challenge. I was still not used to unlimited wealth. I had never had that much money in my hands before.

"AND," he said, his eyes sparkling, "you have only one hour to spend it,"

One hour! I had definitely never spent that much in an hour before.

Even at ten years old, I had already become a professional shopper, all thanks to Gary's training. He had a lot of money, and he loved to spend it, but mainly, it was about seeing the people he loved smiling and being showered with everything we had ever dreamed of. That meant that I had all the department stores at the Aventura Mall nailed down—closest entrances, best sales, and most importantly, the "Pretty, pretty please?!" (just in case I ran out of money or wanted something extra special).

Of course, if I did get something special, Gary would make sure everyone got something special, too. For example, if I got an extra thousand, everyone else did—and, of course, my mother would get five!

I shopped in the adult women's section of Bloomingdale's, choosing adult styles such as skintight skirts and heels. I remember the day I got my first Burberry heels. I wore them around, click-clacking against the stone tile floors. I was so proud. They were three-and-a-half-inch heels from the pink cream Nova collection. I walked in them as if I had been doing it for years - because I had. I secretly broke into my mother's closet countless times to practice wearing and walking in her heels. My favorites were her orange heels. They were thick, tall platforms with transparent straps and a bow on the front. Once I could walk in those, I knew I was ready for heels of my own.

"Gary," my mother exclaimed when she saw me in the Burberry's he bought for me. "Nicole is way too young for those!"

He didn't disagree (he knew better) but he did distract her by purchasing the gorgeous hat she wanted, which got her mind off of me. I got to keep the heels.

Now, facing a shopping spree challenge, I laughed in delight. "Nooo problem!" I said, knowing I would win that challenge.

Gary did the countdown: "Now 1 ... 2 ... 3 ... go!"

I ran as fast as I could to the stores that I loved most and that were the most expensive. First to Bloomingdale's, then Koko + Palenki, and then others. I shopped SO HARD, my friends. I chose all the best clothing and accessories until I ran out of money, as instructed.

"Congratulations, CoCo!" he cheered loudly as I proudly dropped five thousand dollars worth of items on the shiny mall floor in front of him. I leaped into his arms with a big hug, and he squeezed me back, positively thrilled to see my happy face.

I was worried that because Linda was more careful and methodical than I was, she might fail the challenge. But then she appeared from around the mall corner, her hands filled with shopping bags.

Afterward, we went to Bella Luna, our favorite restaurant in the mall, for a nice family lunch. It was often packed with patrons, but Gary's mere presence would have the staff springing into action without being asked. One server would make space at a table; another would clean it and set our places for us. It would all happen smoothly in the blink of an eye. Gary wasn't the kind of person who waited for service. He also wasn't the kind of person who thought twice about tipping $100 USD to each staff member who stepped up to help.

Seeing Gary's influence on the community around us without even asking for it left me in awe. He demanded respect without saying a word. It took my breath away and made me want a little bit of that for myself someday.

When the server came to take our order, I would order my favorite meal: "Beef Carpaccio, extra capers, extra Parmesan, and a Caesar salad with shrimp, please!"

Linda would get the same thing, but sometimes with chicken instead of shrimp.

Dad always ordered chicken Parmesan (without red sauce), and french fries, and my mother would either order the carpaccio or opt for a salad.

Linda and I chattered excitedly, showing Gary and each other the items we had chosen. We thanked him profusely, hugged him, and smothered him in kisses.

To finish off the lunch, I would always have chocolate lava cake, a tradition dating back to my earliest childhood memories when we would go to Il Panino for the treat.

We did many shopping spree challenges over the years. I got very, *very* good at shopping.

You see, Gary was happy when we were happy. At moments like that, he would positively beam like the sun.

These moments were such highs. They made me feel like I was living in a dream, and in it, I was invincible. It was hard to believe it was happening. Just as I started to relax into the pure joy of those experiences, something would stop me in my tracks. It was like in the space between those exhilarating moments, if I blinked too long or if the air shifted in a certain way, I would feel Carlos's sweaty hands on me. Just for a second. A flash, and then it was gone, dropping me back into reality, covered in goosebumps, my own hands trembling. My family hadn't noticed. They were talking and fussing and eating and laughing.

What was this life I was now living?!

There were only a few things that brought me back up for air.

My father stopped sexually abusing me when I was nine years old, but the effects of my trauma continued to spread like cancer and determined, in many ways, the course of the rest of my life. It distorted the way I thought about myself, my body, my value, and even my ability to love and be loved … all the basic human emotions most people take for granted became out of reach for me. It felt like they were for everyone else but not for me. I started looking to fill my desperate need for love and attention in ways that I was too young for.

BULLETPROOF

Linda and I made our way down the stairs at the sight of our ride arriving. I was thirteen. One of our bodyguards pulled up in front of the school in an intimidating black Cadillac Escalade ESV (the only one in the country), its body gleaming in the sunlight.

Notably, it was also a bulletproof vehicle, with thick windows that didn't roll down more than a few inches for security reasons. Our car drew attention for its undeniable presence amid the sea of typical family minivans and sedans driven by our friends' parents. When our vehicle pulled up, everyone knew who was inside. Our grand exit made us a spectacle in the after-school crowd. On the one hand, I would feel a burst of pride at being the subject of luxury and attention. On the other hand, it was overshadowed by an ever-present insecurity I worked hard to hide.

As most of my classmates eagerly sought their parents' familiar faces, mine were often busy, replaced by the polite but empty expression of our bodyguards. Don't get me wrong … the guards were friendly enough, but it was obvious that we were a job to them. They worked for our parents. They weren't there for us or by choice.

I flashed a smile and a wave to my grade 8 classmates and stepped up into the front passenger seat of our tall black chariot. The leather was cool and cushy.

I would look back to see our maid sitting in the seat behind, hands neatly folded into the lap of her beige, starched-cotton pants. My sister Linda followed, climbing up and into the seat next to our maid.

She was smiling and singing "*Hooo-laaa*" to them both. I would ask, "*¿Como estas?*" while my eyes fixed on a chat thread on my Blackberry, not hearing my sibling's answer.

I was immersed in conversations with my boyfriend Leo and also trying to keep up with texting whichever boy "friend" I had at the time. If I wasn't careful, I would text the wrong message to the wrong guy—a mistake I had already made more than once and did not feel like dealing with ever again.

The twins were the next to join our journey home. They clambered excitedly into our car and leaped into their own respective seats beside each other. To keep them occupied, I put my phone down, turned around in my seat and played games with them. Tiffany was like a wild child, with her shaggy dark hair and constant chatter. Little Gary would usually stay mostly in his seat, quietly watching everything and everyone. His dirty blonde locks framed his curious blue-green eyes. When I wasn't playing games with them, we'd chat about their day at school. If I was lucky, I would get a pasta necklace or a piece of art as a gift after their day at school.

Although I was well-traveled at the young age of thirteen, I still loved that Costa Rica is one of the most beautiful places on Earth, with its mountains, tropical rainforest, and beautiful coastline.

As we set out on our thirtyish-minute drive home through the Costa Rican countryside, I eventually placed my Blackberry down beside me, plugged my white iPod into the vehicle's sound system, and turned up the music to our favorite artists—The Frey, Nickelback, Ednita Nascario, and Bacilos—belting out some truly fancy vocal harmonies as if we were auditioning for American Idol. Even our bodyguard could be seen nodding his head in rhythm from time to time.

PURA VIDA LIFE

Driving through the Costa Rican countryside toward our home was like entering a world of its own. The country is unlike anywhere else. Although you can't see the coastline while driving, you are reminded there is a whole other world outside its borders, but you also know that this one is better in many ways. Imagine driving a modern luxurious Escalade ESV down a small road, past someone riding a horse—their primary mode of transportation. Then you head up into the mountaintop road to find a three-million-dollar home with all the modern American finishes.

But to truly know Costa Rica is to know the people. That's what I loved and will forever love about my country. We complain, we have a temper, and we don't like to pay for anything, but we LOVE the "PURA VIDA" life. We love to say *mae* to represent "dude." We are *ticos* to the core, no matter where we go. Our unique Latin accent can be distinguished by another Costa Rican anywhere in the world in seconds. It was where I was born and where I was raised. And when I was in the car, in the passenger seat, even at a young age, I appreciated the little things that I knew, one day, I would walk away from.

With each familiar turn, my anxious anticipation grew as we approached the long drive leading up to our house. Minutes before reaching the property, we passed by Daddy's office with guards standing outside who would then signal with walkie-talkies to those at the house to open the huge iron gate upon our soon arrival. Once we reached the front door, we'd be greeted by another guard standing there with a rifle slung around his torso. It is easy to tell how seriously he takes his job by the stern look on his face. I had come to accept the fact that he was part of my regular landscape. His presence served as a reminder that security and safety must be taken seriously, no matter where you are or who you are with.

The moment I saw our dogs, Yaya and Coca, racing toward the car, any lingering unease from the day evaporated. They would wag their excited tales and jump up and down until Linda and I scrambled out of the car. We couldn't even wait for the bodyguard to open the door for us. A small chihuahua, black and white, that was beautiful in our eyes but oh so *not* cute. Coca was this beautiful golden retriever, slim and tall, and she had a hip problem, so you could tell despite her fast run from the guard house to the entrance of the house where we would park, she was in pain. Yaya was always inside the house and sleeping with us, and Coca became more of our guard dog.

The enthusiastic, furry welcome committee never failed to erase any negative thoughts by smothering us with cuddles and affection.

Once we were in the house, our two diligent maids would quickly swing into action. Backpacks were promptly tidied and stowed away, and we're ushered to wash our hands. But that's where their involvement in our school life ends. Our desks, situated in our individual rooms, become our solitary study sanctuaries. Since our homework is in English, the maids wouldn't understand even if they tried to help.

When it was time for lunch, Linda, Tiffany, Little Gary, and I were directed toward the familiar six-person table in the bustling kitchen. The grandeur of the big wooden dining table in the adjacent room, connected by a sliding door, was reserved for our parents or for rare occasions when we were invited to join them. If we were directed to the larger table, it was a special occasion, and we were expected to be on our best behavior.

But in the kitchen, we'd be drawn like a magnet to whatever the maids were cooking up, following the tantalizing aromas of *pastelón*, a beloved Costa Rican specialty that filled the air with its intoxicating blend of sweet plantains and spiced beef.

Amidst the chatter of my siblings around the table, I found solace in their presence. We shared stories of our day as we savored the delicious meal before us. The clinking of utensils and the occasional clatter of dishes created a symphony of family connection.

After our meal, we left the remnants of our feast on the table, knowing that the diligent maids would soon arrive to clear them away. As the twins were taken away under the watchful eye of the babysitter, it left us with a brief respite.

Linda and I would have time to hang out, play, jump on ATVs

A NEW LIFE

(which were bought for us after my mother and Gary realized that we loved them so much when we visited Carlos), play tennis, or any number of other extracurricular activities that helped burn off energy and stress.

Later, at my desk, my eyes became heavy from the weight of homework. I needed a distraction, so I reached for my Blackberry and called Mom.

She answered right away. "*Si, ¿alo?* Hello?" in her Puerto Rican accent.

"When are you coming home?" I asked, wanting to see her but also feeling that familiar pang of anxiety and desperation. For what reason, I never really knew.

"I'm coming up the driveway," she said. "See you soon!"

"Okay, Mami. See you soon," I said and hung up.

I pictured her in her sleek black Porsche 911 Turbo gliding along the roads of Costa Rica, trailed closely by a Lexus carrying her ever-watchful bodyguard.

I picked up the phone and quickly dialed 101 (we had phones with direct lines to each other), the extension for the kitchen, eager to announce her arrival, and then 108, my sister's room.

"Mom's almost here!" I'd tell her.

"Okay ..." Linda would respond as if to ask what the big deal was. She was busy doing her homework—already effortlessly being perfect.

My sister and I were like night and day, from our appearance to our personalities to our relationships and experiences. Linda, my sister, always seemed to be the shining star in everyone's eyes, whether it was family, friends, or even my mom's acquaintances. Growing up with a mom as stunning as mine already brought its own set of expectations but having a sister who appeared flawless in every aspect, not just in looks but also in behavior, added even more pressure. I can't recall a time when my sister wasn't held up as the epitome of perfection. She never talked back, always followed the rules, and even when she slipped up, she did so discreetly, masking her mistakes so flawlessly that nobody could catch her missteps. But that wasn't me. I was the spirited one, the rebel, the one who couldn't help but speak my mind, the one with a larger-than-life personality. I was the troublemaker, always pushing boundaries, always at odds with my mother, even though all I ever wanted was her approval.

So, when my mom was nearby, I felt as if I had to do more to be noticed.

The twins burst out of their room and raced into the kitchen, their tiny feet pitter-pattering across the tiled floor.

When the front door swung open, and my mother appeared, she was dressed to the nines, as always, after a leisurely lunch with her friends. Her presence commanded attention. It was a testament to her social status.

She put her bags down and said hello to everyone. Then, her eyes focused on me. "You're still in your uniform?" she exclaimed with disapproval. "Go take a shower and change into something presentable." I winced at the implication that I was a slob, but I knew we had an image to uphold, so I did as I was told.

Mom chatted with Linda a little bit before moving on to spend time with the twins. After a little while, the babysitter was called in to whisk them away, freeing her to retreat into the sanctuary of her own room.

As the clock neared 4:30 p.m., we received the notification that Daddy was on his way home. He drove himself, refusing the protection of a bodyguard. His four-door black Mercedes glided into the driveway.

He would park his car beside my mom's in our three-car garage. The third space would be filled with our ATVs and golf carts.

Daddy's attire would be impeccable, as always. His Zegna dress pants, shirts adorned with shining cuff links, and meticulously coiffed hair dyed a dark orange hue, with just a hint of roots showing, were meticulously put together—down to his black alligator skin dress shoes. Growing up around my mother and Gary gave me an admiration for good fashion and the respect it demanded.

Once I had showered and changed into a new outfit at my mother's request, I rejoined my siblings. "Daddy!!" we exclaimed as we all eagerly greeted him. We showered him with hugs, kisses, and excitement. It was a ritual that had become second nature to us.

"How was your day?" he asked with genuine interest. Even though I had begun to detest school by then (for different reasons), I still loved it when he asked me about it. He would question me on what I learned, what it meant, and what homework I had, just as he had when I was still just learning my English words. I liked that he still worked so hard to encourage my curiosity and education. It helped me focus on my studies a bit more, even though dating and friends were far more exciting and had already begun pulling me away.

Gary wanted the best for us. He wanted us to make smarter choices than he did in that he wanted us to be on the straight and narrow. Even though he may have had "unusual" business practices, he didn't drink. EVER. And the thought of his daughters being distracted with that type of nonsense just didn't seem like a concern for him. He expected—assumed—better of us. I suppose that is why I worked so hard to hide it from him. If I let Gary down, it would crush me.

Having an excellent education was expected. Gary would make me vow to focus and do better. "You're the smartest one, Nicole. You have so much potential. I know you can do better," he would say, partially scolding me but mostly encouraging me with his pure belief that I was meant for something more.

He recognized my rebellious attitude and looked at it differently than anyone else. He saw it as leadership potential. He would tell me, "If only you could use your amazing leadership skills for positive change, you would be amazed at what you can create and the impact you can make!"

His words always made me vow (and want) to do better.

"I promise, Daddy!" I would say, and for a few moments, I would forget who I was and how damaged I was. But soon, reality came crashing back in, and I knew the vow was going to be broken.

My demons would start to try pulling me under, offering me escape and relief in the worst ways. And they were way stronger and louder than anything he ever said.

Once Daddy settled himself in the living room, he would turn on his six plasma television screens displaying various sports games, news updates, and his favorite entertainment shows like *CSI*, *Law and Order*, and *Desperate Housewives*.

The bedtime routine for the twins began around 7 p.m., and I often found myself getting involved, reading them stories, and tucking them in before 8 p.m. It made me feel good to take care of them. These were normal family things to do, and I felt normal doing them.

After helping the nannies with the twins' bath time, I would sit down and rock each of them with their own bottle. We would watch *Bear in the Big Blue House*. I had all the songs memorized, especially the farewell song. I sang softly in their ears as they swallowed the milk in their bottles so quickly. The twins were the biggest part of my daily peace, and they didn't even know it. Hell, I didn't even know it at the time, either.

SEX BY CHOICE

When my siblings were down, I'd fill my thermos and race to the bedroom to text with Leo. Leo was the first guy I lost my virginity to (by choice) and my first serious boyfriend.

Leo and I went to Javier's house (my sister's boyfriend at the time) for an end-of-the-week Friday night party. Leo wore jeans and a black tank top that showed off his muscular arms. He was definitely the best-looking guy at the party. Pretty much the entire high school population was there. Plus, me. An eighth grader. The only reason I was even allowed at the party was because it was clear that I wasn't like any other eighth grader. I had money, I dressed and looked older than my peers, I drank, and I was dating a very popular, very hot senior in high school. Plus, my sister was dating the other most popular guy in school, who also happened to be Leo's best friend.

A NEW LIFE

I was wearing skinny jeans, Converse, and a casual top. My hair was down with a natural wave. The only makeup I wore was heavy eyeliner beneath my eyes (a CoCo signature look).

Leo and I drank, flirted, danced, and made out. He looked so gorgeous that I couldn't keep my hands off of him. He had a beard at the time, which I loved. It made me want to run my fingers through it. When it was clear that we couldn't get enough of each other, we went into another room. I ran my hands over his body and immediately wanted more.

"Sexy Movimiento" by Daddy Yankee was playing somewhere in the background. I could hear it through the buzz of countless rum and cokes. The alcohol put me at ease, and I felt safe.

"Are you sure we're allowed to be doing this here?" I asked breathlessly, worried that Javier would get pissed off but also wanting more.

"I already cleared it with Javier," he said as we got undressed.

I hadn't been planning to have sex that night, but it was clear that Leo had.

"You're so wet," he roughly whispered.

I was always wet, always craving sex.

We tore each other's clothes off.

"Are you sure?" he asked me.

"Yes, I'm sure." I didn't want to stop. This was my first consensual sexual sex. It didn't hurt. I felt safe. It felt good. It gave me the escape I had been yearning for.

We heard a creak in the floorboards outside of our room, so we decided we'd better get back to the party. We both slipped back into our clothes and returned to the crowd downstairs, both wearing big smiles on our faces. We danced and kissed and reveled in the glow of sex and alcohol.

And once I experienced sex on my own terms, I had to have it. I craved it.

Leo and I met most often during school breaks. That was our

way of spending more time together and for me to get away from my middle school life for a little while.

Once noon approached, I'd shoot him a quick text:

COCO: *Gate?*
LEO: *Already here, baby.*

And like clockwork, there he'd be, leaning casually against the school entrance, looking effortlessly cool, even from a distance.

The chaos of lunchtime at my middle school cafeteria was a daily ordeal I opted out of. The endless tables filled with giggling students from my grade were a scene I didn't fit into. Most days, I didn't have the appetite to eat there anyway—it wasn't just about the food, but the sense of isolation amidst a sea of familiar faces.

The atmosphere across the street was an entirely different world. It was charged and more alive. Here, they were less afraid to break rules. Their laughter was louder, their conversations deeper, and even the way they moved seemed more defined and more secure. Stepping onto the high school grounds always felt like getting a sneak peek into a world I wasn't quite ready for but desperately wanted to be a part of.

Leo and I, sometimes joined by a friend or two of his, would queue up to place our orders. I insisted on covering the bill and held out my cafeteria card—an account that my parents automatically filled up every week with enough money to easily feed ten or more people. I'd insist on covering the bill. Not only did it make me feel more mature, but it was also a subtle attempt to buy some approval. I was, after all, an eighth-grader hanging around high schoolers. I didn't want Leo's friends to see me as the younger kid trying to fit in.

One of them, the "head" of the group, Umberto, just did not seem to like me, and that shut down my opportunity with everyone else from the crowd. You would think that my sister dating Leo's best friend Javier and another one of the group would make it easier, but these fuckers wanted nothing to do with an eighth grader.

After lunch, the journey back to my school felt like a trip back in time. I could feel my classmates' eyes on me, their glances a mix of curiosity, envy, and judgment. They didn't understand, and I didn't care to explain. I walked with my head held high, my confidence fueled by the stolen moments just shared with Leo.

We had a lot of fun together but were only together for six months. Leo was leaving Costa Rica to go to college, and I felt like I was drowning in secrets, doing my best to hide the real version of myself and a lifetime of baggage that came with me. Leo knew some of what was going on, but I couldn't tell him all of it. He offered to stay for me, but truthfully, as much as I wanted him to, he would have been giving up his future for someone who was more messed up than he would ever know. I wished I could have been different for him, but it would have been too much pressure. I was facing my past with my father and my trauma-induced hypersexuality. Adding to my secrets, I had begun binging food throughout the day and then throwing it up in guilt and shame afterward. Bulimia was yet another side of myself that I was trying to hide. Eventually, the secrets created too much distance between them. I found myself lying about many (so many) more things. Leo despised lying. I mean, who didn't? And he deserved better. We decided it was best to break up before we made a complete shit show out of the relationship and ended up hating each other.

I wished I knew then what I know now about myself and why I did the things I did. Maybe it could have been different.

After Leo and I were done, I spent my weeknights Skyping with Daniel and Sebastian. I felt good talking, giggling, and flirting with them, all of which was made a lot easier with the help of my freshly made signature drink.

Daniel and Sebastian were my support system, my lifeline. I couldn't get through the day without them. They were best friends to each other and had grown to become my best friends, too.

Sebastian was my boyfriend as far as he and everyone else was concerned. He was sweet, he adored me, and I loved him for that. He didn't like that I drank. He would try to keep me talking in hopes that it would slow down my drinking. If he annoyed me enough, I'd hang up on him and call Daniel.

Daniel had complex family issues like mine. He carried the weight of public scrutiny on him. His father had been charged with a crime he didn't commit, and it was everywhere on the news.

Our classmates' parents forbid their kids to socialize or be friends with Daniel after the lawsuit. I could relate. And I didn't give three shits about the rumors swirling around his family. Honestly, neither did my family. With my mother in the spotlight (for her beauty and her television career) and a father who was renowned for his wealth and power, people's eyes and their judgment were often on me wherever I went.

It was hard to find ways to be with Sebastian in person. His parents didn't like me coming over, and his mom would complain if he was Skyping me too much. His mom never liked that "supermodel Lynda Diaz" was my mom. You see, my mom was loved by every single husband and gossiped about by everyone else.

Sebastian's family was straitlaced and Jewish, and here he was, spending time with a wild child from a family they didn't trust. Sebastian tried to fight his mom on this, but it was definitely one of our biggest issues. So, at first, I didn't get to see him as often. But he was so handsome, so romantic, and head over heels for me, making me fall hard for him.

Daniel's household was much more casual and came with a lot more privacy. He lived in a big, white, beautiful mansion on a hilltop with his dad. My parents, including Carlos, all got along with his dad, so going over to his house was something I was allowed to do during the week. Daniel was more of the well-behaved, rule-following guy that everyone thought was too good to be "corrupted by that crazy CoCo" so it all seemed safe.

As we started to spend more time together in person and through Skype, we got really close. Going over to Daniel's became an easy, safe escape for me. I felt fully safe with Daniel in that I trusted him not to reject, judge, or hurt me. Although Daniel lost his virginity to me, we were never serious. Sex was just something we did casually to fill a need—no strings attached.

He made his own rules most of the time. It was easier for me to visit. So, when Sebastian wasn't available and I needed sex, Daniel was there. I think Daniel knew he was a convenience, and he was okay with that. He wanted it, too. We enjoyed each other's bodies when no one was looking. That was all. The rest of the time, we were best friends, or at least I would like to believe we were.

Whatever happened with Daniel, my feelings for Sebastian weren't diminished. I guess I was greedy to want them both, but sex was a need for me. Like air. Like food.

I knew Sebastian deserved so much better than to have his girlfriend and best friend running around behind his back. I don't think he allowed himself to see how fucked up I truly was. Sex meant something different to me than to everyone else. I felt like I had a neon warning sign hanging around my neck, but Sebastian didn't see it.

I could feel the change in my behavior and decision-making from the moment I had sex with someone that I *chose* to have sex with. It's like once I realized I could be in control of it, choose when to allow people to love me—people who weren't forcing themselves on me—everything changed.

IT'S ALWAYS SOMETHING

The morning after an evening of Skype calls with Sebastian and Daniel, I often woke up with my stomach lurching and my head pounding.

Fucking mierda. Ow.

I stuck my hand out of the fluffy duvet to reach for my water, but there was none left.

Fuck. Could it be any worse?

My stomach hurt. My body never did like alcohol. It felt hot. Angry. Painful. I grabbed my hairdryer and flipped it to cold air, which would give me immediate release of the inner boiling sensation I woke up with. My body, especially my stomach, has been trying to talk to me my entire life. I just wasn't listening.

Once the ache subsided, I'd have a shower, jump into the bed, and dry beneath the covers, naked, with the dryer set to hot this time. The blankets filled with warm air and surrounded me like a hug. I closed my eyes and soaked up the heat.

I wanted nothing more than to cocoon myself away like that, buried in a sea of plush, warm blankets, and avoid the world for a bit longer.

I reached for the phone on my bedside table. "Manuela," I said in a low voice so as not to hurt my own head. "Can I have a papaya smoothie for breakfast? In bed, please."

"*Buenos dias*, my Nicolita. I'll make it right away," she'd say.

"Thank you, Manuelita. You are the best," I'd say, grateful to have her in my life.

She'd appear shortly after with my liquid breakfast and sit on the side of my bed. When I felt sick, she caressed my back and my head. Sometimes, if I was sad or couldn't sleep at night, she'd lay down next to me just to keep me company.

Eventually, she would be one of the maids who stole from my parents (which wasn't difficult; there was money everywhere in our house, rooms, drawers, and shelves). But I know she loved me anyway. I have kept my loving memories of Manuela separate from the theft issue I was told about.

As I sipped back my smoothie, I could hear my mother's vivacious voice in the hallway. She was talking to Daddy, the staff, or my siblings, maybe about the day's schedule or where she was headed off to. As she approached my room, I heard her Jimmy Choo heels clacking on the tile floor.

"Nicole!" she exclaimed and swept into my room without knocking. Her expensive perfume, Samsara, breezed in after her. "Why are you still in bed?!" she asked, not knowing (or maybe pretending not to know) that I was hung over. "You should already be up and getting ready!" She waved her hands around emphatically as if to motion for me to get up. "Every day it's something new with you."

I sank down deeper into my bed and toward the loud, hot hair dryer, trying to block out her voice.

"I don't feel good, Mami ..." I moaned.

"You're never happy in the mornings, and you never say good morning. It's horrible manners, Nicole."

She opened the curtains, which let in enough light to make my head feel like it was being squeezed in a vice.

"Why do I have to be the first to say good morning, Mami. Or pretend to be happy and smile when I'm not happy?" I'd ask in exasperation.

She'd ignore my questions. "I don't know why you are so disrespectful. I'm raising a *mocosa*!" *Mocosa* is Spanish for brat.

I sat up and watched her check her makeup and outfit for flaws in my full-length mirror.

We seemed angrier at each other in the mornings. I hadn't had a chance to fill or spike my thermos yet, so dealing with my mother's disappointment in me was not in the cards.

I bit my tongue to prevent myself from blurting out something I would regret. This was something I had become good at throughout the counseling appointments my mother had agreed to send me to. They were one of the first attempts by my family to find an explanation for my anger and behavior.

She returned to Linda and the twins, and I got ready.

By 7 a.m., I was in the car, with my uniform proudly displaying the embroidered words "CoCo" on my right sleeve in my favorite color turquoise. My last names then were Solano-Diaz. In Latin America, people usually use two last names: first their father's and then their mother's. I was often called by my last name, Solano, in school.

While most of my peers at school would wear the pants required by our school dress code, I flaunted dark blue American Eagle jeans—my little act of rebellion. On my feet were either my worn-out Converse

All-Stars or black and white checkered Vans, depending on my mood. Tucked neatly inside my Gucci tote (which I preferred to any standard backpack) was a note "from my mother" excusing my fashion choices for the day (I had become an expert at doing her signature).

As the car pulled away from the mansion, I smirked at my small fashion victories and minimized the dread of another day at school with a big sip from my thermos.

BLUE KAMIKAZES

By the time it was finally my turn to go to high school, I was already way ahead of the class in every manner of the word. High school was a whole new battleground. The whispers grew louder, but I had earned them. Teachers exchanged pointed glances when I passed, exchanging similar thoughts of contempt and distrust toward me. They knew what I was notorious for. And their vigilance around me was palpable.

"You're on thin ice," Mrs. Anderson, my grade 9 English teacher, once warned after a particularly wild weekend, her eyes narrowing as she spoke. "You might be smart, but don't think you can just slide by on your parents' name or your little … gatherings." The teachers and parents hated me because their kids were spending weekends getting shitfaced at my parties.

My parties were known by just about everyone from grades 9 to 12 in my school.

Van Gogh was my bar of choice, at least in the beginning. I got to know the owner, Moshe, very well, and he would let me slide in the kids from my school despite them being underage. And not just a few. I mean, I would help over a hundred kids get in. He welcomed the money he knew I would spend while I was there. His bar would make an entire weekend's worth of bar sales in just one CoCo-style party night. The students of Country Day School would take up the entire VIP room.

I'd buy drinks for everyone and circulate forty or fifty cups at a time filled with liquor of all different kinds. Before anyone arrived,

A NEW LIFE

I'd already pre-ordered fifty trays worth of blue kamikaze shots for everyone so they'd be ready to get passed around, along with five more trays of Jäger shots, Miguelitos, and Mamaditas. As people piled into the bar, everyone would get served and get wasted. They had fun when I was around. We danced and drank and made out or found dark corners to do other things. I wanted to be known as the life of the party. I wanted to be accepted and looked up to.

Even my brother came to Van Gogh with his friends.

Come Friday, my phone would be blowing up with calls and texts from people wanting to get into the party. Everyone wanted to get a shot, get in the VIP room, and get drunk for free. I would dance and smoke hookah all night with all the people who I know talked shit about me behind my back. I mistakenly thought these parties would make them want to get to know me—the real me.

Friday and Saturday, I was on top of the world. I had value, I was wanted, I was cool. On those nights, I was accepted, but come Monday, I could count on one hand how many real friends I still had. It was a blow to the stomach that sent me spiraling into a black hole of depression.

Worse, because I was wasted, hooking up, fighting, and fucking up in front of half my school on the weekends, my behavior would be fuel for rumors throughout the week at school. I was everyone's favorite topic of conversation.

When I wasn't partying, I was getting in physical fights with whatever bitch had offended my friends (I've always been a very loyal, very protective friend) or my family. As much as I argued with my mother, if someone else said something nasty about her, I lost it. If people said something about my mom, it would usually be something along the lines of, "She's a ho that only shows her ass," or, "She only married Gary for the money. She's a sugar baby."

My rule was to hit hard so no one could hit you back. I made sure to know the owner of wherever I was—whether it was Van Gogh or another bar of my choosing—so that they'd have my back.

And those fights got worse as I got older. Alcohol brought out the rage in me if anyone dared step in my way.

I remember one time I choked this girl Cristina that used to be my friend but fucked my best friend's boyfriend behind our back and called my mom a prostitute. I went crazy on her. The school would bash me for it. I didn't feel bad or ashamed. Simply very fucking angry.

When I got in trouble for fighting, my mom would get so mad.

"How could you do such a thing?!" she would yell. "People will think Lynda Diaz is raising a crazy daughter!" Anything that had to do with a negative public image was a big no-no for her.

I soaked up the attention and temporary popularity that my parties brought me. I loved having all eyes on me. It felt like being bathed in acceptance and friendship. I enjoyed that so many people wanted to know what I was planning and where I would be.

It gave me an exhilarating high that drowned out some of the darkness—until I was home again, curled up in bed, the world spinning, and my heart breaking as I came to terms with the fact that most of my school just used me to get what they wanted … and I asked them to. *What was wrong with me?*

Some nights, I passed out in my clothes, sometimes I fell asleep crying, and many nights, I was filled with so much fury or frustration at myself that I dragged my perfectly manicured, very sharp nails across my chest, causing immense pain and relief. When I look at photos from those years, my eyes go directly to the bright red lines of angry skin and small scabs that gave away my self-punishment practices.

Aside from scratching open the skin on my chest and arms, I also burned myself. It was a practice that began by accident when I touched the metal grate of my hair dryer to my skin, leaving four extremely painful red burn lines behind. The burning and scratching of my skin were the two primary methods of self-harm that could be done in my moment of desperation and pain. Sometimes, it felt as if I could scratch the skin off my chest; maybe then I could breathe again. But it never worked. The hair dryer burns were exhilarating. They would take my pain to an all-time high, giving me a shock that would calm me down when nothing else worked. These became marks that others—teachers, friends, family members, and my mother—recognized after years. Every single one of them boiled it down to a call for attention—a desperate cry from someone who had no reason to complain and no reason to be in pain. I look back on this and I just can't comprehend how they didn't see my pain. Why would they have thought it was just all fake? It all just meant I was lonelier. And no one was going to save me. No one.

I dove deep into a cycle of binge drinking, hooking up, surviving hangovers, and other ways of harming myself.

It got to the point that if I was alone, I would have to be drunk, or I would be manic.

The point is, Monday came around, and I felt used, alone, hungover, depressed, and a little crazier.

FIGHTS & FUCKUPS

Dating both Daniel and Sebastian at the same time meant they inevitably found out the truth. Once inseparable, now they had a rift between them with my name on it. Their cold stares were a reminder of the path of damage that my cheating on Sebastian with Daniel had left behind.

The hushed conversations, the side glances—it all seemed like the world was betting on my downfall. And so was I.

A voice in my head repeatedly told me, "These people don't want you here."

It felt like I was trapped in a tornado of my own making, and as I spiraled, those around me were sucked into the vortex. Relationships became transactional—using and being used. Money, power, anger, control—they became tools in my arsenal, weapons to guard against vulnerability.

But in the pursuit of love and validation, I unknowingly sacrificed authenticity.

It's the one thing I wanted more than anything else—to be able to be me, be authentic, be the real CoCo, and still be accepted. Yet every day that passed, every fight, hookup, drunken fuckup, lie, betrayal, or hurt that I inflicted or received, erased another piece of me, one by one, until all that was left was an image I never wanted but couldn't seem to stop chasing.

How could I stop something when I didn't even know how or why it had begun in the first place? So, the unraveling of my soul continued, and I just let it happen. I toasted to popularity as the real me disappeared.

I became so good at being this different version of myself that it got to the point that when I looked at myself in the mirror, I couldn't tell who the real me was anymore. I had erased her. Scratch that. I slowly killed her.

When I was alone, my self-harm frequency increased. I would lock myself away in my bathroom and burn myself with the hair dryer more often, holding it to the skin on my leg for as long as I could—one place, and then another, and another, leaving scars that would last for years.

I have to imagine that many of the friends I partied with saw that I was destroying myself, but they didn't want to say anything for the risk of getting themselves cut out of the party scene. Yet, beneath the surface of every self-destructive act was just a five-year-old girl, trapped in time, making a desperate attempt to escape.

For me, the worst moments were when the hazy buzz went away, the music stopped, and the lights came back on.

I knew I was blessed in ways that others would have given anything for. From the outside, I must have looked like a spoiled, rich girl who was busy trying to blow up her life. I had money and a beautiful home. I had the fairytale. But the reality of it all was that my heart had been broken for a long time. Then my image. Then my family. In reality, the mansion felt like a beautiful prison.

Worse, I couldn't see through the haze of liquor that things were deteriorating between my mother and Gary. Maybe it was their age difference catching up with them or the fact that their personal interests and how they wanted to spend their time had dramatically changed. You could tell that the fairytale love story had ended, and my mother was dreaming of her next fairytale, while Gary fell into complacency, happy to stay home with the family and his wall of televisions.

I chose to stay in my own world—with the help of alcohol, drugs, sex, and parties—believing in the fantasy and stories I created in my head. But my refusal to look at what was unfolding before me didn't stop the reality of what was about to happen.

For reasons that I can't get into right now, my mom and Gary's divorce was heartbreaking, not so much for the fact that it *had* ended, but more due to *how* it ended.

CHAPTER THREE

GOODBYE GARY

It all blew up. In the blink of an eye, the only true father figure I'd ever had was walking away. Catastrophic changes take only seconds, but I hadn't seen it coming so quickly. My mother and Gary were getting a divorce. Everyone was devastated. I adored Gary and I couldn't imagine life without Gary in it. No one had ever been there for me so consistently as he had. While I was busy screwing up my life, the only constant was being able to go home at the end of the day.

I felt sad for Gary, too. I could see that he was sad and angry.

When my mother saw how upset Linda, the twins, and I were, it was almost as if she was confused, as if she wanted to ask, "What's the matter?" As if dads are just interchangeable. The same man that seven years beforehand, she encouraged my sister and me to embrace, to love, and accept, she was now encouraging us to let go of and move on from.

My mother found a new apartment and we were moving. Out of Gary's mansion and into a new life our mother was creating for us.

"Just think, there will be no more guards, no bars on the windows ..." she said.

The thought was a little bit encouraging, but we loved Gary and would miss him.

"I deserve to be happy," she explained. "I deserve to be with someone who likes to go out and enjoy life, and someone who can travel." At that point, Gary was having issues with his passport and couldn't travel.

I wanted my family to be together but also, I was old enough to know and understand that the things she said were missing, were actually missing.

Everyone deserves to be happy, in my opinion. So, I tried to prep my heart for the change that was about to unfold.

Every time I started to feel at ease about the change, I would think of Gary being alone in his big house without us and tears would start to stream down my face.

My mom hyped up the idea of our new home in a gated community. "Nothing will change. We will have each other. You can still see Gary whenever you want," she told us. That was the part that made me feel like I could handle this change. As long as I got to keep Gary as a father …

We somberly packed up our things. We had long outgrown the circus-style playroom but were still sad to leave it behind. We took things that didn't matter—clothing, tech, accessories—and left behind the man who had loved us unconditionally for the best part of our lives.

We unpacked and settled into the new house over the course of a few days. I had gone from my beautiful prison to all the freedom in the world. But with freedom came the sad reality that my mom had started to date. I didn't feel ready for a new father figure in my life. Andres, her new boyfriend, started sleeping over a lot. Within three weeks, he was moving all his shit into our house. I am pretty sure the quick transition is part of what broke Gary. And my heart broke for him.

We never had our new beginning with Mom. We immediately needed to share her with Andres. We went from living in a mansion with guards to having all the freedom in the world, and yet I often found myself longing for my old reality with Gary.

It wasn't long before I hated Andres—not because of who he was, but because of his relationship with my mother. It was volatile and destructive. They would either be head over heels in love and partying every night – she was so free and happy in those days - or they would be fighting. Like really fighting. Screaming mean, cruel things at each other. Sometimes it would even get physical. Once it got bad enough, she kicked him out, put guards at the door to keep him away, and then spent days in bed out of grief over the breakup. She swore never to spend another minute of her time with him. Life at the house would start to become normal, and then Andres would show up again and it would start all over again. Linda never saw any of this, because she was preoccupied with her boyfriend and soaking up the last six months she had in high school in Costa Rica before moving to LA for college. She was there, but she was already mentally checked out. Even though she did try to fight back when she noticed the culture had become dark between Mom and Andres, Linda did what she did best; stay quiet and keep the peace.

Mom went from ecstatic and blissful to the depths of despair. It just depended on the day. And the twins and I were stuck in the middle. I started becoming both sad for my mom and angry at her. When she was sad, I would try to take care of her and make her happy. When she was happy and in control of her life, I would escape and go find my joy at parties and with boys.

With my increased freedom, I started drinking and partying more than ever before. There was nothing and no one to stop me anymore. No guards, no rails across the windows, and little to no supervision.

After one of my mother and Andres' biggest fights, they split up yet again. Not just for a day or two that time, but for a while. Mom declared that she, Linda, and I would all be going on a cruise together. Finally, we'd have the girls-only time we had been hoping for.

I was so excited to have more of my mom and sister to myself. It was an insane vacation. We tanned, swam, talked, drank, and partied. At least during the times that she left her phone out of sight. Andres has started texting and calling Mom, making her feel guilty for having fun without him. They'd argue and then my mother would be sad and distracted.

But because I was under eighteen, according to ship rules, I wasn't allowed to go out of my room or be seen wandering around after a certain curfew—and I definitely wasn't permitted in the nightclubs or casinos that Mom and Linda were going to.

The age issue divided our activities. In the evenings, it ended up being Mom and Linda going out, leaving me to entertain myself with my new teenage friends. It was one of the first times I spent time with kids my own age, because they, too, were on their own while their families enjoyed the ship's nightlife.

I wasn't about to be on a cruise and not party like my mom and sister. If we were at home, we would have been partying together. So instead, I did what CoCo does best; I paid for food and drinks for all my new cruise friends and came up with mischievous hiding spots so that we could have parties with our own rules—curfew or no curfew. Everything was charged to my room. I knew what I was doing wasn't right but at this point, it had become a habit I couldn't seem to stop.

After the cruise, my mom got the bill which included the astronomical amount of extra charges I'd run up. Once we were back home, I could tell things were going to be bad. My mother had already managed to forgive him and get back together with him, yet again. He was asking where she was while I racked up charges, and she knew the answer would upset him.

So instead, the conversation became entirely focused on me.

I could hear my name coming from their heated discussion in the other room. I heard Andres say, "Lynda, you need to see that Nicole is completely out of control! If you don't put some limits on that girl, it's all just going to get worse!"

"I know she's out of control, but I also don't have proof of—"

"You don't *need* any proof. The fact that there's money missing from your purse is enough! When are you going to stop letting this little girl disrespect you?!"

I could hear my mom go downstairs to call Carlos and tell him about the situation.

I frantically opened my door and ran as fast as I could down the stairs, enraged by the version of the story I could hear her telling him.

I scream at her, "You're lying! That's not the way things went down so *stop lying*!"

"I swear, I'm going to beat this girl," she said into the phone while staring at me with fury in her eyes.

Seeing her so disappointed in me and looking at me with such disgust, froze me in my tracks for a moment. It was one of the first times I'd seen that look on her face, but it wouldn't be the last.

Before I knew it, all my feelings—hurt, disappointment, rejection, shame—turned into pure rage.

"If you feel like you want to fucking hit me so bad then fucking do it! Hit me!" I screamed as I stepped toward her, getting inches away from her face.

I heard the smacking sound before I saw her hand move. She was fast and angry. I just glared at her, refusing to acknowledge the pain that was spreading over my cheek.

"I want to fucking leave this house," I blurted out.

"Carlos, you need to come get your daughter. I don't want her in this house."

I found myself furiously packing my shit and feeling heartbroken because my mother was so, *so* angry with me. I also knew that when my mom was mad at me, everyone on her side of the family would be made to be angry too, even my sister. I knew I wouldn't be seeing the twins again anytime soon. Not without going through my mom first.

Andres, who had been texting my mother throughout the cruise, trying to get her to come back to him, clearly succeeded in his efforts. He was moving back in as I was moving back out.

* * *

I know how messed up it is to write this down in black and white (NOTE: although that's *not* how I feel about it now), but when I was at Carlos's house, I felt safe from judgment and ridicule. It felt like that place—once a source of horror—had now become a real home, separate from the one in my memory. I was blind to the damage he had caused and focused on how it felt to be with him now. I had a curfew, rules, and support.

I lived with him several times in high school when my mother and I were fighting. There was no one to subtly imply that I was an embarrassment, or to look at my "trouble areas" when they talked to me to make sure I knew they could see my flaws. There were no comments about how a skirt hung off my curves, implying I needed to lose weight or change.

Instead, Carlos offered support. "How can I help you, Nicole? Do you want a personal trainer? Do you want me to go on a diet with you?" He was willing to be there for me in any way that I needed. And he wasn't offering this because he agreed that I was fat. He just wanted to help me see myself as beautiful and to strive to be healthy. It felt like he saw me for me.

* * *

The first time I met Juan in person, I made an impression. I walked into the bar area of the high-end restaurant where he was waiting for me. I'd only seen a photo of him before that day, but I knew I wanted him to see me as a powerful, sexy, grown woman.

He was sitting at the bar with a Long Island iced tea. I remember walking past Juan in my brand new, super cute, super short BCBG baby-doll-style dress with lavender flowers, silver 3.5-inch Gucci heels, and my sky blue Balenciaga city bag. Both the dress and the heels showed off my long legs. I hopped up onto a barstool beside him.

"Hey Johnny," I said to the bartender and winked at him. I put a ten thousand colones bill on the bar (the equivalent of roughly twenty American dollars).

"*Hola*, CoCo," he said, smiling mischievously as he poured me a Black Johnnie Walker on the rocks. He knew who I was, and he knew my go-to drink. I ordered a pack of Virginia Slims as Juan just watched in fascination.

"Wait, you know CoCo?" he asked Johnny.

"Of course, Juan," he laughed. "I've been taking care of CoCo and her family since we opened."

I was impressed that the bartender quite obviously also knew Juan. Having reputation and status enter the room before me was usually my thing.

"You must be Juan," I said and touched his muscular arm. He immediately smiled and tilted his head to the side as if to ask, "Who *is* this girl?"

I could tell that he liked that I was so forward.

I picked up my drink and looked at him. "Ready?"

We found a table where we talked, ate, drank, and flirted. He wore a tight button-down dress shirt with the top buttons undone like many Latino men did then. His smile was beautiful, and his teeth were perfectly white. He wore dark skinny jeans with a Ferragamo belt.

Leo had certainly never dressed like this man in front of me.

We had an amazing time. We talked about his family and how he had moved to Costa Rica from Colombia in search of a safer life. Families with wealth were better off—safer—living in Costa Rica at the time.

We talked about my family, our ex's, pretty much everything. I admired his silver Rolex, and he admired my Cartier. We had about seven Long Island iced teas and a couple of shots each. After four hours of some of the best conversations and connection I'd experienced in my life, I knew this was going to be something more someday. But I didn't want him to know that. I wanted him to take me seriously.

Once our date was over and the server brought the check, we both tried to grab it. The check was 75,000 colones (about $125 US). I wanted to show that just because other women in Costa Rica may not have been able to afford such a bill, I could. I didn't need to be indebted to a man. This was a signature CoCo move on first dates. I paid my own way, thank you. I was tired of how many men whined that dating was an investment for them, but that it wasn't for women.

At the end of the date, I'd decided I wasn't going to kiss him, but I wanted to give him a taste of who I was. I stepped close to him so that our lips were almost touching and looked him in the eyes.

"I know you're dying to kiss me right now, aren't you?" I asked.

He grabbed me by the waist to pull me in for a kiss, and within a second, I turned my head and kissed him on the cheek.

He seemed surprised.

"It's not going to be this easy for you," I said. "But you'll get your chance."

I shook my head, took his watch off of him, and swapped it for my Cartier.

"I'll make you a deal," I said as I closed the clasp of his Rolex around my wrist, "the next time I see you, we'll exchange watches and I'll give you a kiss."

It wasn't long before Juan and I got our watches back. Once we started seeing each other more seriously, we became inseparable. I met his mom, cousin, and younger siblings and started to grow close to them. I snuck out of school so that Juan could pick me up and we'd spend time together. We'd drink together, of course, but we'd also cook together and be there for each other. That time in my life was also the safest I've ever felt. It was good. Juan had been through a lot with his own demons, but together, we were both doing better than we ever did separately.

RACING

Living with Carlos was so different from living with my mother. He had different rules and he was very supportive of me. He would talk to me and listen to me. I don't know if it was a competition with my mother for my love, or if he was just trying to be a different, better, dad, but it was nice for me at the time.

Carlos had me make a deposition to say that living with my mother was harmful to my emotional health. In return, he would no longer be paying her child support for me, and he instead began building out a wing of the house for me so that I would have a big, beautiful area to live in.

My brother lived with Carlos when I moved in. He was still the golden child at Carlos's house. I tried to ignore the feeling that I was competing against my brother. Instead, I focused on being happy to have the chance to grow closer to Andre. It was nice. I missed him when I was at my mother's.

Andre spent most of his time racing Formula 2000 cars. I followed him to the track many times until he finally introduced me to the sport. Normally I didn't like sports, but *racing* was exactly my speed.

Once I felt the power and freedom of flying around the track at up to 150 miles per hour in open-air, open-wheel cars with nothing more than a helmet to protect my head, I was in love. He and Carlos offered to help me learn how to race. We had all grown up racing ATVs and go-carts around the property (which is how many racers get a taste for the sport), so racing felt like it was in our blood. I was starting ahead of most of the beginner drivers because of it.

So, while my mom and sister were working on their modeling careers, Andre and I were working on winning races. And let me tell you, racing was the best feeling in the whole damn motherfucking world. Beyond sex and alcohol, there is nothing else like it.

My brother was one of the best race car drivers in Costa Rica. Everyone knew him on the track. That meant there was some serious pressure on me to either prove myself or get off the track altogether. But Andre taught me well.

We would get up early in the morning and hit the track, then stay there all day to train. I studied every move he made and was captivated by every lesson he gave me. He had always been closer to my sister growing up, so I relished this time to build a closer relationship with him.

The first time I raced, it was just for practice. Carlos bankrolled my racing education, beginning with paying for me to get my seat molded to my body. The experience was similar to when you go to the dentist, and they make you bite into the plaster to get the exact dimensions of your teeth.

My brother gave me his old helmet, which meant a lot to me. He had won so many championships wearing that helmet that it felt like good luck.

Whenever I talked to my mom, I'd be filled with the excitement of the track and try to fill my mother in on the details. She was not impressed. She went from aloof to annoyed to angry.

She made the effort to come to one race. I hoped she would see how good at it I was and how happy it made me. But instead, she was disapproving. "Nicole, if I knew I was raising you to become a race car driver like some man, I would've cut you off completely a long time ago."

Oh, they know I'm not a boy, I thought.

It was just another reason for her to furrow her eyebrows and look at me as if I were someone else's child—surely switched at birth for a lesser, crazier version of a daughter.

Racing gave me such a feeling of power. It was an adrenaline rush. I worked hard to improve my skills. Inside my helmet, I had a microphone so that I could get messages from my pit team. Someone would wave a flag, signaling the start of the race. Getting off to the right start is everything. If you don't do that, you'll lose for sure.

Once I hit the gas, I would never look back. I never worried about how fast I was going or who was near me. There was a number on the dash that told me what gear I was in—first, second, or third—with a line that would show RPMs, so I'd know when to shift up or down without losing speed. But Andre taught me how important it was not to rely on a computer, and I understood why—computers can quit, leaving the driver in the dark.

It was easier for me to rely on my ability to listen to the sound and feel of the engine instead. It gave me more control. I didn't rely on numbers or lights to tell me what to do.

The car spoke to me. Roared at me. And I listened. I became

accustomed to the sound of the engine when it needed to switch gears. I never looked at the dash.

I just flew.

Once I started racing, everyone could see I showed promise. I could see it, too—and I wanted more. I could feel Andre's excitement toward teaching me begin to falter a little bit. Racing was everything to him and my participation potentially ran the risk of lowering his budget to fit the expense of my being on the track too. Racing was expensive and Andre enjoyed being spoiled by Carlos. His lifestyle was fully bankrolled, complete with new cars when he wanted them. I didn't blame him for not wanting that to change.

On the day of my most significant race, a racer named Ben caught my attention. His eyes were dark and menacing and he winked at me when I looked in his direction, telling me everything I needed to know. I crushed my personal best in that race. It was exhilarating. It seemed only natural to go to the after-party.

I took Juan with me to the party, and we celebrated my victory. The drinks were free flowing and there were a variety of other substances to choose from.

As the night wore on, the world got blurrier, and I got happier. Ben looked me up and down several times and I knew I had it in the bag. He didn't seem to mind that Juan had his arm around me and his hand on my thigh. It was bold. Risky. When Juan left the room in search of another drink, I stood up, took a moment to find my balance, and then led Ben by the hand up the stairs.

About halfway up, I stumbled a bit. Ben caught me and I giggled.

We chose a room, locked the door, and got what we wanted—fast, hot release. When it was over, Ben zipped up his fly and I was immediately disgusted with myself. My stomach lurched and I had to take long breaths to keep myself from emptying it there on the floor.

"Um, are you okay?" Ben watched me awkwardly.

Tears started streaming down my face. Ben didn't know what to do and he didn't sign up for that, so he left me there. I was fine with that. I was done with him.

What was I doing?! I hated that I could let someone be so close to me—literally on top of me—and still feel empty.

I had lost my grip on my life and reality and was now busy trying to lose Juan, even though I loved him. I was destroying everything, including myself. *And I could not stop.*

I stumbled downstairs, looking for Juan, only to find he had taken off. I somehow made my way home, locked myself in my room, and found my hair dryer.

Each burn sent excruciating pain and simultaneous release all at once. It was punishment for my actions. No one was harder on me than myself.

I could feel myself spiraling, my actions chaotic and unmanageable, screaming silently for someone, anyone, to pull me up from the abyss.

Finally, about nine months into racing, my mom forbade me to continue. She said it was too dangerous and it gave people the wrong impression. "CoCo, people will think you're a man," she said. "It's not what properly represents a Diaz." She pulled the plug on the only thing I had learned to love more than being intoxicated.

My mother wanted me to come home. Carlos had just finished building my new room as he promised.

"You need to come home," my sister said. "I don't want Mom to be alone with the twins when I'm gone to college."

I was also fighting with Carlos's current arm candy. She wore my clothes when I was out and used my purses without asking, and Carlos allowed it.

But the biggest reason I went back to Mom's was that Andre was doing so much coke and partying, I was getting caught up in it. I ended up doing it right alongside him. Sometimes I'd wake up in the morning and not remember how I got home the night before.

That was the first time I truly worried about my brother. That was the first time I was introduced to a whole other level of substance use and the manipulation and lying it took to not let anyone on the outside, including our parents, find out. If they had known what we were doing, would there have been repercussions? Would we have lost it all or would they have turned a blind eye because drugs and alcohol were as much a part of the culture of Costa Rica as the beautiful landscape?

Although Andre's friends were getting wasted and crashing cars—one passed away and left his friend in a wheelchair—Carlos couldn't or wouldn't see any of it.

Things were out of control. I had to get out of there.

FAMILY

Once I had moved back in with Mom, it wasn't long before Linda was off to FIDM (fashion design school in LA). She was excited to start her whole new life and I was excited for her. She was moving into her first beautiful apartment complete with a new convertible Lexus. Her future lay ahead of her, a blank slate. One I desperately wanted for myself as well. I was proud of her for breaking free and pursuing her dreams. I was still in high school, doing online learning, living with my mom who was now engaged to Andres (yet still caught in an endless loop of dating and breaking up with him).

I couldn't even stand to be in the room with Andres. He was bad for my mother. He would be all over her one moment and then cruel the next. Their fights were still huge and loud. And then she would forgive him, and it would begin again.

When they weren't broken up, my mother was out with Andres a lot. She would leave the twins with Juan and me. With me doing online school, it made it easy to spend time with Tiffany, Gary, and Juan. It was nice. It felt like we were a little family. It was what I had always wanted.

Similar to the dynamic between my mother and Andres, Juan and I could be toxic to each other at the worst of times and inseparable at the best of times. When things were good, they were really good. He was romantic, attentive, and fun. He knew how to make me smile and feel loved. He would rent a room at the most expensive hotel and have the floor and bed covered in rose petals. He had a way of taking my breath away and making me feel special. He would make me breakfast in the mornings, pick up my friends from school, and stay overnight at my house a lot on weekends. He had become a part of the family. He had even learned to love sleeping in a bed heated by my hairdryer.

Something we loved to do as a couple was travel together. Any chance we had for an escape such as a little weekend getaway, or a once-in-a-lifetime trip to Hawaii, we took it! We were together at all times. I couldn't bear to be away from him. He had become my safe place. Even when I drank, I knew he would be there to take care of me.

But when we were at my mother's house, Juan and I would take the twins to Tukis—it was like a Costa Rican version of Chuck E Cheese, and we had a blast playing on the machines. Then we'd all go to the movies.

Sometimes we would stay in and play Monopoly. It was the twins' favorite game, and I was the champion of the house at the game and the twins would always try to beat me at it!

My grandmother, Mamita, stayed overnight a lot when my mother was away on trips. She was very supportive that way. Mamita had always been full of life, carefree, an excellent cook, and just a warm loving person to have in my life. Despite the trauma that she had been through with my grandfather, she was still full of love.

We would spend time together playing cards and just sitting and talking for hours. Also, her rules were very casual so, being the crazy teenager that I was, I took advantage of that and did pretty much whatever I wanted to when she was "in charge." Once the twins were in bed, either Juan would be sleeping over or I'd be out getting drunk and partying with him.

I remember one day, my mother was on a trip to LA to visit my sister and my phone rang.

"Nicole Diaz?" It was Country Day School. I was on the emergency contact list for the twins so if they were calling, something bad had happened. I felt my heart pick up speed.

"Please tell me everything is okay!"

"Gary has been injured and needs to go to the hospital," they said. "He has hurt his arm. It may be broken."

My mother was a thousand miles away, Andres had moved out, and Gary wasn't reachable. So, Juan and I hopped into the car and sped to the school. When I saw Little Gary, his face was blotchy from crying, and he held his arm at an angle that told me it was most definitely broken.

"Oh, Gary! Look at what you did to yourself, sweetie!" I rushed over to his chair in the nurse's office. He looked so scared and innocent. I kissed him on the head and carefully led him out of the office and into the car.

It didn't take long to get to the hospital. When the car inevitably went over bumps in the road, he would let out little screams of pain and say, "Where's Mommy? I wish Mommy was here!"

My heart melted for him. "It's okay, Gary. I've called Mommy and she's trying her best to catch a flight back as soon as she can. She'll be here soon."

I was determined to make sure that he felt safe and taken care of, even without his mother.

"I'm sorry! I'm sorry!" I'd say, knowing that each pothole we drove over was jarring his little arm. "We're almost there, I promise!"

Juan and I stayed with him in the hospital and through the tests. We were told he needed surgery. My mother wasn't there to give consent, so she called Andres who, as a doctor, had connections at that hospital. That made things very awkward for me, but baby Gary didn't seem to mind. And here was Andres, my now stepfather, giving instructions on the care of little Gary.

The surgery went ahead, and by the time my mother arrived back from her trip, it was all finished and Gary was in recovery. She swept into the room and took over his care, leaving Juan and me to head home and leave our temporary parental roles behind us as if they had never happened.

REMEMBERING

The phone rang one night at the house I was living in with my mother. It was my sister. I was probably seventeen or so at the time. I was doing homework and was grateful for the interruption. Especially from my sister.

"Hi, Linda!" I answered, happy to hear her voice. I missed her. "How are you, sister?" I asked.

"CoCo, I have to tell you something." Her voice was weird. Something about the way she sounded made me feel sick to my stomach.

I fell back onto the couch with the phone in my hand. "Okay …"

"I saw a movie a little while ago that was about the sexual abuse of a child by her father. It triggered something in me. I remembered things. Awful things." I could hear that she had been crying.

I waited for more as memories of my own abuse flashed before my eyes.

"Then I started having panic attacks. I've been having them for a few months now." She was sobbing now.

"Why didn't you tell me?" I asked, immediately wishing I could hug her.

She continued: "And I know … why all of … this is … happening," she said, her words coming out in between sobs. I could almost feel the atmosphere shift. "Dad … I mean Carlos … sexually abused me when we were kids. He did it for a long time."

My heart stopped beating. I tried to parse together the memories of my sister being so completely adored by our biological father, with the fact that he had done this to her.

She began to share details. As she did, I felt the world start to spin before me. The more she talked, the more it became obvious that my father looked at his abuse of my sister as if it were some twisted romantic love affair he was in. His abuse of me was more as if it were a punishment for being bad.

Linda then proceeded to ask me if anything like that had happened to me with Carlos.

"Absolutely not, Linda. Never," I said adamantly. "Wait, don't say anything else. I need to get Mom," I said and called my mom.

"Nicole, what do you want?!" she yelled down. I'd woken her up. "It's Linda, you need to come to the phone."

I heard her footsteps as she raced down the stairs. She could tell by the panic in my voice that something was very wrong.

I handed the phone over and listened to her side of the conversation.

It felt like I'd forgotten how to breathe. I raced through my memories of our shared childhood, looking for signs and memories that would reveal how and when Carlos could have done this to Linda.

Tears and anger and then a hushed angry discussion followed between my mother and Linda. When my mom finally hung up the phone, she turned to me. "Did Carlos abuse you, Nicole?"

"No!" I snapped. For reasons I can't explain, I couldn't tell the truth. Even though this would have been the perfect time to confide in my mother, I didn't.

"I just want to go to sleep," I blurted out and headed to my bedroom.

I had put that part of my history far, far behind me, and tried to never think of it. Especially now that I was getting along with Carlos. The person who had abused me when I was five was not the same person that I knew as a seventeen-year-old young woman. I had completely compartmentalized his actions and behavior into another, different version of a human that was long gone, buried forever in the past. My visits to Carlos's house were fun. He supported me emotionally when I would fight with my mom. He supported my love of racing. I felt like I could talk to him about almost anything. Most of all, it was like now he loved me the right way. And I wanted that. I wanted that kind of relationship with him. Not the traumatic, abusive one.

I felt safe and loved now and keeping my abuse in the past kept it that way.

From my room, I called Juan. "You need to pick me up," I said, my voice quivering. "Like *right now*. I can't be here."

He could tell something was wrong and came right over. He likely assumed I had just had a fight with my mother.

I spent the night in Juan's bed, crying and shaking. He pulled me close and held me. "Everything will be okay … I promise," he whispered, his warm breath on my hair.

I never felt the need to get revenge for my abuse—maybe I didn't think I was worth it—but when I thought of Carlos abusing my sister, it made me furious and sick at the same time.

That night, my sister and my mom decided to sue Carlos, to hold him accountable for what he did to Linda.

She spoke with her lawyer, started proceedings, and one week later forbade me from ever seeing my biological father again. "And no more seeing or talking to Andre anymore either," she added.

"No, Mami! Why Andre?!" I asked, shocked. I loved my brother.

"You can't see Andre without it involving Carlos, so you can't see Andre." I could tell by her tone that it was not up for debate.

My mother didn't think Linda had any chance of being believed in court if I was still having a good relationship with Carlos.

The next morning, I woke up, still in Juan's arms. I went straight for the shower, turned the water on as hot as it would go, and stood beneath it letting it nearly scald my skin. I raked my nails across my chest and sobbed. Juan stepped in behind me, holding my arms to stop me from hurting myself and kissing the back of my head. We stood there for a long time before finding solace in each other's bodies. Then I texted Andre and arranged for a secret meetup at the community clubhouse where I lived. As much as I understood why my mom didn't want me to see Andre, I had questions I needed answers to. It was hard for my mom to understand that there was more than one life crumbling into pieces.

As soon as he got there, I filled him in on everything that had happened.

He just listened. His face was unreadable.

Then I realized why he looked so weird. "Did you *know* about this?" I demanded.

Andre looked at his shoes in shame.

"Andre, tell me!"

"Linda did say something to me once, but I didn't believe her … She was drunk when she told me. We were at a party and things were crazy. I just can't imagine my dad doing something like that …" He shook his head and looked nauseous. "Can you?"

I understood how good at manipulation Carlos was, so it wasn't a surprise to me that my brother, being the golden child, couldn't even picture the father he had on a pedestal, doing something of this horrible magnitude—especially to Linda."

I said nothing. We hugged and went our separate ways. I knew that was going to be the last time I'd be able to hang out with him for a long time. I had grown so close to him that it felt like I was losing a father and a brother on the same day.

As he walked away, I thought about the countless times that Carlos had beat the shit out of Andre and I when we were younger. Whether it was for something we did in school, for a lie we were caught in, or something else, I quickly learned to layer up when a beating was coming. Carlos would call on his way home, letting me know to meet him in his room. His voice would tip me off to what was coming. I'd run to my room and put on multiple layers of underwear and shorts, and multiple sweatshirts. That lessened the pain and bruises.

One time, he beat my brother in his room so badly that I had to plug my ears against the sounds of his screams. Carlos had used a belt. When Andre came down the stairs, he looked crushed and in agony. I'll never forget that moment.

We had both looked at Linda as the good kid. She never raised her voice. She had been the perfect daughter and yet her abuse went on so much longer than mine did.

I remember one of our favorite games to play was hide and seek. Carlos would count to ten as I screeched and scurried away to the furthest area of the house, burrowing deep into a closet or wooden chest or beneath a pile of blankets. I came to find out that he would abuse my sister during those times. She would hide in the attic and he would find her. We'd all be hiding, waiting, while my sister was suffering at the hands of Carlos.

Linda said there were weekends we would go to the beach. Carlos would rent a nice hotel room. Andre and I would be either playing on the beach or swimming in the pool, and Carlos would be abusing Linda in the hotel room.

If that happened to me, I don't remember it. My abuse was different. I don't wish anything bad on my sister. I love her to death. But the fact that my abuse seemed more aggressive, as if I were being punished, has messed with my head for a long time. What is so wrong with me that it made him want to hurt me, and be so brutal to me? What did I do to deserve that?

When I listened to my sister's accounts of what happened, I would try to comfort her and let her know how much I loved her. Several times, she asked me if Carlos had abused me. I always said no. My sister would give me a look. She had a knowing in her heart that would eventually be confirmed.

I wasn't ready. And also, I was the bad girl. I was known for misbehaving. It felt as if no one would believe me.

I wonder if my sister didn't tell me when we were a bit younger because she knew I'd tear things up, go to war for her. I was known for standing up for my friends. If someone ever needed me, I'd have their back, no questions asked. I couldn't help myself. If I saw someone in pain, I had to stand up. I would like to think that I stood up for others in the way that I wished someone had done for me.

CHRISTMAS

With my sister's abuse out in the open, things were raw and awkward with mom, with Linda, and with life in general. Especially because I kept my abuse to myself.

When Christmas Eve came around that year, it was just Juan and I alone. It used to be a cherished day for Linda, myself, and my brother to spend together with Carlos. Obviously, that had to stop once my sister revealed her abuse.

We were curled up on the couch when my phone rang.

When I heard Carlos's voice, it sent shivers down my spine. I hated that voice, loved that voice, missed that voice, and swore I'd never speak to that voice ever again. It was as if he was speaking to me from what felt like another dimension.

"I couldn't let our special date go by without me calling you," he said as if he was simply doing his family duty to keep in touch. "How are you doing?"

I didn't know what to say. It was as if he didn't realize that a world of litigation, betrayal, and trauma now separated us.

"I'm fine," I said, trying to sound emotionless. "You are not allowed to call me."

"It's Christmas Eve, CoCo," he used my chosen name for the first time. I could hear his false warmth hiding a world of things he wanted to say. "Come up to the house. Come see me," he suggested.

I wanted to know what he had to say about all of it. I wanted an apology. For me and my sister. I wanted my childhood back. I wanted him to be a normal dad.

I knew I wouldn't get any of it, but I went anyway. I felt a sick pain set in my stomach at the thought of keeping even one more secret meeting with Carlos to myself. I was tethered to my abuser and he knew it.

I told Juan about the call.

"Are you sure you want to go?" he asked.

"Yes …"

Juan asked, "Do you want me to come with you?"

I shook my head. "No. I need to do this by myself. I'm telling you just in case …"

I knew my brother would be there, so I didn't feel too afraid.

I drove up to his house in the mountains. Andre opened the door to greet me when I arrived. The second I saw him, I threw my arms around him and squeezed as hard as I could. I realized as I hugged him, just how much I'd missed my brother.

Carlos approached us to greet me. I looked at the floor as he said something to me. I don't think I heard a word he said. And I didn't hug him. He motioned for me to sit down.

I remember feeling like all the oxygen had been sucked out of the room. We awkwardly sat on opposite couches.

Why am I here? What can I possibly get out of this?

"Everything Linda has said is a lie, you know," he said. "I would obviously never be capable of doing anything like that." His face was expressionless. "It wasn't like that. She's not remembering the way things really were," he continued.

As he retold "his version" of history, I listened. "Your mom has always had a personal vendetta against me because of the way our marriage ended."

My heartbeat was deafening.

The way he spoke made his words sound so genuine. He was convincing, as he tried to gaslight me—reshape my memory of what actually happened into his version of it all. I started to panic that I'd accidentally remember everything horribly, horribly wrong. I started running through a childhood's worth of horrific memories, searching for clues that I mistook what had happened for something more innocent. Carlos had me questioning myself, my own reality, my own sanity.

Did I make up all the abuse in my head?

Did I ask for it?

Did Linda?

Did it really happen? Was it just innocent hugs and kisses?

It was hard to comprehend how my biological father could be so sure and so adamant that it was all just a lie while looking at me straight in the face.

Carlos denied the abuse to his core—and still does to this day.

I got up, said goodbye to my brother—that was probably the last time I hugged my brother—and left.

I drove to Juan's house for my first Christmas Eve without my mom, Gary, Andres, the twins, my sister, or anyone. Juan's small family went to great efforts to create a peaceful, supportive Christmas Eve for me. I started wondering if I should even go to Aspen to see my family. I was trying to process what had just happened.

ASPEN

Things with Mom and Andres were falling apart and she was desperate to repair the relationship. Mom decided that this would be accomplished by moving to Aspen. It had been her dream to live in Aspen since vacationing there countless times and falling in love with the small town's skiing, fashion, and restaurants.

I probably should have felt abandoned by being left behind in Costa Rica, but I didn't. It was more of a relief than anything. With Mom away, I'd have less pressure to keep up with my lies and my behavior. I didn't want to be around her and Andres when they were fighting.

My mother put the clothing brand she had been building into my hands to either grow or shut down. She was done with it and had her sights on bigger priorities. She was focused on building a new life in Colorado with Andres and the twins.

Once she was gone, nothing was stopping me from doing anything and everything that I wanted to. I began to rely on my mom's business bank accounts to subsidize parties that would last for days, sometimes weeks. No amount of alcohol or drugs was enough. I don't know if I was trying to drown my memories or myself, but I was doing a good job.

I loved Juan beyond measure. In fact, I could envision spending my life with him, but I wasn't in a position to be planning my own future, much less anyone else's. I felt like damaged goods, and he was up against a lifetime of trauma.

We cheated on each other. First, Juan slept with my friend. Then, I slept with someone else.

Despite being equally guilty, if Juan dared to go out and not call or text me regularly, I would experience near-psychotic levels of fear of abandonment. Whether it was a meeting or something longer, I would lose my mind.

I'll never forget the way he looked at me in those moments. I hated myself when I saw my reflection through his eyes.

After those big fights, I couldn't sleep, petrified that I'd lose him.

I would call him forty times in a row, pouring nasty messages into his inbox. When he went to the Dominican Republic for a visit, there was no cell accessibility, and I couldn't handle it. I numbed my panic the entire time by spending it drunk, coked out, and Xanaxed—whatever it took to shut down my mind.

My misery and rage had little to do with Juan, but he was the one who would hear about it. I smashed things without any regard to meaning or expense, including throwing a vase at our television set.

This emotional roller coaster started creating distance between us. I could see him spending more time at his mom's house instead of sleeping over at mine every chance he got.

I started going every day, next door to a members-only cigar lounge, right next door to my mother's business.

I cheated on Juan even though he didn't deserve it. Juan found out when he walked in on me having sex with a man in our bed. We had gone partying the night before and I'd completely forgotten that Juan had called me to tell me he'd be stopping by to pick up his suit for a very important meeting that he had.

After three bottles of *aguardiente*, I didn't remember shit, not that Juan had called, and not that I likely should have locked the doors.

I clumsily untangled myself from the man (who meant nothing to me) as Juan slammed the door on his way back out of it. The man knew Juan's family and how much power they had. The second he saw him, I could tell he was scared shitless. Given that Juan hadn't killed him yet, he knew enough to grab his clothes and get the hell out of there.

I chased after Juan down the hall, begging him to come back so we could talk.

"This is what I walk into? This? I knew it! I knew you were doing fucking shit like this. You've been getting drunk and going out every single night. I'm not stupid!"

"Why is everything my fault? I ask you to go out and you don't want to go out. I bring you food and you don't want to eat it. I take you to the Four Seasons and you couldn't care less. What will be enough for you?!"

I looked at him square in the eyes and said, "You say you're not stupid, but neither am I."

Immediately I realized that there was nothing I could say or do at this moment to justify what I'd done. I felt myself start to shake with anger, a psychotic level of anger that I rarely experienced, but when I did, it was almost like a blackout—I was watching myself scream and behave with so much rage that I looked unhinged, and yet I couldn't control it. It was as if I were detached and watching it happen, without any control to stop it.

Juan yelled as he picked up random items as if to pack up and leave the house. I finally grabbed his arm to stop for a second. He spun around and looked at me. I couldn't stand the look of betrayal in his eyes.

"Juan! *Por favor!*" I begged for forgiveness. "I'm so sorry, babe! He's nothing to me!" And it was true. Juan meant everything to me.

Juan learned the hard way that my demons were too strong for me to keep my promises. He knew I would fail again and that it would crush him again.

CHAPTER FOUR

DOCTORS

Losing Juan destroyed me even though I deserved it. And without him in my life, even the smallest amount of accountability to myself or anyone else was lost with it. I partied every day, hooked up with strangers, and passed out at home when it was over. I felt nothing about the sexual encounters I had. They were a means to an end. Nothing more. My body was just a tool for escape and relief, disconnected from my heart or soul.

One morning, I woke up to the sun blaring through the window and felt my stomach roaring. I immediately sprinted for the bathroom and threw up over and over until I was just dry heaving. It wasn't the first morning spent that way by any means. But this morning, it felt worse than usual. My mind spun and there was a deafening ringing in my ears.

After what felt like a lifetime, I was able to stand up. I wiped my mouth with toilet paper knowing my breath must have been awful. But before I could brush my teeth, I threw the toilet paper into the bowl and looked down. The white tissue turned red. There was blood in the toilet.

It was the first time I saw physical evidence, beyond throwing up every morning or mid-bender, that my partying was killing me. I tried all my usual tricks—my hangover smoothies, the dryer-duvet cocoon of warmth—and I still felt awful. The guy I was with the night before, who had slept over, looked in on me in the bathroom. His eyes immediately went to the red-tinted water.

"Woah! That's not good, CoCo!"

I'd heard of people dying in their forties of cirrhosis of the liver from drinking and drugs. *But I'm young*, I reasoned with myself. *Only old people go down like this.* I thought I had more time before doing any real damage.

I made a deal with myself; to cut back on the partying a little bit.

But I didn't cut back. I kept going. Work, drinking, men, passing out, repeat. It got very bad, sending me to the hospital several times for I.V. fluids and medication.

Each time I got cleaned up, I left the hospital feeling hopeful and determined to do better at remaining sober. One night, less than twelve hours after being released from the ER, I texted Juan to ask if he would be willing to meet up. I felt like I had things that needed to be said.

He agreed and we met at one of our favorite restaurants, Il Panino.

He was there waiting for me when I arrived. He was in a light blue dress shirt and his usual dark-colored skinny jeans and Gucci shoes I had bought him. He looked good. After some small talk, we got into what really mattered. I wanted him to understand why our relationship had been crumbling down for months.

"I don't think you understand what was really happening …"

"Okay," he leaned back, picked up his Old Parr on the rocks, and crossed his leg. "Then help me understand.

I tried to find the right words to explain. "I've been spinning … everything with the lawsuit, losing one side of my family, and feeling completely rejected from the other—"

"I know. I've seen how much it has affected you. I don't know what else to do. I've been there for you. My family has been there for you—"

"Well, your family actually hasn't been there. With all my psychotic breakdowns, understandably, they have taken a step back. It's been uncomfortable to spend time together. So, no. I've lost your family too because I can't fucking control my emotions."

He leans forward and takes my hand, seeing my pain.

"Don't you see? I've lost it all. I'm alone. Completely alone." I looked down, trying to hold back my tears. "And I have nobody else to blame but me."

Sadness and guilt flashed across Juan's face. "I know I've also hurt you and taken a step back because I really don't know how to handle all of this. I don't know how to be there for you while still protecting my feelings. And it felt like your drinking was getting worse, you were going out every night, and nothing was going to stop you. My options were to watch you destroy yourself or pray that if I stayed home and avoided going down that rabbit hole with you, you'd still want to be with me. Clearly, I wasn't enough."

"Juan. Don't you get it? Nothing is enough."

I started telling him just how dark things had become.

By the end of our discussion, Juan made it clear that he would always love me and knew he was never going to find someone like me again. And I was clear that I was never going to find someone like him again either.

As we hugged and said goodbye, Juan whispered in my ear, "You will forever be my wife." It was something he used to say to me on our best days together and something I'll never forget.

I walked out of Il Panino and headed back into the eye of the hurricane, 9N (9 North), a members-only cigar bar. That bar was the death of me. It was the beginning of my end in Costa Rica.

I was still working at my mother's swimsuit business, which was located next door to 9N.

I would regularly walk into 9N like I owned the place, dressed in black, dressy leggings, a black bodysuit, some basic makeup, and I'd sit myself down at the bar.

"Johnny Walker on the rocks," I'd say to the bartender. Soon, before I knew it, I was staring down ten Jägermeister shots, all lined up before me, so that I could start to catch up with all the others at the bar.

Everyone at 9N was on their own road to destruction. Even if those roads looked different from each other, there was only one way this ended for any of us. There was no winning and no escaping reality.

We spent endless days drowning ourselves and enabling each other to keep going, even though most of us didn't even know each other's last names, or who our families were. We only knew the worst version of each other. There could be a guy sitting in a booth with white powder in his mustache and on his black shirt, and no one would say anything. There was freedom in that complete lack of judgment. With no one around to hold us accountable for our actions, it was one of the most destructive places on earth.

One morning, after drinking and taking countless other substances, my stomach was screaming louder than ever before. I raced to the bathroom and threw up more blood than I even thought was physically possible. My head pounded and my stomach lurched, and I could barely catch my breath.

This must be what dying is like.

All of a sudden, my feeling of being young and invincible vanished into a world of horrific thoughts. Had I finally done so many substances that I was actually killing myself?

I leaned against the bathroom counter and tried to calm my breathing and my racing heart. I thought about the months leading up to that morning and how the ache in my stomach had been more and more present. It had become my constant companion.

I didn't want to call anyone. With the exception of everyone at the bar, I tried to hide my addiction. I wanted people to see me as a strong, independent, beautiful woman with her shit together. Not a young, fucked up addict.

I managed to pull on some clothes in between dry heaving, mindlessly made my way to my car, and drove to the hospital. I don't remember the ride there.

When I stumbled into the ER, I must have looked like death because they took me right in. I remember shivering as the voices of nurses and doctors hovered over me.

Through the pounding in my head shielding my eyes from the

glare of the fluorescent lights, I heard them talk about me as if I wasn't in the room: "It's too late to pump her stomach."

All they could do was admit me, put me on fluids, and hope I pulled through.

"You're killing your liver," said one nurse as she took my vitals.

"You're too young to face something like this," said another.

To do so much damage to my liver at such a young age was rare, but then so was I.

After a few days, I was still alive. The alcohol and drugs had passed through my system. I'd been meticulously cared for by a medical team that surely looked at me like a spoiled rich girl who was throwing away her life. It was humiliating.

Before I left the hospital, I met with an addiction psychiatrist. He was so different from the other staff at the hospital. He was blunt and honest and also seemed to actually care if I lived or died.

"I can't stop," I whispered, as he sat at my bedside.

"I can help with that if you want me to ..."

But he didn't realize how bad my intoxication habits truly were.

"You don't understand—"

"Yes. I assure you, I do. And I can help ... *if* you want it."

I couldn't imagine ever not feeling like this.

"You have to realize that no one just gets here because they want to be here. There's a reason behind all of this." His voice was warm.

Something about the way he spoke to me flooded me with too many emotions to form words.

He put it bluntly: "But, if you don't stop abusing your body with toxins at the rate that you are, you will surely die."

Would that be so bad? The thought came so easily. In fact, giving in would come easily, too. I simply couldn't even imagine what it would feel like to live sober again, to be coherent enough to have to deal with my thoughts, memories, demons ...

I simply nodded with tears streaming down my face.

He took that as a yes and put me on pills to help me stop drinking and set me up with a therapy appointment.

I was released from the hospital with my new prescription, which I filled right away.

Surprisingly, I found that the cravings weren't nearly as bad as they'd been in the past.

When I got home, I immediately fell into my bed. I buried myself under my duvet and thought about the previous few days and how far I had pushed my body. Instead of turning on my hairdryer and cocooning myself to sleep to the warmth and sound of its little engine, I called my sister.

"I'm in trouble," I whispered. It felt like an admission of defeat.

"What's going on now?!" I could hear the familiar worry in her voice that she often had when we spoke. We both had been partying for as long as I could remember, but I always took it further.

"I think I've ruined my life ..." I filled her in on everything. I told her about Juan, the cheating, the partying, the hospital, the get-clean-or-die status I was facing ... everything.

"CoCo, you need to call Mom and tell her." I could hear her trying to mask her panic.

"No! I can't!" I exclaimed. "You better not either!"

There was no way I was going to tell my mother what was really going on.

But of course, she went ahead and did it for me.

I KNOW WHAT YOU NEED

"You need to come live with us." At this point, my mom had divorced Andres and found herself depressed and alone in Aspen. Gary made a deal with her that he'd buy her a beautiful mansion in Miami, in the same neighborhood as him, and gift it to her as long as she stayed there until the twins had graduated high school. This would mean that the twins and their dad could be close again, now that Gary was also living in Miami.

That was my mother's answer. She insisted on me moving to Miami and getting sober.

"Things will be better in Miami, Nicole," she said, her voice sounding bright and cheery yet somehow hollow, as if trying to convince herself as much as me that her daughter could be saved. "It'll be a fresh start."

A fresh start.

I was all too familiar with fresh starts by then and they never worked out.

"Mom, the psychiatrist and I made a plan. I need to go to rehab."

"No, Nicole, what you need is discipline in your life, a personal trainer, a healthy diet, and to lose some weight since you have let yourself go—"

"Mom, really? Are you actually saying that to me right now?" The sting of her words was a familiar pain. "This isn't about my looks!"

I knew I had put on a lot of weight. Drinking came with countless calories. But this wasn't about my measurements. It was about trying to stay alive.

"Nicole, I know that nobody tells you this to your face, but I'm your mother and will always tell you the truth. I know what's best for you."

Mom also believed that being close to family, getting out of Costa Rica (and the pressure that it came with), and moving to Miami would give me a new outlook on life. Miami had been a second home to me, having traveled there regularly (almost monthly) throughout my life.

I didn't argue. I surrendered.

The thought of getting out of Costa Rica seemed like the best option I had right now. Maybe this would be the move that changed everything.

I agreed to sell my apartment, packed all of my stuff, sold my car, and within a couple of weeks, had vanished from my home country. I didn't let anyone know where I was going. I just left.

I know what you're thinking. Getting sober in Miami? Miami is one of the highest-intensity drug trafficking areas in the US, meaning that substances of every kind are easier to get there than just about anywhere else. Needless to say, people don't usually go to Miami to get sober.

BAD FOR MY HEALTH

I hadn't faced Carlos since Christmas Eve when his gaslighting had me questioning my own sanity, so when my mother asked me to come to my sister's court case against him, my immediate answer was, "No!"

Just the thought of seeing him again made me feel sick.

"I want Linda to win her case, but I don't want anything to do with the lawsuit." I shook my head violently. I'm sure my eyes showed the panic I felt.

I tried to explain to my mother what going to court—to Costa Rica—would do to me: "If I go back to Costa Rica, it will break me. If I have to see him, it will break me. I can't be sober there."

She either wasn't hearing me, didn't believe me, or didn't care. I still don't know which one.

"Your sister deserves your support, Nicole. If you don't come to the trial, you can just consider yourself out of the family!"

It wasn't the first time I had been frozen out of my family because of my mother so I believed her.

"I can't, Mami!" I said, my voice rising with panic.

"Why on earth can't you just support your sister, Nicole?! You're just going to leave her alone on the stand without your support? Go through her case alone?"

I didn't know what to say.

And then she paused, and asked softly, "Is it because he abused you?"

I shook my head and stared at my fingernails as if to inspect them.

"You don't have to go into detail. Just did he, or didn't he?" she offered, as if that somehow would make it easier.

The silence between us was deafening.

"Nicole, just tell me," she demanded, growing more frustrated.

I gritted my teeth and stared hard at her: "You already know the answer, so why are you even asking me?!"

She looked at me. "I *knew* it. I fucking knew it." Her eyes grew dark as I dissolved into tears. "That motherfucker is going to burn in hell and he's going to pay for this."

Tears turned to heavy sobs, and I buried my head in my hands. I felt my mom's arms wrap around me in a hug.

She began to ask me for more details, like how it happened and how many times, but I didn't want to answer. I wasn't ready.

"We can talk about this later," I said. Mom's boyfriend Brian was in the house at the time too, so I wasn't about to be more specific at that moment. "All I can tell you is yes, it did happen, and it was horrible."

I felt shame and anger start to build as memories of the past came closer to the surface and I tried to push them back down.

"Why don't you want to be part of this trial since he did that?" she asked.

I shook my head again.

"Why don't you want to make him pay? Your testimony could give your sister a better chance of winning!" She pummeled me with questions, and I could feel myself wanting to disappear into the floor.

"Mami, stop! It's not that I don't want to support you and what you or Linda need to do, but it's not what *I* need to heal."

She started to protest, "But—"

"I don't need to go to court to get closure. It won't give me the peace I need. Quite the opposite. It will break me. I know it will. I've worked so hard to be sober."

My mom frowned and asked, "Are you still afraid of him? Is that it? I just understand why you don't want to help us put him—"

"No!"

"So, you're just going to turn your back on your sister and me and make us do this without—"

"No! It has nothing to do with you. Nothing to do with Linda! This is the problem, you guys always make it about you."

I had just told her what happened to me and she wanted more. She was angry that I wasn't giving her what she wanted.

She straightened her back and looked down at me. "Well, you need to understand that you can't just let what happened to you control your life forever."

What did she just say?

She continued, "You can't be this damaged person for the rest of your life. I realize this is traumatic, but you can't make poor choices forever."

I immediately regretted telling her. I had turned into some sort of secret key to making the trial stronger, a trial that would surely be the death of me if I had to take part.

"Going to the trial would be a poor choice for me!" I tried to explain. She didn't agree. She felt she knew better. And no matter what I said that day, it was obvious that I was going to be a part of the trial.

"Listen," I said. "If I go to this trial, I am going to need support, otherwise I will relapse. I need support before, during, and after so all my hard work doesn't go to hell." I needed my family to stop me from going back down a dark path as a result of facing Carlos.

The four walls of Carlos's home held secrets that no one outside could ever fathom. To the outside world, he seemed ordinary—maybe even enviable. He was the charismatic one, always the center of attention at events and gatherings. But behind closed doors, it was a very different story.

Soon we were on a plane and then in a creaky, wood-paneled courtroom just mere feet away from my abuser. The court case brought the nightmare of what he did to my sister into the light, where she had no choice but to face it. It also forced me to admit, on the public record for the first time, that he also abused me.

The look of shock on the faces of the judges (Costa Rica trials often have multiple judges) was nothing compared to the literally burning glare I felt from Carlos as he stared at me.

At the end of my testimony, one of the judges turned to me and asked, "Is there anything you'd like to add before you step down?"

My mind raced through a lifetime of trauma, trying to conjure the right words for this opportunity that may never occur again. I had been fighting the urge to look at Carlos throughout the entire trial, but now, I felt a rush of courage to finally look him dead in the eye, raise my index finger to point at him, and say, "All my sister and I have ever wanted was for you to say you're sorry. And you couldn't even do that."

The room went silent until one of the judges finally broke the silence: "Tell her you're sorry, Carlos."

My abuser shook his head and then stared at the floor.

The façade my father had so carefully built crumbled before the world. The testimonies made in that courtroom changed all of us. My father began to be exposed for who he was. And so were we. I'd often find solace in my sister's presence, feeling a little less alone knowing she understood the pain, the shame, the rage. The secret we held was like a ticking bomb, and we knew that now that everything was revealed, our lives would never be the same.

Listening to my sister's depositions and accounts of what happened made me sick to my stomach. I wanted to go back in time and protect her. It didn't matter that no one had been able to protect me.

My father denied everything in court. He often attended with his girlfriend who, at the time, looked exactly like my sister.

Various girlfriends also appeared to testify on his behalf. I recognized some of them from the past.

The last person who testified on Carlos's behalf was my brother. I knew that if there was anyone who wanted to be there even less than me, it was Andre. His answers were angry and short. He gave as little information as possible, likely to just be done with it. I couldn't blame him. If there was anyone that could understand how he felt in that moment, it was me.

The media hounded us for comments and information, taking

photos of us going into and out of the courthouse. Headlines screamed the story of "the Diaz daughters" doing this or saying that.

In between sessions, the OIJ (the Costa Rican equivalent of the FBI) contacted my mother to inform her that we were in danger. Carlos had put a hit out on us.

He wanted to save his reputation and his money while also silencing our pain, our voices, and our truths. He thought he could erase the very evidence of his sins with a lump sum payment of God knows how much to some hired gun. He wanted to ensure the secrets we held died with us.

Luckily, the hit man he hired, perhaps plagued by his own conscience or motivated by some other reason, recorded a conversation between himself and Carlos, in which Carlos complained that we weren't dead yet.

"They have been in town all day," he could be heard to say. "Everyone in Costa Rica knows it. Yet they're still alive. Why?" He was pissed off and continued by saying, "I'm not paying you one more cent until they're gone."

The recording was undeniable proof of who Carlos was and how expendable he considered us to be.

It felt like a cruel joke. How could a parent, regardless of his crimes, wish death upon his own flesh and blood?

The realization that our lives were in danger meant that fear was a constant companion. Again. After all those years.

The OIJ put us under their protection every time we were in Costa Rica. Bodyguards and bulletproof vests became our daily routine throughout the trial, a heavy but necessary reminder of the life we were forced to lead.

The man who had my sister and me living in fear and shame throughout our childhood was in control again. He had us scared again. That's how he liked us. We jumped at the sound of squeaky floorboards in the night and the sight of an unfamiliar face that might be a hit man. It became a living, terrifying hell and just one more reason I never wanted to return to Costa Rica.

This was just the beginning of six years of trials and appeals, and yet it already felt like I'd been put through the wringer. I wanted to numb out more than ever before. I knew that I would feel that way.

Once I was back in Miami, a couple of days later, we received the call. We had lost. My sister and my mom immediately swore to appeal. I dreaded the thought of going through it again.

My mom suggested I call my sister to check in on her.

As I walked out of the house and got into my car, I dialed my sister's number. It went straight to voicemail.

Within minutes, I found myself at a bar, ordering a Black Johnnie Walker on the rocks and letting my mind race with the events that had just taken place.

The crushing weight of unresolved pain and overwhelming fury, exacerbated by a stressful trial, and replaying terrible memories can push resilience to its limits. The trial, each moment leading up to it, and its aftermath, played on an endless loop in my mind. Seeing my brother so disheartened added to my frustration. I understood why everyone supported Linda, but where was the support for me? Was it, maybe, because I didn't share my whole truth?

Heading back to court was against my better judgment. I had expressed my fears about going there; I knew it could potentially drag me back into the depths of despair I'd fought so hard to climb out of. And it did. When I needed her most, my mom appeared indifferent. She let me walk out the door without asking about my wellbeing, it felt like her concerns centered solely on my sister—that she didn't see me.

Whenever I dared to voice how isolated and overlooked I felt, I was quickly dismissed as playing the victim, lying, exaggerating, or being dramatic. It made the loneliness and the pain even more acute.

In that moment of intense vulnerability and silence, where nobody seemed to see or hear me, I turned to the familiar yet destructive comfort of alcohol—it seemed the only thing that wouldn't turn me away or invalidate my feelings.

These were not just moments of weakness but cries for understanding and support that went unheeded.

So, I stayed quiet and did what I knew best: Order one drink. Then another. Then a line of Jäger shots.

I fucking *knew* this was going to happen.

Finally, the numbness started to set in, and I could breathe again, blurring the past and drifting into an easier, hazier existence than the horror of the Carlos trial, easier than the feeling of being invisible to my family.

To make things better, I took someone home with me.

In no time, I found myself buying rounds of drinks for many faceless "friends" who hung around to see what "badass CoCo" would do next. The party was wherever I was. And because I had to hide my drinking from my mother, I would rent bougie hotel rooms where I'd stay for days and weeks, partying, all at my mother's expense.

I used the money that Gary sent me to help subsidize my spiral. I would tell him I was taking five classes but was really just taking two. And because Gary always dealt only with cash, there was very little record of where his money did or didn't go.

Making matters much worse, I started dipping into my mother's personal bank account. Because of her divorce settlement with Gary, she had more money than she could keep track of. I knew I would get in serious trouble for stealing, but at the same time, I didn't really care.

You have to understand: I didn't care if I lived or died, so why would I care what my mother thought? At this point, anyone and everyone had become collateral damage, including myself.

I began throwing up blood in the mornings again and trying to hide it from the household.

It was when my mom was going through my room (probably searching for evidence of drugs) that she found receipts and bank statements showing that I had been taking money from her account. She *lost* it.

It was one of the only times I was truly scared of her.

"Give me your keys!" She screamed louder than I'd ever heard her. "You are CUT OFF, CoCo! I'm done! I can't do this anymore! You are never getting anything from me ever again."

I remember her face filled with fury and hurt.

"How could my own daughter do this to me? What did I ever do for you to treat me this way?" she screamed.

Then I lost it. I was infuriated at myself for what I had done and I knew this was going to be the end. I had pushed things way too far and I didn't even recognize myself.

"Give me the keys, Nicole ... Now!" she said, stepping closer to me and staring me in the face. "I don't even recognize you anymore, Nicole. You look like the devil to me!"

Instead of handing over the keys, I ran out of the house, jumped in the car I was supposed to return, and started driving. If I could have driven off the face of the earth, I would have. I couldn't get the look in my mother's eyes out of my mind. She would never talk to me again. I'd be cut off from everyone I loved again.

I raced through streets blurred with the tears that poured from my eyes uncontrollably. I sobbed and screamed at the world and hit the steering wheel at how stupid I had been to throw it all away again. Everyone would know I was cut off because I was a horrible person.

What am I going to do? Where can I go?

There was nothing for me in Costa Rica, and now nothing for me in the US.

I don't know how long I drove, hands shaking, mind racing over my options, only to end up with the obvious answer: *It's over. There is no coming back from this.*

SUICIDE WATCH

I found myself at the Miami airport, pulled over, and started punching the steering wheel as my mom called over and over, screaming at me to return the car.

I took my key out of the ignition and dragged the hard edge of its metal up my arm, from my wrist to my biceps, splitting my skin open and immediately covering myself and my seat in blood. Then I did it again and again until chunks of flesh began to come off of my arm.

I texted my friend, Christina, and said "I need you. I got kicked out."

My phone rang instantly. I winced as I hit the answer button.

"Coco! Where are you? What's going on? What happened?" she asked.

"Chris," I blurted out in between sobs. "I've fucked up worse than ever before and I think my life is over. I don't know what to do! Can I come over?"

"Of course. Do you need me to come and get you?"

"I'm okay to drive. I'm fifteen minutes away. See you soon." I hung up, pulled my sleeve down over the gruesome gash, wiped the blood off the key, and put it back into the ignition to drive in Christina's direction.

I have no idea how I avoided putting the jeep into a ditch, but I eventually ended up at Christina's. She met me at the door, and I fell into her arms and cried. Christina and I spent our entire friendship battling our own demons, but never at the same time. When I was down, she was there, and vice versa. We had known each other since high school. If there was anyone who understood my full story, and who had always been there for me without judgment, it was Chris.

"Why do I keep making the same mistakes over and over?" I screamed into the air, to no one in particular. Christina made me some tea as I sat at her dining room table, still hiding my wounds.

She came over to me with a big steaming mug of chamomile tea in her hands and rubbed my back and hair as I fell apart before her.

"I keep screwing up, hurting people, hurting myself! There is no point to anything anymore!"

I released every emotion I'd been holding back for God knows how long, and Christina sat with me as I did. I told her everything that I had done, in detail, finishing with the fact that I had no money, no car (because I had to return it), and nowhere to go.

"I can't do this anymore," I whispered and laid my head on the pillow of her couch. "I don't want to ... It's all too hard ..." I made horrid sobbing sounds in between words.

She led me into her guest room, grabbed her hair dryer, and invited me to curl up into the bed.

I reached my arm out to take the dryer, and she saw the blood on my sleeve.

"What the hell?" she asked and made me pull my sleeve up.

In embarrassment, I showed her the horrid-looking gash. "It's nothing, really." I shook my head.

"That," she pointed at my arm, "is not nothing. You are *not* leaving me, CoCo."

I sunk into the bed, closer to the dryer, feeling the shame of cutting myself.

Chris sat beside me and ran her hands through my hair which was wet around my face from tears. "This is *not* the end. It'll get better. I promise ..."

She brought me bandages for my cuts and tissues for my eyes. I surely had mascara and eyeliner running down my face, but I didn't care.

"Please don't leave me," I said hoarsely. I'd lost my voice from screaming. "I'm going to kill myself if you—"

"I'm right here. I'm not going anywhere, and neither are you."

Christina saved my life that night and I'll love her forever for it.

TWELVE STEPS

After she took time to process everything that had happened, my mother was willing to talk to me again. I begged her to pay for me to go to rehab. I craved having a different life. An end to my substance abuse problems. I wanted to know what it felt like to have my feet on the ground again.

"Please, Mami, I need this."

"After everything you've done, you're asking me to spend more money on you?!"

Gary agreed to pay for half of my rehab which helped my case. My mom begrudgingly agreed to pay the difference.

The rehab was in Clearwater, Florida. It was pretty modest at the time, but it was exactly what I needed. When I was there, it was the first time in a long time that I was truly happy. I loved rehab! I loved the people, the therapy, the honesty of it all, and the inspiration of seeing others beat their addictions. It gave me hope. I felt like a different person there. It was liberating—not something you would expect from a program that required you to give up no less than anything and everything you had come to rely on to feel good.

But rehab was like a protective bubble, and I felt safe there.

There was group therapy, journaling, medication, and above all, forgiveness. I shared space with others who had experienced things that were as bad, sometimes worse, than I had. It was so refreshing. It is strange to say, but rehab was the first place I didn't feel like a screw-up. Everyone was there by choice to get better. And the team at the center was there to help us be successful in that.

This was the first time in my life that no one knew or cared who I was or where I came from, but only who I wanted to be and where I wanted to go.

In the first couple of days, I kept trying to call my mom, but she refused to answer. I began to write letters to all the people I had hurt. I found myself taking responsibility for my actions. And although I didn't know how people would react, or whether they'd forgive me at all, I was focused on the now and on really taking in the experience as much as I could.

Every night before we turned in (boys in one wing, girls in the other), we would all meet by the beach volleyball court and play "mafia," a fun and energetic game that was quite frankly perfect for people who knew all about manipulation and lying. Not that this was something to be proud of, but it was so much fun!

We also played countless games of cards and smoked countless packs of cigarettes. That's the one good thing about rehab, we were allowed to smoke as much as we wanted.

As family weekend approached, I finally got a hold of my mom and asked her if she would come and be a part of family weekend. Family weekend meant spending time with family members, doing therapy together, and re-establishing healthy connections.

My mom wasn't going to come. In fact, no one was going to come. So, I decided to invite the one person who was always there for me—Christina. Not only did she come, but she drove twelve hours to see me for two or three.

I was so excited to see her pull in. She parked her car, got out, and saw me coming toward her. She is super tall, bright eyes, light skin, angelic looking, and she emits a feeling of peace and calm whenever you're near her. I was afraid at first because she was the first person from the outside world to see me. I was worried she'd hate me for something I had done while drunk in our past.

As soon as she smiled, I knew it would be okay.

She brought me Ferrero Rocher chocolates, which we ate while sitting at a picnic table and talked about everything. I confided in her about how happy I was in rehab. I didn't feel pressured to do or be anything but myself.

"I can see that you're doing better," she smiled and grabbed my hand. "I am so happy for you, CoCo. And so, *so* proud!" I could tell she meant it, and that she was relieved. She had also been working on her own demons, which was good.

I talked excitedly about what I had learned and the books that helped me. I wanted to teach her everything I had learned.

"When do you think you'll be going home?" she asked.

I looked down at the wooden tabletop. "My term is almost over, so I could technically leave in about a month, but I wish I could stay longer. I feel like I have so much more to learn and have so much more work I could be doing …"

"Well, I'm proud of you. I love you."

My visit with Christina gave me hope that the rest of the outside world might not be so bad.

Rehab goes in three-month "semesters" and before I knew it, it was my three-month graduation. I couldn't believe it was already over. I was doing really well, and it was good for me. It was common knowledge that many addicts needed to stay at least six months for any hope of lifelong change.

I had a phone call with my mom as the graduation date got closer.

"Mami, I am not ready to leave, please let me stay here. I need this," I pleaded. I knew if I left too early, I'd fall right back into bad habits. But I also knew that rehab was expensive.

My mother decided, likely for financial reasons, that three months was enough.

"I'll make you a deal. If you promise to stay clean, get a job, and go to college, you can move back in with me and we'll get you a cheap car since we've already sold your jeep. You have to go to AA meetings, and pass drug testing whenever I feel like it."

I didn't know how to say no. I couldn't say no. I surveyed the safety of the rehabilitation center's walls around me with the phone in my hand, trying to imagine being in the outside world again. My stomach lurched at the thought.

I tried to imagine a life of education, freedom, and sobriety, all at the same time and I couldn't. But Gary wasn't going to pay anymore, and my mom certainly wasn't either.

"Okay Mami," I whispered in agreement. I wanted her to love me again. I wanted to be a better daughter and a better person. I didn't want to lose the feeling of acceptance and forgiveness that cocooned me in rehab. I hoped to God that I could stay clean.

"Love you," was all I said, and hung up, feeling like I might have just sealed my fate and ensured the demise of my sobriety.

Once it came time to leave rehab, a car picked me up and I got my phone back. It was like a car ride back to reality. My phones were filled with messages from people wanting to party, asking where I was, all things I didn't want to hear. I was dropped off at Tampa airport, took a flight to Miami, and was met at the landing gate by Gary, my sister, and her boyfriend, Bobby.

I was so excited to see Linda after everything that had happened. I was really happy to see Gary, who was quite obviously so proud of me.

My mother was not in the vehicle. At rehab, they prepare you for the fact that not everyone is going to be ready or willing to talk to you or forgive you. Especially right away. As rehab patients, we have the advantage of having been working on figuring it all out and processing the past. On the other hand, our friends and family didn't have that same opportunity, and many were likely still very angry or hurt.

My mom is never going to talk to me again, I thought to myself, but before I let that thought get away from me, the carload of people I loved began asking questions about anything and everything.

I told them about therapy and the mafia game and writing letters and facing our demons. Then I played what I call "the rehab song" for everyone in the car. It was a song that the girls and boys at rehab would sing (or scream, because we were separated by half a football field's worth of grass as we stood in front of our gender-specific wings) at each other at the end of each day. The rehab song was actually "Lean on Me," by Bill Withers and it filled me with so much peace and hope. It came to be a song that I would play to myself in my darkest moments. It still brings tears to my eyes to this day. The lyrics meant so much to me. "*Lean on me ... when you're not strong ... I'll be your friend ... I'll help you carry on ...*"

Gary drove us in his big SUV back to my mom's house, where my mom and her boyfriend, Brian, were. She greeted me with a quick kiss on the cheek and a clipped "Hello, how are you," letting me know she was still very angry.

We all sat together—Gary, my sister, Bobby, my mother, Brian, and me.

"So, what do you have to say for yourself?" my mother started, letting me know she was not taking any bullshit from me. She wanted answers. Promises. It was what I imagined an intervention might feel like. Luckily, rehab had prepared me for moments like that, so I tried to keep my cool, put a lifetime of mother-daughter turmoil behind us, and do my best to answer her questions. I silently reminded myself she deserved that much and more.

"I want to apologize," I started, and then began listing the things I had done that I knew hurt her and betrayed her trust. I started explaining that I had changed, I was a different CoCo. I had learned so much in rehab and wanted to share the lessons I took home with me, but my mom cut me off before I got very far.

"What are you going to do now?" I could hear her barely containing her anger. "How do I know that you can live here and not go stealing all my—"

"Lynda, give her a chance," Gary said softly, treading dangerous waters.

"Don't you *dare* tell me to give her a chance!" my mother snapped. "*I* am the one who has had to swallow all the repercussions of Nicole's behavior for as long as I can remember. *I* am the one that is going to have to sleep with one eye open. *I* am the one who is going to have to lock the closet. Because I don't know what she's capable of anymore."

"But Mom, I've done a lot of work to be better. I am not like that anymo—"

She laughed coldly. "You were in there for twelve weeks. Are you telling me you're totally different after only twelve weeks?"

I tried not to react to her rejection the way I would have in the past. I tried to find words that fit the situation without blowing everything up. "Why did you send me there if you weren't going to believe me when I got back, that I have changed?

"How are you going to prove it? How am I going to trust you?!" She had begun to yell.

Linda stood up. "CoCo, why don't you go for a walk with Bobby?" She knew that space was likely the best idea for everyone at that point.

"Yeah, okay," I agreed and pulled my cigarettes out of my purse.

"Oh, so now you're smoking?!" my mom asked incredulously. "What else have you started doing?"

"No Mom, they allow cigarettes in rehab. It's nothing compared to the damage being done from the other substances we were all addicted to, so they allow it."

I took a long, grateful drag on my Virginia Slim as I walked through the neighborhood with Bobby. *Thank god for smokes.*

"Don't give up, CoCo," he said as I smoked with tears running down my face. I didn't want to fall apart this soon after getting out of rehab. I wanted to believe I could hold it together. "Listen to the positive voices in your head, ignore all the rest. This is going to be hard but do your best to do well and make smart decisions." Bobby was wise.

When I got back to the house, my mom said I could live with her again, but there'd be strict rules and if I didn't like it, I could leave.

"You have to get a job. You can't go out. I will *not* be giving you any money."

I didn't have anywhere else to go and no friends except Christina, who my mother decided was bad news and wouldn't let me see.

She didn't know any of my real friends, so she just assumed Christina was one of the bad influences. I got a new phone with a new number to leave the actual bad influences behind me.

I started doing really well after landing a job at Express. I saved up and got myself a little red Mini Cooper. I moved out of my mom's house and into an apartment with a roommate. I was doing well, making nearly 50K, and the closest thing to alcohol that I drank was the odd Red Bull or a virgin raspberry mojito. I felt great being sober. I didn't miss the alcohol in those days.

It felt like a brand new life. My friends at work didn't care where I was from or how much money I came from. They just liked me for me and respected that I earned my money.

That was my first full-salary job, and I loved it. I quickly grew to be really good at my job, earning a position as the youngest manager in the company, managing a six-million-dollar store. Work kept me busy and fulfilled.

I would sometimes call Gary to check in with him. When I told him how well I was doing at the store, he was proud of me. It felt good. I knew fashion and I knew what looked good on people. I could spot a trend a mile away. When I worked, I worked hard. It is nothing for me to work around the clock for an upcoming promotion or to hit a sales goal. Solving problems was a rush for me. If there was a problem at work, upper management would say, "Give it to CoCo. She'll figure it out." And I always did. Gotta hand it to a lifetime of traumatic troubleshooting to make problem solving second nature to me.

Not having a lot of money meant that I couldn't screw up as easily as I had in the past.

I got a great new job working at Kate Spade that came with a big raise (I'd now be making 75K) and soon met Zach.

He worked for the same company. Technically, I was his boss. He was handsome and seemed sweet, so we ended up hanging out at my house and soon began dating. I took him to Cancun for the weekend. He seemed to fall in love with me right away, but I wasn't as sure. Eventually, a few months and one rotten boyfriend later, I found my way back to Zach. He saw me for me. And we soon became everything to each other. My brother and Carlos were off-limits, my sister was in LA, my mother and the twins in Aspen, and Gary was remarried to someone I couldn't stand.

Soon Zach's family became my family. We would rather hang out with them on a Friday night than go out. This was a change for Zach, who without me being there, would never have spent that much time with them. Our relationship made him realize how lucky he was to have a family that was there for him. His Mom was grateful to be seeing Zach more than ever before.

We had fun together. Everyone was supportive and loving toward each other and toward me. It was the kind of family life I'd always hoped for.

Zach and I could talk about everything. We shared our lives, memories, faults, and proud moments. He didn't have a lot of money, but he helped me when he could. We had great sex, and we could laugh and tease each other.

I remember teasing him about loving an older woman since I was a couple of years older than him.

"I've always liked older women," he winked. "But none were as hot as you."

"Oh yeah? Prove it! Who else did you date?"

He began talking about a friend of his mom and how they would mess around when his mom was out. He was eleven at the time, and she was over thirty. As he told the story out loud, filling in details, I could see understanding cross his face, now that he was looking at the past through different eyes. I don't think he had even realized it was sexual abuse until our conversation that day.

"Zach ... You didn't 'like older women' when you were eleven. You were too young to make that decision ..."

He frowned.

"Imagine I told you that when I was eleven, a thirty-year-old man had sex with me. What would you think then? Did I just like older men? Or was I being sexually abused?"

I remember trying to find the right words to soften the blow. But there weren't any.

I could see him processing the information with a look of disgust on his face. We talked for a long time, and I watched as he replayed his life with this new knowledge and perspective.

"I'm so sorry," I said, wishing I could protect him and make him feel better.

Over the following weeks, he began falling into depression deeper than I'd ever seen. He smoked a lot more weed, stopped going to work … I tried to be there for him, listen when he needed to talk, support him when he needed advice, and just love him.

And we started drinking.

He didn't want to leave the couch.

I knew from experience there was no magic pill for abuse trauma. *If there was, I'd have already found it.* I tried everything I could think of to pull him back out of the dark hole he was being swallowed up in.

He was very receptive because he knew what I went through when I was young. We talked it through in detail and then I helped him talk to his mom about it so they could start to deal with it as a family. More than anything, I think it was just helpful for him to have someone there who understood, and could listen without judgment, as he was processing all of it.

I took him to some counseling sessions so that he could talk to a professional. I hoped and prayed that all of this would lead to him being able to confront his past and work through it in a healthy way.

TIJUANA

It was mid-2017, and I was feeling restless. I wasn't happy in my own body. Zach loved my body, that was nothing new, but it felt as if I had hit a wall. Dieting wasn't helping, I hated exercise, and I was ready to love what I saw in the mirror again. I was sick to death of being compared to my model sister and beauty-queen mother, only to fall miserably short. I was sick of feeling like the bad, ugly daughter.

I laid my head in Zach's lap one afternoon as we hung out on the couch he hadn't moved from in hours. I looked up at him and said, "I need to do something about my body, Zach. I can't take it anymore."

He looked down and growled. "You do not need to lose weight. You're perfect and I love you."

"You're sweet. And I love you too, babe, but I've had it. I'm going to take my mom's offer."

If everyone saw me the way he did, I wouldn't even be considering it. But in my family, measurements and weight meant the difference between being valued and being ridiculed.

I picked up the phone and called my mother, who I knew would have no shortage of advice.

"Mami, I am going to take you up on your offer of paying for weight loss surgery."

We talked about the diets I'd been trying, and then she agreed, it was time for surgery. "I will take you to get you the gastric sleeve, Nicole," she said.

Frankly, I had been defeated by the trial, by falling in and out of sobriety, and at that point, surgery to solve my problems sounded perfect.

"Where? In Costa Rica?" I asked, knowing the price would be lower there than in Miami.

"No, no. I'll take you to Tijuana," she said.

"Huh? Why?"

"Thousands of people go to Tijuana for gastric sleeve surgery," she said. Knowing all the best beauty secrets was her superpower, so I believed her. "There's no waiting six months to be approved, it's less money, and it's their specialty," she said.

Where a gastric sleeve might be twenty-five thousand dollars in the US, it was the equivalent of maybe nine thousand in Tijuana.

My mother and I got busy making plans.

Zach was not happy. "CoCo! Why would you do that?! You're beautiful right now. What if something happens to you there?"

I parroted my mother's words: "People get this surgery there all the time. It's their specialty. It's perfectly safe."

The decision was made.

My mother and I were on a plane within a few weeks. It wasn't until I saw the modern clinic that I realized how anxious I had been. We were given a full tour of the medical facilities. It looked pretty much like any other medical building I'd ever been in.

Surgical patients were put into cohorts of four at a time. We would all go through the procedures on the same day and then recover in the same hotel together. I liked that. Having company took any remaining doubts out of it. Plus, my mother was with me.

When I came out of anesthesia, I didn't feel too bad. Nurses came to the hotel in the evenings to take care of us. Nausea was my biggest complaint, but also, one I was familiar with.

I liked being able to talk to the other patients.

We healed up pretty quickly and were released so that we could hop flights to our various countries of origin. There was one girl who didn't leave at the same time. She ended up in the ICU for months, from what I heard. It sounded like her complications were more about the fact that she was extremely anorexic before the surgery. Her body wasn't as strong as the rest of ours, because of it.

In the US, that likely wouldn't have happened because she would never have been approved for the surgery in her condition. From what I heard, she couldn't eat for months due to pain and other symptoms. I felt so bad for her. To this day, I still think about her and wonder if she's okay.

FIXED

After being back in Miami for a few weeks, I started seeing pounds falling off and it felt good. I wanted more of that feeling. Because of the surgery, my stomach could only handle very small volumes of food. If I had more than a few bites, I would feel full to the point of being sick. Throwing up came far too easily, whether I wanted it to or not, having battled with bulimia off and on for years.

The vomiting and extremely small number of calories I took in gave me a body that was starting to be more like that of my mother and sister.

Mom showered me with compliments over my appearance as it changed. I couldn't remember how long it had been (if ever) since I'd felt so accepted by my mother. We shopped together more often, and I found myself sponging up the positive attention and my mother's approval.

Suddenly, she was asking me to come with her to lunches with her friends, at which she would say, "Doesn't Nicole look gorgeous?" and "Nicole has lost so much weight! Look at her!"

Something about my weight loss sparked hope in me that maybe I did have the power to change my life. That kind of hope was new to me. It felt amazing. I looked like a different person, so now I wanted to actually be a different person.

The problem was that if I had any chance of real change, I knew I needed to get the hell out of Miami. There were no limits here. All of the richest cultures, the widest variety of people and drugs, the wildest parties, and the biggest fortunes came together in Miami. I could lose days, weeks, even months of my life in a blur of luxury and intoxication there. My relationship with Zach, as much as I loved him, didn't help.

We started a self-destructive pattern that probably had nothing to do with each other and everything to do with where we came from. It was awful watching something that could have been magic turn to dust.

Somehow, I always knew Zach had demons too, but I didn't realize how deep they went until we uncovered his childhood abuse. Similar to the way an addict can see another addict a mile away, so can someone suffering from trauma see another one in pain. My darkness had seen his darkness—and they didn't get along.

Zach dulled his trauma with weed. I began dulling mine with everything else.

CHAPTER FIVE

SWEET HOME ALABAMA

Once my weight issues were taken care of—I went from almost 250 to about 180 in a few months—I got a taste for more dramatic fresh starts. I wanted to get myself together in other areas of my life too. Now that my body was "fixed," I wanted to fix other areas of my life. I scouted for cities that would allow me to keep working for the company I loved. Because I was a top manager at a high-volume store, when I asked for a transfer, they quickly agreed. They wanted the volume and were happy just to keep me in the fold.

I was looking for a store location that would let me continue to earn big commissions but without the big Miami life.

In grade 7 I had been obsessed with the movie *Sweet Home Alabama*. I watched it over and over again, picturing myself as the character played by Reese Witherspoon, who came from the sweetest small town in Alabama. Even though she didn't want to at first, she just fit in there. She was part of its history. She was notorious in the town for being the screw-up, but everyone loved her anyway. The people in the town knew each other's names. They'd gone to school together, raised their kids together, argued, and made up together. It was a slower pace and the little things in life mattered there.

There I was, at twelve or thirteen, living in a huge, beautiful home surrounded by all the best that money could buy, wishing more than anything in the world to live a *smaller* life, a *loved* life. Because if anyone cared to look at me all those years ago, past the barred windows of my pre-teen bedroom and the headlines of my bad behavior, they would have seen me, sitting in my room, alone, dressed in expensive designer clothes, with my thermos of Bacardi and designer Gucci, wondering why I felt so empty.

Out of all the locations the company had, many were either in cities that were too big or small towns where volume would be so low my commissions would be next to nothing. The closest thing I could find to my Sweet Home Alabama setting was Frisco, Texas. It was a small town, but it was an up-and-coming one. The mall where the store was located was busy and promised decent commissions if I hustled, which I always did.

A transfer to Frisco, Texas, would be a belated solution to a lifelong search for home.

I put in for the transfer and began preparing to go. I was excited and scared, all at the same time. I was also sad because I was worried I would lose Zach.

I tried to convince him to come with me, but he wanted to stay where he was. If I was at work and didn't answer the phone, then he would phone me twelve times. It reminded me of how I'd been with Juan—caught in fear that I was going to lose the person I loved.

"We could have a calm, peaceful life," I told him, trying to paint the picture of a world outside of the chaos of Miami.

"So, you really are going?" he asked, as if surprised.

"Yes, Zach, I'm going. Come with me!" I urged, wishing I could get him to see the vision I had for a new life.

Zach was afraid of taking a risk on making such a big change if it didn't work out. I understood. I had the same fears, but I was set on going anyway.

We both cried as I packed and on the day that I left, we were both afraid it was the last time we'd ever see each other.

He engulfed me in his arms. I looked up into his eyes and whispered, "Come with me."

He kissed me long and hard. "I promise you I'll come get you," he said. "We're going to have our happily ever after."

The next time I saw Zach was a few months later, in his obituary photo after he died from an accidental overdose.

NEW NORMAL

When I arrived in Frisco, it was Fall, and the air was crisp and cool—not what I had expected. When many people think of Texas they think of cowboys and heat. But it was so much more than that.

The sun was bright, illuminating the sky lighting up the purest shade of blue that I'd ever seen. After the twenty-hour drive from Miami, I pulled up in front of a house that screamed order and precision based on the neatly trimmed boxwoods alongside its pristine pathway.

I double-checked the address on my phone just to confirm I was in the right spot. Everything was so perfect and orderly.

And *quiet*.

That's when a realization struck me—*I am a stranger in this place. Literally, no one here knows me or my family.* That was the real definition of a fresh start. In a place like this, I had an opportunity to blend into a life where my past doesn't define me.

This is what I need.

Sure, the setting was a far cry from the high-class world I was used to, but that is exactly why I was there.

I lugged my suitcases up the steps, gave a warning knock, and opened the front door to a sea of beige. I found my way to a sleek black sofa in the middle of the space. Everything was neat and in its place. It looked like a model home.

I spent about ten minutes taking in the space before throwing my luggage into my room and hitting the town to explore. It almost immediately lived up to my imagination. Most people passed me with a smile or a hello and I could immediately feel that the tempo of life here was much slower than in Miami. My heartbeat felt as if it relaxed into a slower rhythm right along with it.

Is this what peace feels like?

As I was walking down the street, the sweet aroma of freshly baked goods caught my attention. I turned my head to see a colorful, quaint little bakery with rustic charm, and couldn't resist the urge to step inside. Without hesitation, I pushed open the door, and the tinkling of a bell announced my arrival. The warm scent of sugar and cinnamon enveloped me, and I felt instantly comforted. The interior was cozy, with exposed brick walls and vintage decorations adorning the shelves. Behind the counter stood a woman with a warm smile and all the Southern charm I had heard about. She looked up at me and greeted me with a friendly, "Hi y'all!"

"*Hola*! Sorry, hi!" I replied with a smile, remembering I was no longer in Miami where I could speak my native language with most people.

"I'm new in town and was just passing by when the smell of your bakery lured me in."

"Well, welcome to our little town," the woman said as she wiped her hands on her apron. "I'm Mary. What's your name?"

"CoCo," I replied, as I extended my hand to hers.

Mary shook my hand with a warm grip. "Nice to meet you. Where are you from?" I knew my Miami wardrobe probably looked out of place. I'd already counted about a dozen cowboy hats in my short travels down the main street so far.

"I'm from Costa Rrrrr-ica," I replied, exaggeratedly rolling my *Rs*, with a smile and wink.

Mary's eyes widened in surprise. "Well, welcome to Texas! I hope you're enjoying our little corner of the world."

"I just got here but everyone seems so friendly," I said.

"That's what we aim for," Mary said with a chuckle. "So, what can I get for you today?"

I glanced at the display case filled with an array of pastries and baked goods. "Everything looks so delicious. What do you recommend?"

"Oh, you have to try our pecan pie! It's a southern classic and a personal favorite of mine."

"Great. I'll take a slice, please." I said with a smile and reached for my credit card. Then, filled with a familiar urge for more, I corrected myself: "Actually, make it, two."

Old habits.

I would only manage to eat a couple of bites, but she didn't have to know that.

As Mary packaged up two generous slices of pie and handed them to me, I was grateful for my first interaction to be so sweet and warm.

I knew that I had made the right decision to come here, and I couldn't wait to see what other surprises this place had in store for me.

I stepped out of the bakery, holding my tightly packaged pecan pie, and wondered if I should get a bottle of something to go with it.

After all, my new beginning in this wonderful town was a cause for celebration. I noticed a quaint little liquor store a few doors down from the bakery and couldn't resist the urge to take a peek inside.

POR ARRIBA

I was greeted by a man with a thick Texan accent, who called me sugar and asked me if he could help me find anything.

"I'm new in town and looking for something to go with my pie," I explained, holding up my bakery bag.

He pulled a local bourbon from the shelf, assuring me that it would pair perfectly with pecan pie.

"Well, I actually prefer scotch whiskey, but I'll give TX a try, sure!"

I left the store and wondered who I would share my pecan and bourbon new-town celebration with. I wondered if my roommate would be interested.

I picked up my cell and dialed his number. "Hey, Andy! I was thinking about celebrating my move to Texas tonight with some bourbon and pecan pie. Join me! I feel like we haven't even had a chance to get to know each other yet." I explained, following that with the many reasons why he and I should eat and drink together, including how fun I was to hang out with. "You'll see!" I promised.

I had worn him down with my excitement and after only a moment of hesitation, he agreed. I was immediately relieved. I wasn't used to having to work this hard to share a drink with a friend.

Early in the evening, Andy came home, and we sat down at our kitchen table. I poured us each a glass and watched as he seemed to slowly savor the smooth, smoky taste.

"Come on, Andy, are we toasting or what?" I teased, trying to lighten him up.

He looked like he was trying to figure me out.

I continued, explaining, "In my country, we say, *por arriba*!" I flashed him my cutest smile or mischief and saw a glint of amusement flicker in his eyes.

Giving in to my enthusiasm, he mimicked the gesture, said, "*Por arriba*!" and we clinked our glasses together.

"*Por arriba, por abajo, pal' centro, pa' dentro'*," I said, demonstrating by guiding my glass through the motions.

I brought the glass to my lips, bracing myself for the assault of flavors, and took a reluctant gulp of bourbon. *Ugh*. It tasted awful. The bourbon was completely different from what I was used to. And that's exactly why I decided I *loved* it, despite its weird flavors.

A few nights later, we were back at the kitchen table, and I was busy trying to find a way to party in my new small town.

Andy and I had been having shots.

I let the amber liquid spread its warmth throughout my body. I leaned back in my chair, took a gulp of a Sprite chaser, and let out a contented sigh. Everything now felt a bit lighter, more fluid. Easier. I couldn't deny the comforting sensation it gave me, or the fact that due to my weight loss surgery, it was hitting harder than ever before.

I'd been given strict instructions by the gastric bypass surgery professionals not to drink alcohol because of my body getting adjusted to my new stomach size and faster digestive system. In layman's terms, it makes you get drunk faster and can create alcohol dependence, even in those who have never had a problem with substance abuse before.

I could feel the worries and stresses of the move fade away and be replaced with a sense of calmness and joy. That's the easiest way to describe it. Joy. It was as if the weight of the world had been lifted off my shoulders, and I could finally breathe again. With each passing sip, I savored the feeling of the drink.

I started drilling Andy for what people in Frisco did for fun.

"Uhhh, I don't know," he hedged. "People here kinda just go around and stuff."

"What is, like, *the spot* to go to?" I pushed, wondering if Texas was filled with honky-tonk bars or if that was just a stereotype from movies.

I could see worry flash across his face; he was obviously not one to go to any kind of spot on a regular basis. He must have been wondering what he was in for as I pulled him out of his comfort zone. "Don't worry! We'll just look for some good old-fashioned Texan fun!"

I could tell this was going to be awkward at first, but if there's anything I know how to do well, it's talking a person into going out. We chatted more as we drank, and I worked away at his shyness, helping him to open up.

We finished our drinks and made our way to a honky tonk bar. I chatted away, trying to keep the mood light and easy. I told Andy some stories about my wildest experiences in Miami, and he shared some stories of his own from back home in Nigeria.

The live music and lively atmosphere were contagious; we ordered a couple of tequilas and joined the crowd on the dance floor. Andy started to let loose and have some fun and we both found ourselves joining the line dancing, attempting (badly) our best two-stepping. We bopped around to "7 and 7" by Turnpike Troubadours, a song I'd never heard before that night. In fact, I'd never listened to so much country music in my life before that night.

I found myself scanning the crowd for cute guys. Part of my *Sweet Home Alabama* story was to find the love of my life. My gaze landed on a guy who appeared to be about six feet tall with blonde hair and striking green eyes. He had a light scruffy beard that made him look charming. I could see evidence of the six-pack beneath his T-shirt. He looked every bit the modern cowboy as he leaned against the bar, sipping on his beer.

I nudged Andy and pointed the guy out to him, excitedly whispering in his ear about how cute he was. I watched Andy's face fall with disappointment when he realized I would not be going back home with him, in the non-roommate way he hoped for.

He rolled his eyes but cracked a smile at my enthusiasm.

To catch the charming cowboy's attention, I sent over a tequila shot, CoCo-style. Once the server had delivered it, I sauntered over to him and struck up a conversation.

He was a bit awkward at first, but soon we were chatting and laughing, leaning in. I was drawn closer by his intoxicating scent—like leather and tobacco. As I breathed him in, his scent wrapped around me, evoking images of hard work under the Texas sun. There was something undeniably masculine about it. Suddenly, I wanted my hands on him.

As the night wore on, I got lost in conversation with the cowboy, enjoying the spark of attraction between us. Andy seemed content to hang back and watch, happy to see me having a good time.

The clock ticked and patrons began to trickle out, leaving the bar almost deserted. The cowboy leaned in closer, his voice low and tempting, "How about we continue this somewhere more private?" The invitation was clear. I was drawn in.

We left, heading to a nearby hotel, and spent the night together. Once morning came, I knew without a doubt that there was no chemistry with this cowboy. Even worse, I now had a hangover and my stomach hurt from not eating.

So, I went home to bury myself in blankets and sleep away the pain.

PUMPKIN SPICE & MATCH.COM

There is something about the warm autumn sun and the scent of pumpkin spice as it follows me from the coffee shop to my car that tugs at my heart. This season is for families, for love, and for being grateful. When I drove through the streets of Fort Worth, past the rows of stucco-covered houses, I imagined them filled with loving, rowdy, *real* families—the kind that shouted at the television on football Sundays, carved the turkey while arguing with their daughters over politics and then hugged and made up over dessert.

Real families. Real homes. Unconditional love.

I could picture Zach and I in one of those houses, raising a family. I missed him and I wished he could find the motivation to make a change so that we could create a life together. Zach felt like home to me. But in my heart, I knew that he wasn't coming. He had his own demons keeping him away.

The emptiness inside me was almost painful. I wanted a home of my own. Somewhere safe, somewhere I would be loved.

I decided I would take my future into my own hands by setting out in search of love. And where does any twenty-something-year-old go these days to find love?

A dating app.

I set up my profile with no problem. It wasn't hard to find a photo in my camera roll of me looking cute and carefree, flashing a sexy smile at the camera.

Apps made it easy to pick from a list of things I thought I wanted in a man. I never had a problem initiating conversation. I was good at taking that first step and putting my intentions out there.

And that's how I met J. I posted my profile and within a few minutes, he messaged me.

He had the dad look, which I liked. He was real. Not some perfect Ken-doll-looking guy, but still sexy. I loved his hair, and I loved his smile in his photos.

On our first date, the stark contrast between us was hard to miss. He strolled in wearing jeans, a hoodie, and cowboy boots. I wore black skinny pants, a seductive lingerie bodysuit, a sharp black leather jacket, heels, and my hair was impeccably done. He told me I looked like a

Kardashian—his words, not mine. Our conversation flowed so easily. It was as if we were old friends catching up after years apart.

By the second date—which was the next day—I was wondering why he hadn't kissed me yet. Throughout the drive from Frisco to Fort Worth, I stole glances at his rough hands gripping the steering wheel. They looked strong and I imagined what they would feel on my body. I could see by the shape of his jeans that he had big strong calves, which I found incredibly attractive.

We drove with the windows down. The sun beat down on us and I basked in the glow of a perfect day. J's half smile, outlined by his perfectly trimmed scruff and strong jawline, was enough to make my heart skip a beat.

I felt my cheeks flush as I adjusted my hair from behind my neck and checked my lip gloss in the side mirror. In that moment, with the hum of some sultry southern love song on the radio, everything felt just as it should be. J was the missing piece of the puzzle that I had been searching for and being with him made me feel complete.

We had our first kiss that night. I remember J pulling away sooner than I expected. I was used to Miami guys who were very outgoing and sexual. J's standoffishness had me on my toes. I didn't know what to do with that. This was new.

On our third date (which was the third day since we had met), we walked through the streets of The Stockyards of Fort Worth, and my heart began to race with excitement. The energy of the city was contagious, and I couldn't help but feel like I was walking on the set of *Sweet Home Alabama*. The Stockyards was the heart of the city, and as we entered, I was struck by the unique beauty of the area. The people, the food, and the atmosphere were all so different from what I was used to, and I couldn't wait to explore it all.

On our fourth date, we hadn't slept together, and we'd barely shared more than a few shy kisses. I was a fish out of water. I even started wondering if he just wasn't into me or who knew? Maybe he was gay? He certainly didn't come off that way. I found his demeanor to be very masculine and attractive. But I was set on finding out if this guy wanted to do something with me or not!

We went to a restaurant called 2909 for dinner and drinks. Fort Worth at that time of year had outside patios and twinkle lights everywhere. We sat at the bar, and I tried to order 1800 Gold (a favorite tequila of mine), but you couldn't really get that in Texas. So, J introduced me to another tequila, Espolòn. We had shots of that on the rocks.

Little did I know, J had Googled me. He had learned about my family and some of the drama from the Diaz life. When he admitted he had looked me up, it also made it a bit easier for me. Even though I wanted to be a different person in Texas, I was now allowed to share more of the real me and my history with the man I was falling for. This was a good thing. I loosened up and became flirtier. I opened up a little bit about my abuse. Not a lot but something.

As we were on the way home, I knew I had him. Finally, after wondering whether it would ever happen, we had sex. It was good. Really good. But there was a level of intimacy and connection missing that I was used to.

The next morning, I called my sister.

"You're spending a lot of time with him," she said.

"Dude, it's only been four dates!" I laughed. "But there's something different about him, I can't really pinpoint it." I jokingly added, "Mark my words, I'm going to marry this man. There's something about him."

"Woah. You've never really said that about anyone. You usually run away from the idea of marrying somebody."

There was something different about J. Maybe it was because I had to put in so much effort to get a little bit of intimacy and connection out of him. Our dates always started off awkward, but after a few drinks, we would connect more because he would relax.

BIRTHDAY FIGHT

For my twenty-third birthday, I decided I wanted to hit the bar scene in downtown Fort Worth with my friends, Emily and Angie, so they could meet J. They came in from Frisco for it and we started celebrating. After a couple of hours, J caught up with us. We were in the West 7th Street area, a young hipster hot spot in Fort Worth.

I wore black high-waisted jeans, sneakers, and a black, revealing bodysuit. I wore my hair down and I felt really cute.

Emily, Angie, and I were drinking and doing shots.

When J walked in, straight from work, my heart skipped a beat. He looked good.

"J!" I yelled excitedly, ran up to him, and kissed him on the lips. "Come meet my friends!" I said and led him to our spot at the bar. Even after a number of drinks, I found myself a bit nervous. I wanted him to love my friends.

"Emily, Angie, meet J. J, meet Emily and Angie," I said, making introductions.

"Hey, nice to meet you," he said with a nod and turned to the bartender to order a drink.

The vibe immediately changed. Our heightened, carefree, partying mood was immediately brought down to reality.

I hoped J would relax after a drink.

We all decided to go to another bar. J offered to drive, and we piled into his car. I immediately went for the radio to find a station that played Latino music. I started to dance and sing along to the song being broadcast. That lasted about thirty seconds.

J scowled and said, "I don't want to listen to Mexican music," and switched it to a country station.

I looked at him, insulted. "This isn't Mexican music. It's Latino music, reggaeton."

"Anything south of Texas is Mexican," said J, adamantly.

This is the first time J is seeing me with my friends. I couldn't even bear to look back at my friends and see their thoughts written all over their faces.

I texted my friends, so J didn't know what I was saying.

SWEET HOME ALABAMA

ME, EM, ANG GROUP CHAT: *It's okay. Let's just go with it. We'll get to the next bar and have fun. It'll be fine.*

I hoped the change of scenery would help, but J still wasn't really talking to anyone. I could see something was wrong.

Was it my friends? Were we acting too drunk?

A group of guys at the bar heard us celebrating my birthday—we weren't shy about it—so they bought us a round of drinks—including J. I was used to making friends with half a room full of people, so in true CoCo fashion, I ordered a round of tequila shots and sent it back to the guys (as well as a round for us, of course).

J was visibly annoyed or uncomfortable. I couldn't figure out which. Come 8:30 p.m., he wanted to go home. I had planned to sleep over at his house at the end of the night, but it was too early to leave my birthday celebration!

I led J outside to talk about it. We stood in front of the bar, and I rubbed my arms to stay warm. Texas gets cold after the sun goes down. "What's wrong, J? Did I do something wrong?"

His face revealed his anger as he stared at me. "You literally sent an order of shots to *other men* while I'm standing right there!"

I thought of how that must have felt or looked to him. "I'm so sorry, I didn't mean to disrespect you. I'm sorry!"

J shook his head, "You know what? I just think you need to enjoy this with your friends, and I'll see you another day."

"Wait, you're leaving?" It hadn't occurred to me that he might leave in the middle of my birthday. "The whole reason I came to Fort Worth is to celebrate with you, and have you meet my friends. It's only been an hour and a half and you're just going to leave? You haven't even spoken a word to them. *Please* come back in and spend time together!"

"I'm going home. I'm over it," he said.

I stood there on the street, not sure what to do, holding my breath and trying to figure out what had just happened. Tears started to pour down my face as I watched his car speed away. I pushed through the heavy wood and brass double doors to the bar. I found my way back to my friends.

Emily and Angie took one look at me and ordered another round of tequila "ASAP!" as I explained that J had just broken up with me.

"He's gone. We're done. He's over it," he said. "Like *what* did I *do*?"

Emily's jaw dropped. "You're kidding right?"

I shook my head. "I can't believe it. I've never seen him act this way." I stared down at the floor, catching sight of my body and the outfit I'd felt so good in at the beginning of the night. Now I felt like I had done something wrong or trashy or ugly.

Emily said, "Oh my God he is such a total dick!"

We replayed the events of the night, the fact that he looked like he felt out of place for the little amount of time he spent with us. In the end, we gave up trying to figure out what it all meant. I proceeded to drown my sorrows to celebrate the worst birthday ever.

"Maybe this is karma," I said to my friends. "It's karma for every man I played with over the years, everyone I hurt. I've been telling myself this is going to happen—people have been telling me this is going to happen."

"No way!" declared Emily and handed me another shot. "You do not deserve to be treated this way."

Yeah right, I thought, as my mind raced through all the awful things I had done to men who loved me over the years.

With a sleepover at J's off the table, I ended up in a hotel in Fort Worth. I was too trashed to do anything else.

In the morning, I was due back to work early, so I got up, called an Uber, and headed back to Frisco, trying not to cry. It looked like I had to start over. Again. Just the thought of it made me feel sick.

My phone buzzed in my hand. I looked down. It was him.

J: *I'm sorry about last night. I don't want to let you go.*

To my dismay, a rush of relief washed over me. I should be furious with him.

> CoCo: *You said you were over us.*
> CoCo: *To me, that means we are done.*
> CoCo: *Why would you treat me that way?*
> CoCo: *Why would you leave like that?*

How could I show my face to my friends again after last night if I took him back?

> J: *A lot of things were said yesterday. I'm sorry. I really want to make things work.*

I thought of how I must have looked, sobbing in a bar in front of strangers. And then I thought about how he was the cause of that.

> CoCo: *But why did you act that way, J? You wouldn't listen to my Latin music. You wouldn't talk to me or my friends. You left me on my birthday!*
> J: *I know I'm sorry. I'll never act like that again.*

I didn't know what to say. I wanted him to forgive me. I wanted to forgive him. I couldn't shake the intense need I had to have his approval again. I had never been this intolerant of anyone this early into the relationship before.

What's wrong with me? I wondered. *What is so different this time that I'm willing to take him back?*

We went back and forth, and by the end of my forty-minute Uber drive, J and I were back together and I was filled with the excitement of new love once again.

THE J CHARM

I have always loved Christmas. J knew I was a little bit sad this was going to be the first Christmas without my family. J took me to the most beautiful Christmas display I've ever seen. It was at the Gaylord Texan Resort—tens of thousands of square feet filled with Christmas lights that twinkled overhead, casting a warm glow on everything around us. The music, a mixture of country and holiday tunes, floated through the air, adding to the magical feeling of the night. J led me from one spot to the next, pointing out the best restaurants, the coziest bars, and the most interesting shops.

As we walked, laughing together, my arm swinging to brush against his, a wave of contentment washed over me. He presented me with thoughtful little gifts each time we were together.

We approached a bench and I playfully tried to pull him closer to hold his hand. He stiffened and looked around. "I'm not really into the whole PDA thing …"

I looked at him, a little surprised by the brush-off. It felt mean. I wasn't used to being treated that way. Most guys I dated loved having my affection in any way they could get it. The arm's length space that J created felt painful, but it also felt like a challenge.

We stumbled upon a cute little gift shop. The door was locked, but we peered in through the window to catch a glimpse of what was inside. As we stood there, I caught sight of our reflections in the glass. I liked how we fit together. I leaned my head on his shoulder.

This adventure, this night, was everything I had hoped for and so much more.

**

I confessed to J that Christmas Eve was a big night in Latino culture, and in my life. It was the night when we held the biggest celebrations with dancing, food and family. That's the day that included the most traditions that we all cherished. Even when I was with Zach, his family started putting out all the stops on Christmas Eve, knowing I was missing my family. (*To this day, they have a big dinner on December 24th in remembrance of those good times.*)

After The Gaylord evening, I could tell J was trying to make

Christmas special. But when I began mentioning all the little traditions I was excited about—having Christmas dinner the day before, fireworks, making a huge pork dinner, dancing, opening one gift before midnight—he disregarded them as weird.

"In America, we celebrate Christmas. *On* Christmas Day."

When December 24th came, there was no family or dancing or celebration at all. J put on a Christmas movie, we sat on our separate couches, and I drank a bottle of wine. As the night went on, loneliness crept in. Here I was in a relationship, I was supposed to be happy. It was unlike anything I'd felt before. All I knew was I wasn't happy. So, to make it happy, I went to our at-home bar, grabbed a bottle of Espolòn, taking shots right in front of J, until I got drunk enough and thought, *Fuck it. The only thing we have left to do to celebrate is have sex*. So, we did.

On Christmas Day, I woke up determined to make the best of things and approach my new Texas life with a fresh perspective. Maybe I was being too hard on J. Maybe I needed to let go of mine and embrace more of his. Besides which, I had already spent a lot of time and money on shopping for special, one-of-a-kind gifts for J, to show him, more than words, how much I cared for him. J had repeatedly told me that actions spoke louder than words for him. If we were to talk about love languages, his was "acts of service." Mine was "words of affirmation."

I woke up super early and made sure to take out one of the gifts I had hidden. J, like me, was terrible at waiting for surprises, so we had both managed to open and perfectly re-wrap all of each other's presents. But there was one gift I had managed to keep a surprise. I'd used some of Gary's sports industry connections to get my hands on an autographed and framed jersey of J's all-time favorite Longhorn football player.

I'll never forget J's face when he ripped open that paper and saw his present.

I was also so thankful for all the gifts he gave me in return. He showered me with them. It was sweet and it made me rethink the loneliness of Christmas Eve.

***

After the high of the holiday season, I was staying over at J's all the time and was offered a promotion—to become a general manager—at a store that was closer to his house. With Emily being my only friend and spending all my free time with J, it just made sense to move in with him now, as opposed to waiting any longer. I packed up my Frisco life and moved to Fort Worth, into J's house, and we began planning our future. My mother and sister probably thought I was crazy, but I told them about my yearning for love and a small-town life where I could raise a family. They didn't get it, but they didn't have to. This was *my* life now.

Fort Worth wasn't Miami. And J wasn't like any guy I had dated before. He liked to plan ahead. He liked order. He had specific views on what family looked like. J put financial stability as a top priority (something that I had always hoped Zach could have been able to do). He was responsible and gave me a sense of security that had nothing to do with the financial aspect—and he wanted to share his life with me.

It felt like this was my chance.

TEXAS CHIC

Everything about our relationship became extreme, including the expectations we had of each other and the promises we made.

We partied a lot, had a lot of sex, and lived in a whirlwind of romance. It was one of the highest highs I've ever felt in my life, which is probably why I soon came to find out that it couldn't last that way.

We started to fight.

One night I was doing dishes and water started coming out of the bottom of the sink. Something was wrong. J jumped off the couch, came into the kitchen, and pushed me to the side. "What did you do?!" he growled.

"J, nothing. I'm just doing the dishes. Obviously, I didn't do anything!"

He opened the cupboard below the sink and started throwing grabbing items and throwing them behind him, saying things like, "Well, this is ruined, and this is fucked ... what did you do?"

"I didn't do anything bad. The water just started coming out of there!"

He snorted. "Well, I've lived in this house for almost a year, and I've never had any problems with it, so you must have done something."

That was the first time I saw how J reacts to anything that goes wrong. It was one of the first times I felt belittled by him since my birthday.

J started picking fights with me about how much I drank, what I wore, who I texted, where we would party, and how hard we would party. When we fought, it increased my need to win his love. I wanted him to choose me and love me. I dreamed of us being inseparable and him saying sweet things to me. I wanted it so much; I would almost become manic.

What I got instead was rejection, criticism, judgment, and coldness. That is until the fight ended with intoxicating make-up sex.

The next morning, I'd wake with hope and a resolve to do better.

Much of our conflict was over my transition into our new life.

"You have so many clothes, they don't even fit in the closet," he said to me one morning, after I had emerged from the bedroom dressed in black leather tights and a bright pink blazer with a tight black crop top underneath and monster silver heels.

"J, of course I have a lot of clothes. Have we met? I'm a Diaz."

"Well, half of that stuff is from Miami, and you know you're not going to wear most of that shit here, so you might as well get rid of it."

He looked over my ensemble, clearly wishing I had left my bold, flamboyant style behind in Miami. He asked, "Want me to get a black trash bag?"

I don't know if he was jealous of my past or embarrassed by me bringing my dramatic Miami fashion choices to Texas, but his ridicule had me questioning myself. But if I held onto my Miami clothing, maybe I wasn't fully committing to our life together after all. If I was going to live the part, I should probably look the part too, right?

The thought occurred to me that Zach or Juan would never have asked me to do something like this. They loved the way I dressed.

I quickly disregarded the thought. I needed to focus on what was in front of me.

Days later, I found myself standing in the middle of our spacious walk-in closet, surveying the meticulously organized rows of plaid shirts, jeans, gingham dresses, and white linen peasant tops.

The sight before me was a dramatic departure from the colorful, attention-grabbing Miami and Latin-style outfits I was used to. Those shimmering, bold dresses that used to dance with me on Miami nights were nowhere in sight. At J's suggestion, I had willingly boxed up that past.

As I was digesting the contrast of my current attire against the wardrobes of my past, my phone buzzed, breaking the trance. The screen flashed "Linda La."

With a hesitant swipe, I answered and feigned my usual cheer, "*Hola*, Sis!"

"*Hola*! I was just online shopping and saw the cutest sequin dress. Totally your vibe. You should get it for the next family gathering. It's so you!"

I hesitated, picturing the dress in my mind and then looking around at the closet. "Oh, sounds lovely. But you know, I've been exploring a new … uh, more subtle style lately," I stammered, feeling the weight of the pretense.

Linda chuckled, "Subtle? Since when?"

I laughed, "Just trying something new, I guess."

There was a silent pause before Linda finally said, "Just don't lose yourself in all the 'new', okay?"

I knew what she was saying. The wardrobe makeover somehow

felt symbolic of a much larger shift. It was one thing to evolve on my own terms, but another to be molded into someone else's idea of what I should be. Did I willingly step into this new chapter, or was I trying to fit a narrative that wasn't entirely mine?

I stood before the multiple racks of clothes and I reminded myself that I chose this. Each clothing purchase and change I made to fit into this new Texas life held a deeper significance. They became symbols of rebirth and a full life makeover. I was leaving the heavy baggage of the past behind me. It had held me down for far too long.

As I made small and large adaptations to my new life with J, any hesitation was followed by a wave of excitement, as if I were brushing away the remnants of the old CoCo.

I had to admit that the gentle texture of the plaid shirts offered me a sense of comfort, just in a different and new way. The sweaters wrapped around me like a warm embrace, and I liked the feeling of security they gave me. *And I looked hot in jeans*! I couldn't help but delight in the success of my transformation. It was a declaration of my commitment to this new life and this relationship that felt different from anything I had experienced before.

Despite my efforts to assimilate into J's lifestyle and the Texas culture, our arguments continued. I could feel the familiar trauma-fueled anger creeping back into my world. It had followed me to Texas and began to wash away any hope for a good life with this man, much less a *Sweet Home Alabama* one.

J had a clear vision of what he wanted and didn't. He liked going out, but he wanted to be home by 10:30 p.m. He wanted a stable life and required a clean house. He didn't like me going out and partying without him. Yet, he still had no interest in spending time with my friends, even after the birthday fight. He preferred to stay home together and get wasted together with a bottle of wine and go to sleep.

When we fought, I would either go to bed and slam the door or I would storm out of the house in search of a different source of happiness—inevitably causing more problems.

FUCKING CRAZY

After a couple of months together, and probably a dozen massive fights, I started noticing J texting on his phone a lot. I was doing the same, frankly, because I hadn't cut off communication with Zach. Even though he had opted out of a sweet small-town life with me, we still talked. He was still in love with me. I liked the way I felt when he said sweet things to me. So, I keep the connection going.

On our first New Year's Eve together, my suspicions that J was sexting and cheating on me were confirmed. I got a hold of his phone and was scrolling through it while waiting for a cab outside the restaurant. That's when I discovered a series of secret messages, sneaky plans with other women, and sexy messages.

I *lost* it.

My head and heart pounded with a mix of anger, confusion, and intoxication. If J wanted to spend the rest of his life with me, how could he be talking to other women? Was I not good enough for him? Did I not give him everything he wanted? Did I not look how he wanted?

I felt as if I was being rejected once again. In a fit of rage and betrayal, I stomped on his phone with the heel of my boot and enjoyed the sound of its glass shattering.

J came out of the restaurant to the sight of me smashing his phone. "CoCo! What the—"

"Why would you do that?" I spat, pointing down at what was left of the phone. I hated that my voice was trembling. I wanted to look strong under the weight of his stare, not insecure or crazy. "What have I not given you?"

"You broke my phone!" he exclaimed, pretending not to hear my question. "Maybe I should smash your phone every time you talk to your ex-boyfriends," he sneered.

I fought back, my voice rising with each word. "I told you about my past, about Zack, and you claimed to be okay with it. But these ... These are naked pictures of other women!"

"I don't know what you're talking about, CoCo. You're fucking crazy!" he half laughed, half spit at me. "Every guy on earth has photos of naked girls on their phone," he said, trying to reframe reality.

"These are not just naked girls from a Google search, J. They are naked girls you're talking to!" I pushed him in the chest, furious at his denial.

As I went to push him again, he brushed my hands away. "Stop being crazy, CoCo," he fake-laughed as if he was dealing with some clown off the street, knowing that it would make me even angrier.

J had become good at pretending like something was no big deal, when to me, it was a very big deal. This was a development that had occurred early in our relationship. His detachment and complete lack of remorse for how he hurt me was what always crushed me the most. The worst part was that he knew it would crush me and, out of cruelty, did it anyway.

When we arrived back home, I tore out of the cab to escape the suffocating tension and anger. There had been no apology, no resolution, no reaching out for peace.

Inside, I went straight to my closet and started packing my bags. I knew deep down that J and I were at a turning point in our relationship. This fight was my chance to break free, to leave my failed attempt at a normal life.

I heard J slam the front door, stomp to the couch, and turn on the television.

As I jammed my suitcases full of my barely-broken-in Texan wardrobe, I pictured the look on my mother's face when I returned to Florida a failure. Just the thought of it was nauseating. I ran to the bathroom and threw up. I couldn't bear the thought of turning to my family for help. *Again.* I pictured the looks of pity when I was forced to admit that yet another one of my wild plans had blown up in my face. My stomach churned and I threw up again. *CoCo the fuckup.* I wished I could disappear.

I brushed my teeth, returned to the bed, picked up my suitcase, and before I could will myself to put even one more item in it, said, "Fuck this!" and threw it across the room.

I flew down the hallway and confronted J. I swore at him and pushed his buttons as hard as I could. I wanted this fight. I wanted him to fight for me. I wanted him to care.

"No man in his right mind would let his girlfriend text their ex-boyfriend."

"You said you were fine about me talking to Zach. It's not like he's sending me naked pictures!"

"What about the guy from the bar I saw you flirting with and the late-night messages? Who are you talking to then?"

"J, you have no idea what you're talking about. You're just making stuff up. Why do you even want to be with me if you hate me so much!?"

I wasn't just fighting J. I was fighting for someone to love me. I was screaming at him, but what I really wanted to ask was, "Am I unlovable? What is wrong with me?"

J insisted he wasn't cheating, deflecting blame, gaslighting me, and making sure I felt as if I was overreacting. I knew then that this was how it would be. Now and forever, with J.

For me, anger was a double-edged sword, a force that both consumed and empowered me, heightening my senses to an almost unbearable degree.

I went back to the bedroom, scraped my suitcase from the floor, and threw it back on the bed. J followed me into the room.

"Get the fuck away from me!" I wailed. "I am fucking done. I am fucking leaving, J—I am done!"

"You think I care?" J shot back. "You're nothing but a joke!"

I grabbed my face and dug my nails into my face and scalp, filled with the fury of ridicule and rejection. I wanted to find release in the pain it brought.

"What the hell are you doing?" he asked. "You need help," he spat, with disgust in his voice.

In the midst of our confrontation, the world around me faded into the background, dulled by adrenaline. There was a peculiar euphoria in those moments of rage. A cathartic release that coursed through me like a drug. It hurt me more than anyone else, a new form of self-harm. It was all pain.

As the fight escalated, so did J's anger. He hurled an insult at me and punched the wall to make his point—and so that he didn't punch me.

"You think *you* can scare *me*?" I would never let another man scare or control me ever again. And he needed to know that. "Nothing fucking scares me, J. NOTHING." I wanted to believe the words coming out of my mouth, but I didn't. I was scared.

I stared at him, recognizing his cold rage. It was familiar to me. It felt like home. Not the kind of home I ever wanted, but a home I knew. He had become a reflection of myself and my past, a mirror into the darkness I'd carried with me since I was five.

"Stay away from me!" I tore through our closet and pulled clothes down into a heap on the floor.

"You think you can just leave me?" he said. This time his tone was different. "Perfect. Go. I'll go ahead and put your shit on the lawn."

I realized his beast was bigger than mine.

When the fight was over and the awkward silence set in, as it always did, I wondered how much longer I could keep living like this. Physically exhausted, I would often find myself reeling from the sheer amount of energy it had taken from me. The release of words, of pent-up frustrations, left me drained and hollow, as if I had been poured out over our bedroom floor in the process.

Having grown up in a home where displays of anger were commonplace, I was used to explosions and punishment. And in return, I learned to fight fire with fire, even against inanimate objects. Growing up, the smallest challenges always seemed to intensify my internal fury.

Take, for instance, tying my shoelaces when I was a little girl. For the longest time, I just couldn't figure it out. I would get so angry; I'd literally tug at my hair till it hurt. It is such a trivial task that it seemed like everyone else could do, but not me. It made me wonder what was wrong with me. Why couldn't I master something so simple? With every unsuccessful knot, every lace that slipped from my grasp and refused to form a bow, I felt like a failure. Another tally mark on my ever-growing list of personal failures.

J's behavior only reinforced my insecurities. Whenever something went awry at home—a broken vase, a mislaid tool—the fault was mine, even if I wasn't involved or in another part of the house entirely. Instead of questioning him, I questioned myself, believing that maybe I was as clumsy, careless, and incapable as he made me out to be. Perhaps if I were more careful, smarter, or simply *better*, he'd see my worth.

J may not have been an angel, but I had convinced myself that his outward stability would be enough to chase away my demons. For a while, he provided a distraction from my insecurities, and I clung to him like a lifeline.

The following day, like always, I was determined to start fresh. I buzzed around the kitchen, putting the finishing touches on dinner. I heard the sound of J's boots on the wood as he came through the front door. I hoped he'd left the chaos from the previous night behind him like I was trying to do.

It was clear from the moment I saw him that he was exhausted, as if the weight of the world was crushing him. No greeting, no acknowledgment of my presence, just a half-hearted nod before he slumped onto his familiar spot on the couch. The TV flickered to life, filling the room with the mindless noise of sports highlights and talk shows. There he sat, like a statue, his eyes glazed over, detached from the real world. No matter how hard I tried, he wouldn't let me in. Our conversation remained superficial, devoid of any intimacy. This was so different from what I was used to. As a Latina woman, I had come to expect a man who wanted his hands on me, who loved being kissed and hugged, who always had his hand on the small of my back. A partner who wasn't afraid to show that he was as obsessed with me as I was with him.

Despite his public image as a quintessential Texas gentleman—polite, kind, and well-spoken—J had a talent for hiding his true emotions. He wore a mask of politeness, keeping everyone at a distance. He could engage in conversations about current events or shared interests, but when it came to revealing anything personal, he always held back. I was often left wondering who the real J was. Which side of him was the real side, true to himself?

I watched him from the end of the kitchen counter, trying to determine which version of J was the real one—or at least, which one was mine.

It was as if he had an impenetrable barrier safeguarding his true emotions, preventing anyone from truly connecting with him. The surface-level charm of the Texas gentleman masked his emotional distance.

We were trapped in an endless loop of superficiality, never breaking through to the real issues that mattered.

I don't know how much longer I can continue like this, I thought, trying to come to terms that my happily ever after was out of reach again.

GREAT ON PAPER

I slumped on the barstool, staring into my half-empty glass as my friend Emily arrived, sliding onto the stool beside me, her eyes immediately filled with concern.

"Emily!" I squealed and threw my arms around her. "I'm so happy you're here." I'd been missing her so much since I'd hooked up with J.

"I miss you too, girl!" She squeezed me hard. "CoCo, what's up? You look like you've been through hell and back."

I knew she was right. My eyes were red from crying and drinking most of the day.

"Well, damn, thank you for letting me know I look like shit," I teased her, half-heartedly.

"CoCo, you know you always look flawless," she rolled her eyes. "Now tell me what's going on."

"It's J. I honestly don't know what to do. I want to make this work so bad, but I don't know how much longer I can keep sacrificing."

"I don't get him. If he wants you and doesn't want to let you go, I don't understand why he's being so difficult." Emily always tried to root for J and me to work out but it was becoming impossible.

"I don't either," I admit. "One day he is the kindest, most attentive, cutest man. And the next day it's like I'm with a stranger, and no matter what I do, it's all wrong."

"You deserve to have someone who adores you," said Emily.

"When we're drinking, we get along well but if he drinks too much, we fight. And lately, because we've been going out with his friends and drinking a lot more, I'm seeing a side of him I don't like."

"What do you mean? Is he being like Matt?"

Matt was Emily's boyfriend who had been struggling with alcohol after having several family members pass away.

"No, not like Matt. And it's not just him. It's the both of us. When we first start drinking, everything is great, he's flirty, open, and fun. I feel like I can open up to him. It is like he finally relaxes enough to open up to me too."

Well, that doesn't seem that bad—"

"Until the switch is flipped." I interrupt. "He becomes cold, angry, rude, careless, cruel and aggressive. I don't even recognize him when he's like that. And I become unhinged. I get so fearful of the idea of losing him, fearful that I have no idea who he is, fearful of what he's capable of, and most of all, fearful that even though I'm trying so hard to make this relationship work, he's not the one."

Since my relationship with J had begun to break apart, my addictions resurfaced with a vengeance. I was maxing out credit cards and taking out new ones. Late nights blurred into early mornings, colored with liquor—familiar patterns of self-destruction. I'd stumble home at odd hours, sometimes greeted by J's yelling, other times by his cold indifference. I don't know which was worse.

Emily's eyes were filled with concern but without judgment.

"Damn, CoCo, I wish I knew how to help. It's so hard to know what to do with J. He's so great on paper. If only he could just stop being such a dick."

A lump formed in my throat, and I took a shaky breath. "That's not all," I admitted, avoiding her gaze. "My period is late."

For a moment, Emily just stared, processing what I just said. Then, setting her drink down firmly, she said, "We need to know for sure. Let's go get a test. *Now*."

Before I could protest, she was pulling me up, settling the bill quickly. We dashed to the nearest pharmacy, and within moments I was in the restroom, the small stick of fate in my hand. Em and I waited for what were the longest three minutes of my life.

When the result finally appeared, the room was filled with silence.

CHAPTER SIX

FAMILY

For one electric second, a rush of happiness swept through me. The air shimmered and I had one thought—family. All I ever wanted was exhibited in the form of a plus on the stick in my hand. Until I remembered where I was—and *who* I was.

I was pregnant. ME. CoCo Roper. Renowned party girl and fuckup. I mean, who the hell was I to bring a child into this world? How could I be a good mother when I felt like a disaster in every other way? I mustered the courage to call J. I didn't know what I wanted him to say, but I hoped that whatever it was, his words would make it make sense.

My hands trembled as I dialed his number, every ring elongating the anticipation. When he answered, there was a hint of surprise in his voice, not expecting a call at this hour.

"J," I began, hating the sound of fear in my voice when I said his name. "I'm pregnant."

I heard his breath stop and felt his shock and disbelief radiating through the phone. "I thought you couldn't get pregnant," he said carefully. The tone wasn't accusatory, merely filled with surprise.

My stomach churned with anxiety. After suffering from endometriosis and other issues, I was told the likelihood of kids was minimal, if not impossible. "Apparently, the doctors were wrong, J …" I didn't know what I wanted from him, but I did know that for me, abortion was off the table. "This is happening, J."

"What do we do now?" he asked.

"Do we break up? Do we get married?" I remember asking, my voice stripped of any excitement, replaced by grim practicality.

"Well, we've already talked about being together in the future. Maybe getting married is the right thing to do, given the circumstances," he said matter-of-factly.

"Well I don't want you to marry me just because I'm pregnant," I protested.

"I wouldn't do something if I didn't want to do it," he said.

That was how I got engaged to J. No big proposal. No "I love you." No rings. No kiss.

I reasoned with myself that this was better than going back to my mom and admitting that my Texan getaway had resulted in disaster.

Before I had too long to think about what that meant, I was preparing to go to Costa Rica.

DON'T MAKE ME GO

The last thing on earth I wanted was to go back to Costa Rica for the trial and face Carlos again, but I knew I didn't have a choice. I had to show up for Linda and my mom.

"J, please come with me. I can't do this alone," I begged, but he said he had to work. J didn't feel comfortable with the idea of going to CR for a trial, especially with the safety issues in Costa Rica with my dad.

On the plane, I stared at the back of the seat in front of me, trying not to panic. I was pregnant, which meant I had to stay in the mess. There would be no numbing out. I don't remember if anyone spoke to me or who sat near me.

My mind was in free fall at the thought of Carlos burning a hole into me with his glare—and that's assuming I made it to court. Who knows? Maybe one of his hit men would get me in the airport bathroom so I wouldn't have to take any stand at all, ever again.

Once we touched down, I grabbed my bags and went straight for the hotel, wishing I could have a drink, a pill, a line, anything. My phone buzzed against the table, scaring me half to death. It buzzed again, lighting up with a number I didn't recognize. But my stomach lurched instinctively.

"Hello?" My voice was hesitant.

"Is this CoCo?" a gruff voice inquired.

"Yes, who is this?"

"This is Detective Rodriguez. I'm calling about the allegations against you."

I felt the blood drain from my face. I didn't know what was worse: the threat to my life, the sexual abuse trial, or having to deal with legal charges. Costa Rica was different. Influence and money could get you out of anything. But not in Texas.

Not now. Please, not now.

I hung up on him. I didn't know what else to do.

The next time my phone buzzed, it was my sister. "CoCo, the court date is canceled. Carlos didn't show up."

Apparently, he was "so sick" that he couldn't show up for court. We knew this was just Carlos's manipulation of us and the courts. He was trying to waste our time and make us go back and forth, stressing and preparing for court, only for the date to be canceled. He hoped we'd get so exhausted that we'd just drop the case.

I didn't have to testify. I immediately unclenched my teeth and exhaled one very long breath.

Thank God.

I was relieved not to have to face Carlos.

We talked for a few minutes before hanging up. As always, I was drawn to the window, staring at the bustling Costa Rican streets. I adored my home, the vibrant colors, and the people.

There was one silver lining to the trip. My mother was overjoyed at the prospect of becoming a grandmother. She was already shopping for baby clothes. Her radiant optimism was contagious.

My mother and I decided to meet up in Miami and look for some of the things I would need to bring a baby into the world. I loved seeing her pick out blue clothes (she was convinced it was going to be a boy). It brought a fleeting smile to my face.

My phone rang again.

"There's a possibility you could be arrested today." The words sent chills down my spine. It was my lawyer.

"That can't happen," I said firmly.

"I'm working on it," the lawyer replied. "I'll keep you posted."

I hung up.

"What on earth is wrong?" my mother asked when she saw my face. I couldn't speak. "Nothing, Mami," I said and flashed her a fake smile.

I turned away and continued mindlessly sifting through baby outfits as the world secretly crashed in on me.

I packed as fast as I could and met with my lawyer and the police. I had no intention of being arrested, so my lawyer arranged for me to go directly to them. I was honest and begged for forgiveness, promised to repay—with interest—and explained that I'd been battling addiction and had since become sober. My lawyer helped pitch a settlement that made everyone happy, and I readily agreed. Even though, technically, I had to go to jail, it was for mere minutes. With no prior convictions, coupled with my brutal honesty and my ability to immediately repair any financial damage, we were able to reach a speedy agreement.

I was so grateful to have faced this particular demon head-on and be able to walk away with my dignity intact.

THIS IS HAPPENING

Once the legal matters were taken care of, I flew home and changed into a soft, long-sleeved (to cover my tattoos), flowing dress to fit the profile of an idealized version of myself.

J whistled at me as he eyed me up and down. "You look nice," he remarked, matching my nervous energy.

I mustered a smile. "Thanks." We were about to go to dinner with his parents and tell them about the baby and our engagement. This was going to be a big night for us. I was a nervous wreck.

J's family welcomed us in. But as the evening progressed, I waited in anticipation for J to share the news. Every clink of cutlery and polite exchange steered the conversation away from the reason we were there.

I tapped his knee under the table to cue him that it was time. We had to just come out with it and tell his parents what was going on. He pretended he didn't feel or hear my hints.

J, usually chatty with his parents, appeared at a loss for words. As dessert was served, I waited. Every ticking second stretched the silence. But the announcement never came.

The drive back home felt like an eternity, the darkness outside matching the storm brewing within me. The anger bubbled to the surface, and I finally burst: "Why, J? You had so many chances tonight. Was this not the whole point of the dinner? Are you ashamed of our child? Of us?"

He remained silent, his eyes locked onto the road, but his evasiveness spoke volumes. That night, the walls between us grew thicker, and the weight of his unspoken shame was palpable.

Reflecting on the evening, tears welled up in my eyes. The sting of betrayal, the undercurrent of embarrassment, and the layers upon layers of shame added to the mounting pressure—how did our love story, our blessing, turn into such a source of anguish?

J promised to call his parents and set up another dinner. He swore that this time we were going to tell them everything. To our surprise, when the day finally came, we were greeted with joy and congratulations. Sheri even cried at the thought of having another grandchild.

LAST CHANCE

We set a date for our wedding in April. The day before, J and I had a huge fight. I think it was about a debt that he was worried about, but it soon wouldn't be a concern. My parents gave me the gift of a clean financial slate, so J didn't feel like he was taking on my financial baggage.

I woke up on the morning of my wedding feeling sick to my stomach.

It would be the first time our families would meet and spend time together. Even my mother had only met J once before.

Before leaving to get ready, I left J a card and a bottle of whiskey. I knew he'd appreciate the gesture of liquid courage. We were both so nervous. We were trying to do the right thing but the circumstances were less than romantic.

Twenty-five people in total were in attendance at our courthouse wedding. The building was gorgeous.

I went to the hotel where my mom was staying, just a block away from the courthouse. My mom helped me get ready, doing my hair and makeup. My sister was there. The twins were there. The only friends from Costa Rica that I invited were Christina (who couldn't make it) and Tebi (a longtime friend from my less crazy days).

My mother lent me some of her jewelry.

Just as I was about to leave my mom's hotel room, she put her hand on my shoulder. "Are you sure you want to do this? This is your last chance to walk away. You can still say no to all of this but once we leave this room, there's no turning back."

I tried to imagine saying no at that point and was horrified at what everyone would think ... what J would think. I remember thinking, *I just have to go now. This is it. This is the right thing.*

I had planned this day in less than a month. People thought I was crazy for choosing the courthouse, but that's only because they had never laid eyes on it. The building was gorgeous, and it would be gorgeous in photos. Some of my favorite videos are of me making my way up those big steps with my veil caught up in the breeze.

An elevator took me to the floor where our ceremony would be held. As the elevator doors opened, J was standing in front of me. His face lit up. That smile—I loved it.

It was the first time he'd seen me in my dress. I could tell he didn't really know what to say or do, but neither did I. We were both petrified.

The only challenge with a courthouse wedding is that you have to wait for your name to be called by the judge. I remained standing beside J, trying not to think too hard. Even though I was pregnant, I wasn't showing at all.

The waiting wasn't long, but it was long enough to allow fears and self-doubt to begin creeping in. Emily looked over at me and recognized that look on my face. I was about to have a panic attack.

"Why don't we freshen up, CoCo?" she suggested so that I could make a graceful exit.

I nodded, my eyes wide and my heart pounding in my ears. She took me by the hand and led me to the bathroom.

"Oh my God, what am I doing?" I panicked, wringing my hands and pacing in my gorgeous white fit-and-flare Halston gown that clung to my body in all the right ways. But at that moment, I wasn't thinking about how I looked.

Emily took me by the shoulders and said, "Try to breathe, it'll be okay. You're getting married! You're supposed to be happy!"

"I've gotta get out of here! I can't do it, I can't—"

I heard the slap before I felt it. "Ow!! What the fuck was that for?!" I squealed in shock. Emily had slapped me to snap me out of my spiral. I instantly forgave her, knowing that's exactly what I needed to bring me back to reality.

"You *need* to do this. Really. You convinced me this was the right decision and I believed you and now here we are and I'm here to help you say I do!"

She carried on fussing over my hair and makeup and dress for a moment until she stopped and whispered, *"But if you really want to run, we can go. Like now."*

Little did I know, J was in the men's bathroom having a similar conversation with his best man.

I sighed heavily, knowing it was time to get my shit together. "No. I love J and I love this baby already. I'm just freaking out. Let's go get married!"

She winked at me. I hugged her. And I prepared to walk down the aisle.

Emily truly was my ride-or-die and I loved her for it.

We went back into the waiting area and I heard our names being called. My stomach filled with butterflies.

All of our friends and family were already in the courtroom.

J and I took our positions in front of the judge, trying not to look too nervous. I had the biggest smile on my face, hoping it would hide my complete terror.

When I said "I do," I did so with all the hope in the world for our future together.

We put wedding bands on each other's fingers.

"I now pronounce you husband and wife," said the judge. "You may kiss the bride."

We kissed quickly and he said, for the first time, "I love you."

I remember getting a rush of adrenaline when he said those words. I had been so desperate to hear him say that.

J pulled a tissue out of his pocket to dab away the nervous sweat that had accumulated on his forehead. I could tell he was freaking out because he was sweating the entire day.

We had a small reception with our small guest list, but there was no first dance. My sister was acting out of character, tearing up because she wasn't the one getting married. I found myself consoling her and feeling guilty to be the one tying the knot before her. She had never acted like that before so I wasn't sure what to do.

When the party was over, J and I returned home together. We crawled into bed, and instead of celebrating our marriage, J rolled over and went to sleep. I lay awake, tears soaking my pillow, wondering if I'd just made the best decision of my life or the worst.

By morning, I convinced myself that maybe, if I did things right, if I got my shit together, maybe this man who was now my husband (and would soon be the father of my daughter) would love me the way I had always wanted to be loved.

UNFIT

When I announced my pregnancy, everyone seemed thrilled. They probably thought this would make me grow up and calm down. Whereas most expectant mothers are beaming with a maternal glow and show off their baby bumps beneath cute dresses, my experience was different. I was still losing weight and had been ever since getting my gastric sleeve. You can see in my wedding photos that I was probably the thinnest I had ever been.

As my pregnancy progressed, and I still wasn't showing, people began to fuss around me, picking at what I ate or didn't eat, or how often I threw up—as if I had control over that. I could only tolerate one small sandwich per day, which I would eat throughout the day, not in one sitting. J started making grilled cheese sandwiches that were cooked with so much butter and extra cheese that I was able to gain a few pounds. But it wasn't enough.

I didn't want to be sick. I felt like a lab experiment sometimes, but I was used to having all eyes on me and the choices I made. I'm a Diaz.

Whenever we went shopping, my mother's critical eye assessed and dissected the maternity outfits I tried on. I didn't really need them because I hadn't gained any weight. I was still throwing up regularly. "This one might make you look a bit fuller," she'd say, or, "You know, if you just ate a bit more, that dress would sit better."

I'd spent years before my weight loss surgery wanting my mother to think I was thin enough. But now, the narrative was often that I was too skinny. Being that it was less than a year after my surgery, pounds were still falling off and I was still throwing up regularly whenever I ate more than a few tablespoons of food at a time. It was really hard to keep weight on, even though I knew I needed to try to do that for my baby's sake. I could feel people's eyes on me—pitying me for being so skinny when I should be plump with pregnancy, judging me for not being fit to bring a baby into the world.

I felt like an unfit mother—and I hadn't even had my baby yet.

"Come on, baby," I whispered to my belly whenever I had a moment to myself. "You can do this. I love you more than anything in the whole wide world." I'd sing to my baby and talk to her, hoping she would thrive and be the beginning of my family. I was already in love with her and she wasn't even here yet.

By the sixth month, I was still barely showing, No amount of singing or wishing was helping her. Most people gain thirty pounds with their babies; I lost thirty-five. With the weight loss, my PCOS (polycystic ovarian syndrome), and endometriosis, the term "high risk pregnancy" had become a constant narrative and my doctors watched me like a hawk. I was diagnosed with preeclampsia, a potentially deadly condition, and IUGR (Intrauterine Growth Restriction), which essentially meant Ellie had stopped growing because she wasn't receiving the nutrients she so desperately needed.

I am literally unfit, I panicked secretly. I tried not to let my fear show, but I'm sure it was written across my face.

I didn't really start showing until the end of my pregnancy. I cherished that period, because around 6:30 or 7:00 in the evening, she would start moving inside my belly and I *loved* that feeling. I would sing to her and play videos to her. Emily would come over and talk to her too.

Because I couldn't get enough nutrition, I began fainting a lot. At first, J was there to catch me. The more that I fainted, the less worried he became. I could see he was wondering if I was just being dramatic. Thankfully, he didn't say as much. He continued to support me in whatever ways he could.

I remember waking with a headache one day, but I didn't realize where it was coming from.

At first, we thought we would have more time before my daughter made her appearance in the world. But then things got scary. I saw my doctor and my blood pressure had risen to levels that were risking the health of my baby and myself. That meant we needed to start labor now.

LISTEN TO ME

The doctors didn't mince words. I had been begging them to let me carry her just a little longer in the hopes that it would be good for her, but the medical team said no. "You need to have the baby right now."

I was still working as of the day I was about to give birth. That meant I needed to maintain calm just long enough to finish off work tasks and hand over the reins to the new manager taking over in my absence.

My mother jumped on a plane as soon as she could so that she could be by my side in time for the delivery.

The birth of Ellie was difficult and terrifying. My abdominal area had always been a battleground and it seemed that this was no different.

They induced labor with Pitocin, gave me an epidural, and told me to get comfortable. It would likely be about twenty hours before I met my baby. Within a few hours, I felt pressure. There's only one time you feel that pressure, and it's while you're giving birth. It felt like Ellie was coming out. I called for a nurse, who appeared within a few minutes.

"I can feel my baby coming out! I think I'm having her right now!" I exclaimed.

The nurse scrunched up her nose, tried not to roll her eyes, and flippantly said, "You just got the Pitocin. There's no way you could be in labor so soon."

I didn't know what to say as she walked away. J was in the delivery room with me. I looked up at him and felt a strong pressure again. I could literally feel Ellie, always the impatient one, deciding that the time was NOW.

"J, oh my God, call the nurse back!"

J said, "Nicole, the nurse said it wasn't time yet."

"J, you're not the one feeling this pressure coming out of your vagina. It is time. NOW!"

He went to the door, now believing me, and said, "I need someone in here. *Now.*" He wasn't taking no for an answer.

A nurse begrudgingly came in, did a check, and immediately flew into action. "Looks like you're right!" she said.

When the doctor came in, he had to tell me when to push and when not to because my epidural was in full force. I couldn't feel the contractions, just a constant pressure.

They said twenty hours. Ellie seemed to say, "How about four?" Then she was born. Ellie was in the world, her small cries echoing in the room. She was born at thirty-five weeks and was a mere four pounds.

Four pounds ... You don't realize how tiny a four-pound baby is until you see one in person. Ellie was a fragile, tiny being, fighting for every breath and she had my whole heart immediately. At first, despite her small size, she seemed to be doing pretty well. I was able to hold her in my arms. But then her heartbeat became erratic. Her premature lungs weren't fully developed and she struggled with the enormity of life outside the womb. A team of doctors and nurses whisked my baby away. In that heart-wrenching moment of separation, I was distracted by the realization of something horribly wrong happening inside me.

It was an indescribable feeling—a sensation of gushing blood, even when nothing seemed to be coming out. I looked at my mom and told her something was wrong. She called for a doctor or nurse.

They came in, took a look at me, and said, "Everything looks good."

But it wasn't. I was bleeding out. I had placenta abruption which could be a life and death situation. By the time they realized what was happening, there was no time to prepare an operating room. The doctor wanted to try to save me there on the table.

Mom stood on one side of me, J on the other. To this day, I think they are still both traumatized by the sounds I was making and what came next.

Even with an epidural, I felt this. I felt *all* of it. The doctor put her hand inside of me and pulled and ripped out parts of the placenta. Blood was everywhere. The doctor had to keep pulling parts out and then going back in. It felt like the doctor's hand was inside me up to my lungs. With every move they made, it was like being pulled at or cut inside. I knew the doctor was trying to save my life but the pain was blinding. I screamed and sobbed and begged to be knocked out so I wouldn't have to feel it. But again, I was met with, "There is no time for that."

They thought they got all the placenta out finally, and stopped torturing me with the ripping and pulling of my insides. Then, about twenty minutes later, I started feeling like I was bleeding again. It was happening again. The team realized they had to do a full D&C. So they took me away, knocked me out, and removed anything that could rupture or cause more bleeding.

The room settled into an eerie calm, but the impact of those harrowing hours would be felt long after. It was a baptism by fire into motherhood.

Emerging from this ordeal, my first instinct was an overpowering need to see Ellie. In the NICU, a heartbreaking sight awaited me: tubes and cables covered her tiny body, and she had a huge breathing mask on her face. She looked so frail and vulnerable.

We had purchased preemie clothes, but even they were too big for her. She was just so small. Even my mom and Sheri, who had babies before, were nervous to handle Ellie for fear she might break.

Sheri came to visit us at the hospital. She walked in while I was taking care of the baby in the NICU and was blown away. "Here you were, having just finished giving birth and then having surgery, in a wheelchair and surely in pain, and when the nurses asked if you wanted to change your baby and learn to care for her tiny body, you didn't hesitate. You went into full mommy mode. It was so impressive to see you be unafraid and ready to do whatever your daughter needs." Those words of encouragement stayed with me as I faced other challenges.

The nurses urged me to try to breastfeed her. They set me up in one of the rocking chairs, carefully lifted her out of the incubator, and positioned her in my arms just right. It was quite an operation because we didn't want to pull on any of the lines attached to her.

I wanted to breastfeed. I felt like it was a rite of passage, and I could see that it was expected by, well, everyone. I wanted so much to be able to do this magical thing, but it felt impossible—like an insurmountable barrier. Ellie had a hard time latching and, when she did latch, it soon became obvious she was allergic to my milk. After each attempt to feed her, she would break into bouts of vomiting.

Through no choice or fault of her own, Ellie rejected my milk.

She needed to grow and hit certain milestones before she could come home. Every rhythmic anomaly in her heartbeat was like a cruel echo, ringing in the dread that it wouldn't be anytime soon. Each time her heart or oxygen levels dipped below the safe threshold, the clock reset. Another day, another setback. A rule was in place: she needed fourteen consecutive days without any such drops before they would allow her to be with us at home. This was a good thing. If we hadn't put that rule in place, I would have lived in constant fear at home of her passing away in her sleep. I wanted my baby but I was eternally grateful for how much care the medical team gave us.

The advocacy for breastfeeding continued to be passionate at the hospital, perhaps excessively so. Every professional's urging felt like a chain tethering Ellie to the NICU. It was agonizing to acknowledge that the very nourishment I was providing was causing Ellie's extended stay. Throwing up my milk and being hungry all the time was making her sick. I knew that asking to give Ellie formula was some sort of cardinal sin, but she needed food.

It took all my strength not to scream out, "Just give her formula!!" But instead, I kept trying and pumping and trying and pumping. In the end, I watched thirty-seven bags of my pumped milk being discarded because it was unusable. Then we switched to formula, like we should have done from the moment we saw that my milk was making Ellie sick.

I was released from the hospital long before Ellie was, which seemed cruel. Returning home without Ellie was awful. The silence was deafening, nothing like I had envisioned.

The distance between J and me became more pronounced during this period. I watched as he hesitated, visiting Ellie sparingly, mere minutes that stood out in stark contrast to the hours I spent gazing at our daughter through the glass of her incubator.

Once the day came to bring Ellie home, J and I were ecstatic; yet, we were so scared that we might do something wrong. J had so much trepidation that he didn't want to pick Ellie up. It broke my heart but I understood. I could see the fear and caution in his eyes every time he looked at our fragile daughter. He would confess, voice laced with a mixture of guilt and fear, that he didn't know how to touch her, fearing he might somehow harm her.

At home, the watchful eyes of nurses were conspicuously absent, as were the monitors that assured me Ellie was alive. It was so quiet ... I spent countless hours straining to hear and count Ellie's breaths, second-guessing if she was alright.

She cried off and on all night, making it impossible for me to sleep. She had no routine yet, and the hospital NICU routine had been fairly active at all hours due to round-the-clock vitals checks. There was no sleep schedule to speak of.

I was running on fumes when she was crying for attention. J grew frustrated. He didn't understand why I couldn't soothe Ellie or do whatever a mother should do to make her baby happy. He thought that since I was on maternity leave and he was working, I should be able to just handle it.

I spent evenings in the rocking chair with Ellie in my arms, crying to myself as she fought sleep. J thought I should have some magic power to get her down to sleep on a normal schedule. He yelled at me, asking me what was wrong with me, which made me cry harder.

Tension built day by day until one night, after hours of Ellie crying because she couldn't go to sleep, J lost it. "Why can't you just be a mother and take care of her?!

I knew he was just frustrated and exhausted but his words struck a nerve. I was a failure. I didn't know what I was doing. Ellie wouldn't stop crying. She couldn't take my milk. I couldn't even give her the nutrition she needed in the womb. J feeding into my insecurities was just the sour icing on the cake.

There were days when I couldn't function. I wasn't sleeping or eating. I felt helpless. That's when I realized, one night at 3 a.m., I could put Ellie in the car, and we could escape for a few hours if I just got in the car and drove away. The motion put Ellie to sleep. If I wasn't in the house, no one could judge me or yell at me.

I'd use the time to go out and get something to eat or drink, and when Ellie settled down I would just sleep in peace for a few hours in the driver's seat with it reclined. We'd come back in the door before J left for work.

All this paved the way for postpartum depression.

All I had ever wanted was a family and a home, but it felt like I was screwing it up. I had imagined a little face with my hair and J's eyes looking up at me with unconditional love, and me protecting them with everything I have. But I couldn't protect Ellie. The relentless challenges surrounding Ellie's birth and J's growing detachment were chiseling away at my strength.

I do have to commend J. Whether he wanted to or not, he really stepped up at this time. I thought I would have more support. I envisioned my mom and sister staying longer and being around to enjoy those early months of love and chaos, but it was just us.

The pressure was off the charts: pressure to be a good mom while being flooded with hormones that were making me feel crazy; the trauma of my abuse; the trial; going from "you eat too much" to "you can't eat" (after the weight loss surgery) to "you are not eating enough; your baby's gonna die" (pregnancy) to "eat more or you won't produce enough milk" (motherhood). And through it all, I was trying to resist this inner battle of worrying that I'd get fat. *How insane is that?!* I would find myself looking in the mirror and seeing an overweight woman staring back at me, even though I was the opposite (or so I'm told). It was an endless mindfuck.

FAMILY

***

There's a saying about addiction—that even in periods of sobriety, it's just outside "doing push-ups in the parking lot," always ready to strike harder and fiercer. My previous battles with addiction were resurfacing. I thought I had left them behind the moment I saw the result of my pregnancy test.

It was as if during my time of sobriety, my real addiction was silently gaining power, waiting for a moment of vulnerability to launch its most ferocious attack. And postpartum depression was the perfect opportunity.

Each day became a constant struggle to help my baby be happy and healthy and show J that I wasn't the worst mother on earth. I tried my best to make Ellie smile and shield myself from J's comments on my abilities as a mother. All this on top of resisting the siren call of alcohol was a lot. I would've done almost anything for relief from the emotional turmoil I was trapped in.

The first time I gave in, I reveled in the rush of calm and sense of ease that came with drinking. As always, within an hour or so, calm was replaced with guilt and self-loathing, making me want to go back for more.

As I rocked Ellie, fed her, changed her, and hugged her close to my heart, whispers of escape began to taunt me from the edges of my consciousness. I thought of what life would be like without J criticizing my every move and reminding me that our marriage was broken. Leaving him wasn't just about salvaging my sanity but also preserving Ellie's future. I didn't like the idea of bringing her up in a broken family but I wasn't kidding myself either. Our current situation was unsustainable.

Eventually, Ellie grew out of her crying spells, slept better and longer in the evenings, and began growing into a beautiful little girl. It was incredible how fast time started to pass. J became more comfortable with her and I could see him enjoying their time together.

The first time I heard her laugh, I thought my heart would burst. When she smiled, I felt her joy deep in my bones. There was nothing like that feeling. Ellie's wide-eyed wonder at the world began pulling me away from the demons that tried to drag me back into the darkness. She was six months old, then twelve—crawling, then standing, then toddling toward me, across the floor of her nursery and into my lap as we played with her mountain of toys.

J and I continued fighting. We had no trouble in the physical capacity, but emotionally, there was no connection. And when there was, it was an angry connection. Someone suggested marriage counseling and I jumped at the idea. I wanted an objective party to hear us, to help us, to find hope in our mess.

Within a week, we soon found ourselves sitting across from a therapist, dumping our stories in her lap and begging for answers. J kept most of his thoughts and emotions to himself, whereas I shared every detail that came to mind, looking for someone to make sense of it. We had a number of sessions filled with tears and vulnerable admissions, at least from me. Eventually, the therapist leaned forward and challenged me to make a choice.

Her voice was firm but compassionate when she asked: "What do you truly want?"

"I just want to be loved. I want to feel like the person I'm married to appreciates me and wants to be with me," I said.

"How do you think I don't show you that I love you?" J responded. "You're my wife. Look at everything I do for you."

"Just because I have the title of a wife, doesn't mean you love me. You're rude, mean, you ignore me, and you don't see how it makes me feel."

"Nicole, do you think I want to be all nice and sweet when you get back all drunk from the bar?"

"You and the bar. The bar, the bar, the bar."

At this moment, the therapist breaks into the conversation. "Okay guys, let's go back to what you said, Nicole. What would make you feel loved? What does J need to do to make you feel loved?"

"I think it would be nice to have someone not make me feel worthless."

"Oh my God Nicole, you are so dramatic," J laughs. "Worthless? Come on."

"J, you have to be more understanding of Nicole's feelings." the therapist suggested.

I could see J putting on his good boy mask. "I will make more of an effort to show you more appreciation. But the drinking's gotta stop.

"J, don't you see I drink because I'm lonely and in pain? I'm embarrassed I feel this way, so I drink too much and I can't stop. All I want is some support, some encouragement. But it seems like you want nothing to do with that. It's so nice to think you can just snap your fingers and fix somebody, but it doesn't work that way."

After countless therapy sessions, both of us were breaking our promises to each other. If anything, things were getting worse with the realization that J was never going to be able to give me what I wanted. It wasn't who he was. As much as I hoped he would change, I finally understood I didn't have the power to change him; only he could do that. The realization hit me with the force of a freight train. I replayed our past in my mind—the sessions, the arguments, the loneliness. I had to find a way out, not just for me, but for Ellie too.

I picked a date on the calendar and circled it—the day I would summon the courage to tell J I wanted a divorce. My mother and Gary sent me money so that I would be able to pay the necessary legal fees. The next few days were a blur. The gravity of the situation consumed my every waking moment.

I kept going back and forth from knowing this was what I had to do to wondering if it was all a big mistake.

HOW DARE YOU

I was trying not to lose myself entirely but between the impending separation from J, my insatiable craving to numb out, and my postpartum depression, keeping a grip on life, the future, and my daughter was my primary focus. I knew I was in trouble, so I continued seeing the therapist that J and I had been going to, but this time it was for me. Because of the depth of my postpartum depression, I also started seeing a psychiatrist. She told me that this was just a temporary storm and prescribed medication to help my anxiety and depression.

I was underneath my blankets trying to calm myself down from an anxiety attack when I saw my mom's name appear on my phone. Something told me not to answer it, but it was my mother, so obviously I had to.

"We've been given a date for the trial," she said. Any relaxing effects of the Xanax I'd just taken disintegrated within seconds.

My stomach did a leap and I immediately felt sick. Mom—"

"We need you to come back to support Linda and I in court," she said, cutting me off.

"No, Mom. I don't want to leave Ellie—"

"Ellie will be fine for a few days without you, I'm sure." I couldn't take my baby because of the hit out on us making the trip dangerous.

"But I'm trying to get used to motherhood. I don't want to leave her."

"This will give J and Ellie a better chance to bond," she said, flippantly.

"Mom, this will *break* me. I can't do this. I told you last time I needed support before and after the trial, and I don't want to end up in trouble."

"Why do you need someone else's help just to control yourself?" she asked, belittling my fight against addiction and implying I was just being dramatic.

I tried to come up with any possible reason I could to avoid being faced with the trial, my memories, Carlos ... "This is not good for my health. You know it's—"

"You need to support your sister, Nicole." She said the words with finality. It wasn't up for debate.

I remembered (though no one else seemed to) what the previous trial had done to me, so I knew I was headed for destruction if I went to this trial. My mental healthcare team did too. They increased my anxiety medication ahead of the trip to Costa Rica in an attempt to help me manage it.

But from the moment I got on the airplane, all bets were off. I immediately ordered a whiskey on the rocks. And then another. By the time we landed, I was wasted. I had a bodyguard waiting for me outside the airport who grabbed my bags and took me to the car where my mom and sister were waiting for me.

I got in and slumped into my seat. I didn't notice that I smelled like alcohol but they definitely did. Mom tried to talk to me but I was so wasted I couldn't even form words. My mother was disgusted.

"Why are you drunk? You don't take anything seriously! You're a disgrace. You're a mother now, what the hell are you doing with your life?"

She was going for the jugular. It hurt and I wanted to fight back but I was too drunk to get the words to come out right. I wasn't going to win this battle. Instead, I just leaned my forehead against the glass window so they couldn't see the tears falling and stared outside quietly for the rest of the ride.

I hadn't even faced Carlos yet, and I was already falling apart.

We arrived at the apartment we'd rented. I wanted to just go to my room and sleep it off. I flopped down on the bed and took my medication out of my purse. As I did, my mom followed me into the room to talk to me about drinking and what was going on. That's when she saw me with pills in my hand. Her face froze in fury.

"Now you're taking pills too?" she demands. She grabbed the pill bottle out of my hands. "*Why* are you like this? Why are you acting this way?!"

"Mom, I need them. These are the pills that are helping me—"

"Helping you?" She laughed hard. "Doesn't look like they're doing a very good job."

"I need them so that I can calm my anxiety and get some sleep before the trial. They're prescribed by my psychiatrist!"

"I want to talk to this psychiatrist," she yelled, not believing a word I was saying.

"You can talk to her tomorrow because I have a phone session with her. She knew that I'd need her. She also knew I should not come to this trial. It isn't safe for my mental health."

"And did she want you to take them with alcohol, Nicole?" she asked.

"Just give me my pill so I can calm the fuck down and sleep." I snapped at her.

"Over my dead body are you getting these pills, Nicole," she said. She was so close to my face, I could feel her breath.

That was it. I was done. I jumped out of the bed, filled with rage. I wanted to hit her, shake her, make her see me, make her look at me and what I was going through.

"What's wrong with you, Nicole?! You're out of control. I'm the one that always has to pay the consequences of your actions. No one else has ever taken on the weight of all of your mistakes. Your drinking, your stealing, your partying—I've reached my limit! You need help."

Before I knew it, my hands were pushing her away from me, too fast, and too hard. I had crossed a line.

Linda flew into my bedroom and stepped between us. "Nicole, no!! Calm down!" she cried.

"Oh my God, Nicole. You just punched me. Your mother? How dare you?!" my mom's eyes narrowed with disbelief.

"Mom! You're so exaggerated. I didn't punch you. I just pushed you away. You were in my face. You wouldn't stop."

"You are the ones that made me come here," I pointed at them both. "I never asked for any of this. Not five years ago, not two years ago, not ever!" I was so angry, I felt possessed—by haunting memories and by the trauma I'd been trying to put behind me.

"I was taking my pill, you were in my room, I asked you to leave, you insulted me, you provoked me ..." I paced back and forth, yelling over Linda's head. "You say you don't want me to be like this, but you're the one who is pushing me. How many times have I asked you to just leave me—"

Linda interrupted, "CoCo! You don't realize the way you are acting. You don't understand the way you are."

"You don't understand either. You don't see how my abuse, my experience, and my truth affect me—how broken I am. My feelings are somehow completely invisible, not to be worried about."

Linda shook her head, "That's not what we—"

"This trial is not for me. It's for you and for mom. This psychotic breakdown you're seeing now has happened so many times, you've just never seen it in person. You never believed me when I told you this breaks me. And now that you see the destruction in person, you act all afraid and disgusted and surprised."

Mom fled the room crying. My sister followed her.

I threw myself on the bed and tried to sleep. It didn't work. After some time passed, I went into Mom's room to beg for forgiveness. As I always did.

"You were demonic, Nicole. I even hid all the knives. I'm going to sleep with my door closed. I'm not comfortable being around you." She looked at me in fear.

Linda called me out of the room. "Nicole, you need to give her a minute. You broke her. I don't think she'll ever be the same."

I went to my room, started looking up flights, and tried to find a way to get the fuck out of there. But I knew I couldn't leave, regardless of what it cost me to stay. If I left, my family would never speak to me again. Eventually, I cried myself to sleep.

After that night, we proceeded, one more time, to go to a trial that did absolutely nothing for my healing. I threw myself on the fire for the people who didn't want to watch me burn.

As expected, we lost the trial and I was back on a plane to Texas. I felt like I'd been shredded. It was clear no one was going to help me and I had to pull myself back out of the abyss on my own. I signed up for an online outpatient rehab program called Lion Rock. It was a great program. I was really happy. I was sober. Things were going well. My postpartum depression eventually dissipated, replaced by an unparalleled joy of raising my beautiful daughter. I took my therapy appointments and mental health seriously and did everything I could to put Carlos and the trials behind me.

When March 2020 came around COVID swept the world. J still went to work. I had started a job that was considered an essential service so Ellie still went to daycare. I found myself occasionally drinking at the house or going to Emily's house to grab a drink. The bars were closed so that was our only option. Then I started to crave the alcohol. I looked forward to the moment I could pour a glass of wine each day. But before things could get too crazy, Easter came. And the pain came with it.

THIS IS NEW

I started to have random pain in my abdomen that I couldn't explain. After years of sexual abuse, bulimia, alcoholism, a gastric sleeve, endometriosis, constantly abnormal periods, cysts on my ovaries (that at one point exploded and led to emergency surgery), all followed eventually by a complicated pregnancy, I was used to my stomach having pain. But this was new.

By the time Easter came that year, it was so bad that when we got back home from Easter activities, I was wondering what was wrong. *Maybe I've got COVID* I thought. It was all over my body but ended up centering around my pelvic area. Soon the pain escalated to the point that I couldn't get off the sofa. As I lay there, I started to think of all the unexplainable things I'd been ignoring over the previous three months. When I realized the pain wasn't going to go away, I called my OB-GYN, who quickly booked an appointment for me.

I remember laying on the table with just a paper gown to cover my top half, feet in the stirrups, trying to remain calm as the exam began. These appointments are never enjoyable; however, this one was uniquely awful. Every part of the exam hurt to the point of tears. And it shouldn't have.

"Wow you've been in a lot of pain? For how long?" the doctor asked.

"There's been a lot of things happening that I've been ignoring, like watery discharge that was so bad I've been using tampons. I've been having a lot of pain and bleeding. But with PCOS and endometriosis, I'm used to bleeding. I have noticed the pain during and after sex." As I heard myself voicing the growing list of symptoms, my anxiety grew.

"Do you mind if I bring someone in for a second opinion?"

My heart stopped. I knew that was bad. I waited for three minutes, but it felt like an eternity.

The other doctor came in, took one look at me, looked at my OB-GYN, and said to me, "We can't imagine the kind of pain you must have been going through."

"We're going to take three to five biopsies."

"What's going on exactly?"

"You have cancer."

"How do you know that, you haven't even done a test?"

"Well, at this point it's so spread we can visually see the cancer. Plus, the fact that it's covering your cervix looks *very* bad."

Doctors don't say things like that so I knew it was bad.

The doctor took some samples for tests, each one making me scream out in pain. After the third biopsy sample, I ended up fainting for a moment. I woke up to the smell of rubbing alcohol and the faces of nurses surrounding me.

The doctor repeatedly apologized, waiting for me to feel better, and then resumed taking samples.

My heart raced but I was in too much pain to speak. I'm sure he could see the alarm on my face.

After the biopsies, I tried to get off the exam bed and screamed out in pain. I could barely move. It was beyond anything I'd felt in a long time.

The doctor prescribed me a high dosage of hydrocodone to help me cope. It didn't even touch the pain at first. But finally, the pain decreased enough to drive home. As I drove through the streets of Fort Worth and my pain continued to subside, so did my initial alarm. I thought of how young I was and how I could surely beat something like this. I told myself it couldn't be that serious. I could handle getting a hysterectomy and doing some chemo if that's what it would take.

I called J and told him what the OB-GYN had said. His response was similar to mine—relaxed and confident that I would be okay.

THIS IS BAD

Three days later, I was waiting for my biopsy results. The phone rang. It was the doctor. "We have your results. Can you come in as soon as possible?"

Fifteen minutes later, I was in the doctor's office. I must've driven at eighty miles per hour, but it felt like a lifetime. I was admitted straight into the office without waiting. The doctor sat me down and she had an orange sticky note on her hand.

"You have gastric-type endocervical adenocarcinoma. I've never seen this before. I have already contacted the best OB-GYN oncologist in Fort Worth. She's made space in her schedule so that she can see you tomorrow."

I decided not to tell anyone what was going on before I had a clearer understanding. I didn't want to freak anyone out or start receiving a litany of medical advice from friends and family.

The following day, I walked through the automatic glass doors of the Center for Cancer and Blood Disorders. There I had a physical exam, PET scan, and two MRIs. While waiting for one of my MRIs, I showed another patient my list of exams I had that day and asked them, "Does it usually go this fast? Is this normal?"

Their eyes widened and she looked at me. "I've never had that many tests at once. It took me a month just to get diagnosed."

I spent forty minutes in the MRI machine, thinking about all the things that could go wrong.

Was this my punishment? Has my past finally caught up with me?

After my tests, I drove home. Within a couple of hours, the call came in. "Your cancer is aggressive and has already spread throughout some of your lymphatic system, your kidney, and all of your reproductive organs," the doctor continued as I took notes. "My secretary has already put in an order to get a port put in on Tuesday. Call me if you have any questions." Then I heard the line go dead. That was it.

I looked down at my notes.

Stage III-C2?
Spread in kidneys/lymphatic system?
Port? WTH?
Procedure Tuesday?

As I tried to process the enormity of it all, J walked in. His face, usually a mask of blank expression, mirrored the shock I felt. The news had reached him before me.

We stood there, words failing us. I fell into J's arms and held onto him for dear life. "We can't leave each other now." I was hysterically sobbing. "Our problems, our differences—they need to be put on hold."

He looked at me with an expression I couldn't read.

"J, I'm going to die … I don't want to die!"

CHAPTER SEVEN

I CAN TAKE IT

My cancer was aggressive but I was young, so I asked for the harshest, most powerful treatment I could get. I wanted to survive. I felt like I could take it.

Like many people who are told they have cancer, I had no idea what I was in for.

Within a week, I had a port put into my chest. It was a tube that went directly into my bloodstream to make administering chemo and other medications much easier than poking new holes in me with countless needles in the months to come. I have heard that ports are often used for patients who are very sick or are about to be. Either way, it would make giving me the drugs I needed easier and less painful. They knocked me out to put it in, and it felt a bit weird but otherwise didn't cause me pain. It was covered with clear adhesive tape to keep it safe and dry while I went about my daily life.

When I looked at the port in the mirror, I decided it really didn't look that bad. It said, "This girl is going through something," and I was okay with that.

I chose to embrace it by wearing a pink tank top with spaghetti straps. The top was cute and I liked it. When my mom came to visit the next day, her eyes went right to my upper chest. She gasped and held her hand over the port as if to hide it from the world (or to shield it from herself).

"Mom!" I pushed her hand away in confusion. "What are you doing?!"

"CoCo, go put on something else!" She tried to cover it again and whisper-scolded me, so no one could hear but me, "Why would you want people to see that?"

"It's just a port, Mom. It's what is going to save my life. I'm not going to hide it," I said stiffly, surprised by her reaction. *Was my cancer care now going to be something I needed to be ashamed of?*

"People don't need to know you have cancer! Not everyone knows or wants to see those types of things. It's like you're wanting to show the world that you're going through something difficult. It's like you're victimizing yourself."

"And why shouldn't they know, Mami?" I struggled to keep my anger in check. "I have cancer. This is me. If the people don't like it, they don't really love me, do they?" I knew the comment was a passive-aggressive dig meant for her. I knew I shouldn't have said it, but I couldn't stop myself.

My mother looked as if she had been slapped.

We didn't talk for the rest of the afternoon.

THE LAST POUR

A few days later, on April 25, 2020, I was sitting in the middle of my couch cradling a bottle of Francis Ford Coppola merlot in my hands. The sun streaked through the blinds, casting lines of gold throughout the room and on the bottle. It was a gift from my boss, given to me on my last day, knowing I'd be away for treatment for some time.

Emily came over to drink this last bottle of wine with me.

She fell onto the couch beside me with Ferrero Rocher chocolates in her lap. Chocolate and merlot were a great pairing.

We dug into the bottle, talking about anything and everything, especially my biggest fears about the road ahead of me. I was scared, but trying not to show it.

To the left of the couch, the painting with the trees that I loved faced me. The beautiful painting represented the J I loved and hoped to spend my life with. To the right of the couch was the painting with all the colors that had always given me the worst feeling when I looked at it.

"I want that fucking painting gone once and for all," I said to Emily. "I've always hated it." I couldn't explain why, but it always made me think of the side of J that was angry with me and disgusted by me. And now, the ugly painting also screamed something else at me—cancer. I felt suffocated when I looked at it.

"I'm surprised you still have it," Emily said, eyeing the piece of shitty art. "You've hated that thing for so long!"

"J wouldn't let me get rid of it," I said, annoyed at the words coming from my mouth. The merlot spurred on my annoyance.

Emily asked, "Is this really it?"

I nodded, brushing away the tears. "It has to be. I need to be healthy for this treatment. It's non-negotiable." Inside, my mind was screaming:

I don't want any of this.

Am I ready?

What will life look like now?

I'm sure I looked frozen in place.

"Talk to me," Emily urged, her fingers brushing against my arm, trying to ground me back into the moment.

Being how heavily medicated I was for the pain caused by my spreading cancer, alcohol seemed little in comparison.

Emily squeezed my hand. "You're not alone," she said. And yet I was. I was here in Texas while everyone was living their lives everywhere else. Without me.

For a moment, the room was filled with a palpable silence, punctuated only by the ticking of the clock and the occasional car passing by outside.

"You know," Emily said, her voice soft, "you've always had my back when I needed you."

I smiled and tilted my head. "Of course! You're my friend."

She shook her head, "No. It's more than that. You have a fire, a strength in you. And you're never afraid to use it to protect the people you love. But somewhere along the way, you stopped protecting yourself." I knew she meant the countless blurry nights filled with pills and potions.

I looked down, also thinking of a lifetime's worth of sneaking sips, hiding the evidence, and so many failed attempts at sobriety. I also thought of how unfair it was to be just in my twenties and facing cancer.

"This is your time to find that fire again," she continued, "and beat cancer's ass."

Closing my eyes, I tried to visualize the procedures, treatment, machines, and medical visits ahead of me.

It was surreal.

I looked at the bottle one last time, walked over to the sink in the kitchen island, and emptied it down the drain.

I knew how lucky I was to have Emily in my life.

"It's a new beginning," she said, hugging me tight. I hugged her back with quiet tears streaming down my face.

That night was the last time I got drunk. I think of it as "my last pour."

This time, becoming sober wasn't a decision I was making—it was one made for me. But in that moment, surrounded by love and hope, I felt strong. I knew I was about to face something really hard, likely even harder than becoming sober again, but this time I wasn't alone. And that made all the difference.

That was the day when I started doing things to make myself feel more comfortable, to make my surroundings more comfortable. I know I was about to face the fight of my life and that meant taking control of my health and my life.

Getting rid of the painting was my first executive decision. We threw it out.

Since that day, I might have a sip of wine at dinner with friends, but there's really no point. Any potential buzz from a glass of wine or a line of coke seems almost laughable now in the face of the extreme levels of prescription medications it takes to keep me functioning today.

A day or two later, I was measured for my radiation pod. It needed to be molded and shaped to my body for the best possible results.

"That looks more like a casket," I said. It was white and hard and cold and terrifying. But radiation was part of the game if I was going to beat cancer. The pod is where I would lay for what felt like endless radiation appointments as doctors hit me with radioactive x-rays at the sites where my cancer was deemed to be.

"It's not a casket, sugar, I promise," the nurse said, smiling at me. I am sure I caught sight of a hint of sadness as she measured here and marked there on my body.

Did she think I was going to die?

Did she feel sorry for me? Or did she wonder what I did to deserve this?

* * *

Radiation was scheduled for noon the next day. When I entered the radiation wing, I was first taken to a room where I met with the virtual doctor (because it was COVID times). He asked generic questions as if I was just one of countless cancer patients he saw each month, and as if he was just checking boxes on a list. Then I changed into a hospital gown because I was told my pants and bra would get in the way of the treatment.

I climbed into my custom-made pod and was instructed to lay completely still for one hour while a machine hovered around me, delivering treatment I couldn't see.

It was staying still and entirely silent that was the most torture at first. Not only was it hard to do because of pain, but I found myself trapped in there with my thoughts. I fought more demons while in that radiation pod than almost any other time in my life. Only this time, instead of being pulled down into the water to drown, I imagined myself burning.

Radiation was set for every day thereafter—for twenty-eight days.

Because I'd be there so often, I needed to try to make it the best it could possibly be, considering the circumstances. I decided to approach cancer treatment as a task to be completed, a new routine to adapt to and master. I wanted to know everything there was to know about my disease and treatment. I asked countless questions and made it my goal to befriend as many of the nurses as I could. They were the ones I spent the most time with.

I learned to go in wearing no bra, just a T-shirt and sweatpants on the bottom. This way I could skip the hospital gown. I only had to pull down my sweatpants to my knees. Somehow it made me feel more human.

I brought in earphones and popped them in before treatment began. The music helped distract me and pass the time faster. It also helped drown out some of the darkness.

Every three weeks, I would do chemotherapy at the clinic. I was the first one there at 8 a.m. Other patients would come and go, but I would stay, welcoming the strongest doses of medication I could handle for the best chance of survival. Then after eight hours, when pretty much all of the other patients went home and my first chemo was done, they'd start another one called Fluorouracil by hooking it up to my PICC line. I would be sent home with that running for five days. Fluorouracil was also referred to as 5FU—and many people said FU stood for "fuck you cancer" because it was so strong.

"How are things going?" Linda asked me as I came back into the house after my fifth radiation treatment appointment. She had just picked up Ellie from school and was about to make dinner. I could've made dinner myself but I knew she wanted to help.

"I'm doing pretty good," I said and eased into a chair at the island. The cancer pain was still there, but I couldn't identify many new aches, pains, or side effects. That had to be a good thing, right?

"That must mean it's working!" she said, sounding hopeful.

"I think you're right," I said and flashed her an encouraging look. Anyone who has ever had cancer soon learns that you spend a lot of time reassuring everyone else that you're okay. It hurts to see people worry. So you just do. "And I had my favorite nurse today. I think I'm going to bring her in some treats from the bakery tomorrow. She should be working again."

I had decided to be the best damned patient they'd ever had. I wanted to win this fight and the medical staff were my new community, so might as well embrace it.

After a few more visits, everyone knew my name. I could see that they felt sad for me having to go through this at such a young age. And I think they appreciated being seen in return. I took the time to learn about them and their lives.

I was about a week and a half into treatment when I woke up feeling the effects for the first time. I was hit with a profound and sudden wave of exhaustion. It was as if I had never slept a night in my life. Because I was doing a combination of both radiation and chemo, I was told it could intensify everything. They weren't wrong.

I was hit with diarrhea. Constant diarrhea. It just wouldn't stop. It was pouring out of me. I spent most of my time wiping and trying to stay clean. The longer it went on the more my skin was raw and felt as if it were on fire. It soon became easier to just walk into the shower, careful not to let my port get under the stream of water, and clean my behind with water. There was no way I could handle the agony of wiping with toilet paper or tissues of any kind.

My exhaustion grew alongside my pain. It reminded me of withdrawing from a drug. I had been through that before and it can be awful. Everything hurt. I ended up rolling around trying to escape the discomfort. Time passed by so slowly that I found myself almost wishing to die. I couldn't do anything but be in pain and go from bed to shower to the hospital to shower to bed. I wanted to do things the CoCo way. I wanted to get up and do things, hug Ellie, make dinner, organize the pantry … but I just couldn't.

As the treatment went on, I got sicker. I didn't even realize that was possible. I was battling diarrhea and pain from radiation burns which had begun to appear. My skin was burned in places, especially all around my vagina and behind. I would say it was probably one of the lowest points in my treatment. When I went into the bathroom to pee or have diarrhea, I would scream in pain. The best way I can think of to describe it is this: imagine you have a urinary tract infection, and you are about to pee, and you get that shooting pain that happens when you start and doesn't settle down until you're done. Imagine that, but about one hundred times more painful and it never resolves. It just keeps going, in or out of the bathroom.

My sister grabbed my hand and cried with me.

My mother, who was often a force of nature, a point of strength in the room, would close the door and leave the house. She would sit outside on the porch because she couldn't handle the screaming. I knew it was painful for her.

This time she allowed herself to experience the fear of truly losing me. It wasn't the same as in the past when she'd worry about me driving drunk and putting myself in danger.

In those days, my mother would have little sympathy. She would say: "She's an addict. She is doing it to herself." Therefore I deserved it.

Cancer was different—an uncontrollable, unimaginable, unforeseen thing.

But really, I was in just as much danger with cancer as I was with trauma-fueled self-sabotage. They were equally deadly.

FORGIVEN

When word spread through my friends and family that I was facing cancer, and that it was bad, messages began flooding in by phone, email, DM, and text. Some were from people I haven't heard from in ages, others from people who didn't speak to me because I either hurt them or was hurt by them.

Every single message of love and friendship I received added up until it felt like my heart was overflowing. I didn't realize how much I had been craving that forgiveness, and it filled me with a comfort that no other drug had ever been able to.

Before cancer, when I was sick, most people assumed it was because I was hungover. They didn't give me a lot of thought (not good thoughts, anyway). When I exhibited trauma symptoms such as terrible behavior, chaotic addiction cycles, and harm to myself and others, they assumed it was because "CoCo is just a screw-up."

After my cancer diagnosis, when I was sick, people understood why and came to my side. They wanted to help by baking dinners, babysitting, and visiting me with flowers.

Cancer is a much more acceptable illness than any mental health illness.

I also secretly hoped that my diagnosis would help close the distance between Gary and I. Despite everything they have been through, Gary is still close with my mother. Gary is facing life-altering health challenges right now. My mother and her husband, Anthony, visit him often. They will hang out, watch sports, eat ice cream (Gary always gets the best kind of ice cream), and generally enjoy each other's company. Gary still loves my mother. I can see that. And it makes me love him more. He has a big heart, and I want him to be happy. I feel better knowing Gary isn't always alone, even though we don't talk anymore. He, my mother, and I argued about money several years ago and he stopped reaching out to me after that. Maybe I let him down for the last time.

I miss him.

GOODBYE HAIR

One morning during treatment, I woke up to the feeling of hundreds of needles pricking my scalp simultaneously. My hair and my head hurt. *Is that even possible? How does someone's hair hurt?* I felt for my long ponytail and realized immediately that something was very wrong. I sat up and turned to look at my pillow. It was covered in black clumps of my long beautiful hair. Of course, I had been warned that this could happen during treatment but somehow I didn't believe it until that moment.

I couldn't help but sob. My hair is part of my identity. When people thought of CoCo, they thought of my long gorgeous hair.

I called J in a panic. I confessed how sad I was to see my hair falling out. The conversation quickly turned to Ellie. "What will she think if she sees me with no hair, J? She'll be scared!"

"Ellie's a baby, Nicole," he said nonchalantly. "She's not even going to remember. Besides, we always knew this was coming."

After we hung up, I thought about how careless his words seemed. Once again, I had called him looking for comfort, only to immediately regret it.

Later that afternoon, I heard the front door slam. J was home from work. I looked in his direction and my heart stopped. For a moment, I forgot about the pain. J's thick mane of hair that I had always loved, that I had run my fingers through countless times in the beginning of our relationship, was gone. Shaved clean. In solidarity with me.

"What did you do?!" I asked in shock.

He looked at me with deep brown eyes. His ordinarily stoic expression was replaced with one that gave away a mix of emotions—love, frustration, and hope. After all we had been through, and all the times he had made me feel like we were a mistake, here he was, looking right at me, seeing my pain, and joining me so that I wasn't alone. I walked up to him, my eyes blurry with tears, and touched the top of his bald head. He took my hand and led me outside to a chair that was waiting for me on the patio.

I sat down, speechless as I realized what was about to happen. *He is going to shave my head.* J gently placed his hand on my shoulder and then wrapped a towel around my back and arms.

I turned my phone to face us, and with a trembling finger, pressed "record" on a video that still lives on my Instagram and TikTok accounts to this day.

The shaver buzzed to life, a sound that would forever be imprinted on my memory. As the cold metal touched my scalp, I held the towel close to my face, ready to catch my hair or tears or both.

J started with the sides. The first few strokes were manageable. I looked at my image on the phone and tried to envision what I would look like when J was done. I watched as clumps of my hair fell onto my shoulders and to the ground. As the clippers mowed away my beautiful hair, I felt my resolve crumble. The magnitude of it all hit at once—the unfairness of my diagnosis, J stepping up to help shoulder my pain, and seeing the ground being covered with my hair. I sobbed into the towel.

I have never felt closer to J—before or since—than I did that afternoon.

Once the clippers finally went silent, my head felt infinitely lighter but prickly to the touch. Ellie wanted to see it up close and feel it, so I scooped her up onto my lap and let her run her little hands over my scalp. I couldn't help but smile.

After the shave, J and I went to a full-length mirror, leaned into each other, and struck a pose for our own benefit. We each took in our appearances and matching bald heads. I didn't feel alone in this any longer. Someone had taken a leap of faith with me. And it was J. Despite the crazy fights we had, he was there for me right now. I felt a spark of hope try to ignite within me. For once, I didn't immediately extinguish the feeling. I allowed myself to embrace it.

I caught sight of my "live like a warrior" tattoo I got years before cancer had ever been on my radar.

If this wasn't warrior life, I didn't know what was.

The next morning, I woke up in a haze of pain and the immediate reminder that something was missing. I felt for my hair and it was gone. *Another day that began with tears.* I knew it was silly in the scheme of my life-and-death challenges at the moment, but I immediately missed playing with it, styling it, running my fingers through it; it made me feel pretty.

Bvvv.

The phone vibrated on the nightstand, dancing slightly in its spot along with the sound.

Bvvv ... Bvvv ...

"Something must be going on," I thought. More likely it was my mom or sister blowing up my phone about something.

I sat up in my bed too fast and winced from the pain. Everything hurt today. Even the little amount of sunlight coming into the room seemed to hurt. I grasped for my glasses, momentarily wishing they were prescription sunglasses, popped them on and opened my phone. It was still open to Instagram from the day before. But now it was flooded with a sea of notifications. The head-shaving video had gone viral, along with my account, with hundreds of thousands of likes, comments, messages, and shares. Being the center of attention had always run in the family, usually due to my mother. But this wasn't about mom.

This was all about J, me, Ellie, and fucking cancer.

It was real.

No filter.

CHAPTER EIGHT

VIRAL

I spent hours scrolling through comments on Instagram and TikTok. They were filled with hope and healing from all over the world—in particular, from Costa Rica. Even though I didn't know them, they knew me and were worried about me. It was unlike anything I'd ever experienced before.

My cousin Mario had created the hashtag, CoCoStrong, and everyone was immediately adding #cocostrong to their messages and posts. For the first time, people could see how strong I could be.

The support of the community distracted me from my mounting list of side effects from treatment. At times, it was the only thing that gave me hope.

Different energies were swirling around me based on who was caring for me at the time. J would try to give me a break from life's duties by taking care of Ellie. But it wasn't always a peaceful break. He would make comments or grumble in complaint that he had to do everything, making me wish I could just get up and do everything myself.

When Linda was taking care of me, it was a relief. She brought a feeling of peace, love, and understanding with her. She would prepare food for me, write me sweet little notes of love and encouragement, and play with Ellie so that I could rest to the soundtrack of Ellie's giggles. Recovery time was shorter when Linda was there. She was literally good for my health.

When my mom took care of me, it was a stronger, different energy.

She made me want to fight for my life. And true to the history of our relationship, there was always room for the resentment over unresolved issues between a mother and daughter to surface in various ways.

When I would take my prescribed medication, Mom would give me looks, or make comments, or ask, "Do you really need to be taking that right now?" It was frustrating.

We both tried hard to focus on getting better and leaving the emotional trauma of the past *in* the past.

TRYING

Eating was so hard. Everything wanted to come back up. Solids, liquids, all of it. I had no energy and when I did, I wished for sleep to escape the discomfort. J and Linda were taking care of Ellie, but even with that help, I couldn't find the energy to take care of myself.

During one of my mom's visits, she sat beside me on the bed, where I was curled up in pain and cocooned in my duvet. The hum of the hair dryer was the soundtrack of the morning.

My mother looked at me and ran her hand over my blanket. I tried not to wince, even though the slightest touch felt like being poked by a branding iron. I knew she could see that my skin was sallow, my forehead sweaty.

For the first time in my life, I didn't feel self-conscious in my mother's presence. The heartbeat pounding in my temples drowned out the ability to care about what anyone thought of me.

Linda tiptoed into the room behind Mom. She held a Ziploc bag, inside which was a sandwich, some fruit, and a Gatorade. Tucked beside them was a handwritten note: *You've got this. One bite at a time.*

"Come on," she urged softly, sitting beside me, "you need to eat something."

I turned my face, the mere sight of food bringing a wave of nausea. "I can't, Linda. Every time I try, it just ... comes back up."

My mother squeezed my hand. "We'll figure something out. One step at a time."

Mom was the living embodiment of the Puerto Rican spirit—fiery, loving, and never one to back down. She looked down at my untouched sandwich and said, "How about an egg and a tortilla?"

I wanted to make her happy. And I knew I had to eat. *Maybe this time it'll be different. Maybe this time it'll stay down.* "Okay," I whispered, doubtfully. "Let's try."

Within minutes, the aroma of a lightly fried egg filled the room. A small plate was set before me. I lifted the fork, but a sudden wave of revulsion washed over me.

"Oh nooooo!!" I pushed the plate away, grasping for the bucket beside me. "I can't. I'm going to throw up."

Mom's face fell, but she didn't miss a beat. "Alright," she said with determination. "Let's try something else."

"I'm so sorry, Mami!" I cried.

"It's not your fault, Nicole, don't cry!" she said and set out the direction of the kitchen.

She left and I allowed the nausea to pass, luckily without throwing up this time. I knew I had to eat to live. But I also knew that there was no way.

I had almost drifted back to sleep when the scent of Quaker oats wafted through the room. I could smell that my mother had added cinnamon and sugar, which I loved. I eyed the offering in my mother's hand as my stomach rumbled in protest, but the aroma was too tempting. I nodded and was presented with a spoonful, which I put to my lips. For a second I thought I was going to be able to eat. But just as quickly as the hope had come, it vanished. I brought the bucket back up to my face and emptied what little hope I'd had.

Each attempt to eat felt like a small battle, a war waged between my body's need for sustenance and the violent rejection of anything I consumed.

But Mom was relentless. "A smoothie?" she asked, her voice betraying a hint of desperation.

Linda nodded in agreement. "Let's try a smoothie. Something light and cold."

As I heard the blender in the kitchen spring to life, mixing fruit and yogurt into something I could hopefully eat, I tried to muster the courage to try again. I wanted to do this for her. For me. For Linda. I wanted to be better.

When she presented the smoothie, which under any other circumstances would have made my mouth water, I felt my stomach turn over and I had to look away to prevent vomiting. I felt so guilty. I loved that she was here, that she was trying to help. I had missed my mother.

We tried white rice, toast, and clear soup … and every time, I let her down. Let everyone down.

Somehow, my mother's determination never waned. She tirelessly searched for something, anything, that my body would accept.

Over time, my pain continued to increase. Sometimes I would scream. I tried not to but I couldn't help myself. My pain had gone beyond what anyone could understand.

DON'T STOP

It was a Friday, and I was in the middle of a grueling ten-hour chemo session. I was having an allergic reaction to the therapy. My body was refusing the treatment, and my doctors wanted to stop it. They saw the way I looked and saw my labs. My blood work was dismal, indicating that my body was shutting down from the aggressiveness of the treatment.

"No! We can't stop. We have to keep going," I pleaded, panicking that any delay in treatment would mean I might not survive my cancer. I was young. I just had to push through and then it would be over and I could live.

"You're much too sick, CoCo. You don't have to stop. You just need to take a br—"

"No!" I interrupted. Some people took "breaks" from their treatment and never started again. If I stayed on track, I would have my last day of treatment on my birthday. "Just give me more Benadryl or whatever you have to."

I was already on a long list of medications that helped my body survive my treatment.

The nurse reluctantly pushed 75 mg of Benadryl (which is a lot) through my I.V. and gave me a bunch more nausea medication and something else I don't remember. I was basically passed out for the rest of that day's treatment.

I was well aware of the lethal risks, but I was determined to risk my life that day in order to save it in the long run. Sadly, this is a decision that countless cancer patients around the world have to make on any given day.

The next morning, I woke up to the bleak reality that my pain wasn't any better. It was worse. I found myself imprisoned by it. Neither oxycodone nor methadone was offering even the slightest respite. I tried to remain calm but anxiety began to take hold.

My heart was beating out of my chest. My skin felt too tight and too hot, and every nerve ending was screaming. The muted sounds of J's TV played somewhere in the distance, the chattering voices a stark contrast to my suffering.

How much more of this could I handle? Was I about to die?

I wondered if the disease was swallowing me whole.

Come on, CoCo. Sit up. You can do this.

I held my breath and tried to get up from the bed but was stopped cold with a stabbing pain that shot through my abdomen, hip, and back and forced a scream from my throat before I could stop it.

Ellie was already gone to her grandmother's for the day. *Thank God for Sheri*. If Ellie had seen me in my current condition, she would have been so scared.

J appeared at my door a moment or so after hearing my scream.

"I have to go to the hospital," I said through gritted teeth.

AT YOUR MERCY

At the hospital, I was at the mercy of emergency department doctors I didn't know. They ran scans and tests, all of which were excruciatingly painful (because just laying on a gurney was excruciatingly painful), but they couldn't figure out what was going on. After about twelve hours, the doctors discharged me with orders to call my oncologist first thing Monday. I left in as much agony as I'd arrived.

That wasn't the first time I had gone to a doctor with questions about my symptoms.

Several days beforehand, I reported extreme burns on my skin and increasing pain inside to my radiologist. I knew cancer and treatment was going to feel like nothing I'd ever experienced before, but my instincts told me something was off whenever I received radiology. So I booked an appointment with my radiologist.

When I went in, I was very, very sick, but I was still CoCo. True to myself, I was dressed in a cute outfit, makeup done, hair done, lipstick on. The doctor came in and I began to describe my excruciating, unbearable pain. As I talked, he raised an eyebrow.

I tried to show him photos of my burns, taken with my phone and he didn't seem fazed. "Well you look like you're handling the treatment well," he said and smiled at me reassuringly. I didn't realize he meant my appearance and not my scans until I was home, thinking about the appointment. I realized we didn't even look at or talk about my scans.

I soon came to realize that when I attended appointments looking put together, my pain wasn't taken seriously—apparently, I couldn't be that sick if I was wearing lip gloss. I get that most people choose comfortable clothes when they're sick because it makes them feel better. But what makes me feel better is knowing that my clothes look good and my makeup is done. It's my emotional armor, and I needed all the armor I could get.

My radiologist waved off my reported symptoms and continued

with the highest level of radiation possible. And I continued to allow it. I told myself that if this was the cost of saving my life, I wanted it.

The next day, I was in my bedroom, trying to find positions that would bring me comfort. My insides were screaming. It was indescribable. I didn't care what the doctors said, something was fucking wrong.

Terribly, awfully, wrong.

I tried reaching my regular oncologist by phone, but getting anyone on the phone on a weekend was nearly impossible. Even doctors get to have lives outside of work.

Before J went to bed, he looked in on me. "If you need to go into the hospital, it needs to be now because I'm going to bed."

"There's no point in going, they won't take me seriously anyway." The few responses I did get from my doctors were just to take more medicine, even though I had already tried that and it was miserably ineffective.

I resigned myself to attempt to sleep through the pain. Maybe in my dreams I would find relief.

At about 2 a.m. I was overwhelmed with the need to throw up. I tried to make it to the bathroom but my legs didn't seem to work anymore. I slid off the bed and crawled to the waste paper basket where I promptly threw up, mostly in the basket and partially on myself.

I felt *so* sick. My stomach was raging.

Even though I was light-headed, I decided I needed to get a replacement garbage bag from the kitchen. Somehow I got my legs to carry me to the kitchen island before I ended up getting dizzy and crashing to the floor. I can still remember how much it hurt my knees, which were so bony then, to be on the hardwood floor.

I could feel every vibrating nerve in my body telling me I was in serious trouble. I screamed out as a flash of pain overtook my body.

"J!" I screamed. "I need help! I fell!"

There was no response. I realized no one was coming. J was dead asleep.

I must have looked crazy, crawling around on the floor and

moaning and crying with pain. I knew then that if I couldn't make it to my phone and call 9-1-1, I would die.

Drawing on a reservoir of strength I didn't know I had, I managed to drag myself across the floor and toward my phone. Every inch forward took everything I had. My fingers, strained and trembling, gripped the ground, seeking purchase. Every scrape and graze heightened my awareness of the stark reality—the vast expanse I had to cover, and the profound vulnerability of my position. The chill from the floor seeped through my skin, numbing my senses but sharpening my determination to reach my phone.

Somehow, I managed to reach it and call for help.

Within a few of the longest, most excruciating minutes of my entire life, EMT banged on the door. I couldn't get to it, but thankfully, J heard the commotion, got up and let them in.

They began checking my vitals, trying to find a pulse. My blood pressure was so low they were having a hard time stabilizing me enough to even make the trip to the hospital. They tried multiple times to access my veins to start an I.V. but they were completely shot. They spent forty-three minutes trying. Their frantic voices seemed distant. It was like I was hearing them from underwater.

Once they got levels to a point where they thought I might survive the five-mile ride, I was placed on a gurney.

I couldn't say or do much but I remember grabbing J's hand in panic. I felt like those might be my last moments on earth. I begged him to come to the hospital with me. I was petrified. "Please come, J. I don't want to die alone."

J promised. "I'm just going to get dressed and I'll be right behind you."

As the EMTs loaded me into the ambulance, I passed out.

***

I woke up in the ER (again) but this time, they were taking me seriously. There was a flurry of concerned doctors and nurses rushing around me. They didn't know what was wrong. I just lay there as they ran tests and called doctors from various specialties to look at me.

After about four hours in the ER, J came in. It was 7:40 a.m. He was freshly showered, dressed, and holding a coffee he had picked up from somewhere along the way to the hospital. His crisp attire, his casual sips of coffee as he surveyed my bed, tubes, and monitors ... It was like the world was inside out.

"Oh, so it's bad?" he asked, his voice laced with disbelief more than concern.

"Look where I am, J."

Maybe it was just too much for him.

I was too sick to figure out how I felt about the fact that I could've died while my husband was showering and ordering his morning coffee.

My body was shutting down in slow motion, so they moved me down to my own room in the ICU. By that point, I was vomiting uncontrollably and continued to have constant diarrhea. What's worse, everything coming out of me was pure black. It was like something out of a horror movie.

The doctors ran countless tests before determining what was coming out of me was the burnt, radiated—essentially cremated—remains of my organs. The radiation had done so much damage to my insides that x-rays and MRIs told a horrifying story; the anatomy of my organs from my chest down was almost unrecognizable.

By this time, my oncologist, Dr. Vasques, had called in the best doctors in Fort Worth to consult on my case. Before I knew it, I had the best, most badass medical team anyone could hope for.

Dr. Gray was my surgeon. Dr. Mathe was the head of my palliative care at the hospital, and was now heading up my team. Dr. Kanu was my nephrologist. Dr. Chang was my urologist. Dr. McDonald was my infectious disease doctor.

After collaborating on my case, even with the brightest minds working together to help me, I was given the grim news that I wasn't stable enough to survive the surgery they'd need to perform to address what was going on.

Dr. Gray said, "I wish there was something we could do."

I stared at him for a moment before I realized what he was truly saying.

"This is one of the worst cases we have ever seen and unfortunately, you don't have much time."

Six hours was their best estimate, their guess on how much longer my body could function. Normally, doctors don't like giving timelines, but when you're a young mother with a young child, they try to give you the chance to say your goodbyes.

One nurse who thought I was asleep while she checked my vitals said in a fragile whisper, "It's like her body has been silently burning from the inside and nobody didn't anything to stop it." She was referring to the devastating radiation burns I had from my belly button down..

I grappled with the depth of that reality, trying to fathom how this had been missed just twenty-four hours beforehand in this same hospital.

The smell of disinfectant was a stark reminder of my proximity to death.

It was COVID-19 times so patients weren't allowed to have guests, but all I could think of was Ellie. I no longer cared about my own death. Any thought or pity for myself was replaced with a desperate need for a gentle touch, a fleeting moment with my beautiful little girl. I wanted to feel her warmth, to imprint a final memory in her heart.

Even though my sister, who is very Christian and very spiritual, had been praying for me non-stop since my fight with cancer began, I had always resisted spirituality. Linda would write on my kitchen whiteboard, "Thank you God for CoCo's healing." She would encourage me to pray to God for healing, to pray as if I was already healed, such as, "Thank you for healing me, God."

I loved Linda for her messages and prayers, but I didn't give them a second thought otherwise. I had my reasons. After all, what kind of God lets his children be raped at age five?

But at that moment, with tears streaming down my face, I found my voice, quivering with emotion, forming a prayer:

Please let me stay alive until Ellie gets here.
Give me more time to say all the things she needs to hear.
Let me say goodbye.
I know I don't deserve your miracles, God,
but I will do anything for another moment with my daughter.
And if you see to it to give me a little more time,
I will spend every second of my life making up for my mistakes.

My mother pulled some strings with hospital administrators to find a safe way for me to say goodbye to Ellie. Those were some pretty powerful strings given that it was a global pandemic.

A fifteen-minute visit was arranged. All I had to do was live long enough for her to get there. While I waited in a haze of medication, I tried to formulate what I could say, should say …

How do you wrap up a lifetime's worth of love, memories, and advice for the future in fifteen minutes?

When I saw her little face and bouncy curls I took her into my arms as best as I could. I held her close, the weight of this being our last moments together was crushing me. But joy at the miracle of living to see her also filled me with warmth.

"I will always be in your heart, Ellie, do you know that?" I kissed her forehead and looked into her big, frightened eyes.

She just snuggled into me, despite the sea of tubes.

"Never let anyone diminish your worth. Remember, you are powerful, radiant, and boundless."

Her innocent eyes, looking forward to her second birthday, couldn't grasp the gravity of our goodbye.

I cried as I said, "I'm sorry I'm going to miss your birthday party. But you're going to have a wonderful time!"

She began to cry too, not really knowing what was happening but knowing it was serious.

"Just remember that you always have to be stronger than you think, okay? Promise you will always speak up for yourself."

I started telling her all the things I wish someone had told me when I was her age.

I smothered her in kisses, and she did the same in return.

J gave me a sign that our visitation time was up.

"Where's Mommy, Ellie?" I asked her.

"In my heart," she said and pointed to her chest.

J picked her up from the bed and led her away, back down the corridor and toward a life without me.

I felt a silent communion with a higher power, thankful for granting me that final embrace. Ready to surrender, I was strangely at peace, knowing I'd had the chance to say one last goodbye.

My whole life I've heard about miracles and God making the impossible possible, but I had spent years being angry at Him for everything that had happened in my life. But at this moment, I didn't care. I had nothing to lose. So I prayed:

God, it's me again. I know that you just gave me the biggest miracle, and here I am being greedy and asking for another miracle. I'm sorry I'm this way, always asking for more, but I'm not ready to go. I want to live. I know that I've been reckless my whole life and have not valued being alive, have not been thankful for everything you've given me, all the good despite the bad and the fact that to this day, you've saved my life over and over and over again.

God, I don't want to die. I want to live. I want to heal. I want to change. And if you please give me the opportunity to survive and find my purpose, and become the woman that you have always wanted me to be. I beg of you to please give me a chance to go into surgery and keep fighting for my life. I will spend the rest of my days making you proud and being the best version of me possible.

But even if you don't, I want you to fill me with peace. I don't want to die with a heart filled with heavy pain.

Ellie needs a mother and I want to be able to be there for her. I want to be able to raise her with the unconditional love, peace, and understanding that I always wished I had.

I ask for your forgiveness.

In Jesus's name I pray. Amen.

I truly didn't expect anything to come of my prayers, but I had to try.

Over the following hours, the deep stillness of the ICU was broken that night by a nurse's voice, a lifeline in my numbing world. "Do you feel that?" she asked, as she pushed on points on my body. I realized I could feel a sensation creeping into areas that had been burnt and numb for days. Like a cascade, my vitals began improving, mystifying everyone around. What had been a countdown to my last hours extended unpredictably.

I had asked—begged—for a miracle. And I was given one. Six hours later, I was still alive, stable enough to go into an eight-hour surgery. My medical team was baffled, unable to rationalize my inexplicable recovery.

* * *

Having grown up in an environment where beauty was everything, I had learned that without beauty, I would be worthless. And for most of my life, I agreed with that. My body had brought me nothing but pain and trauma. It had been used and treated like garbage. It almost made sense to me that even though I had always been dressed beautifully, it came to be that I was rotten beneath.

It took my entire medical team to operate on me in an attempt to save, or at least prolong, my life. Like any other person, I needed to have the ability to eat, drink, and expel all of it afterward. But because I was so badly burned, my intestines, ureters, and colon weren't doing what they were supposed to anymore.

It was a bloodbath surgery, or so my doctors said.

I woke up to a sea of overwhelming pain. As my surroundings came into view, I realized my life had changed.

I looked down from my elevated hospital bed to see this thing attached to me. I soon learned that it was my ostomy bag. I could feel the ache of a huge incision and the gauze that covered it. I felt the pain of multiple objects pulling on my back. These would end up being my nephrostomy tubes.

I had a port coming out of my chest and monitors all around me. One of the doctors explained that due to damage to my intestines, kidneys, and other organs, they had to give me a loop ileostomy and replace my damaged ureters with nephrostomy tubes which drained into two separate bags, one on each side of me. The "nef-tubes" were intended to be temporary.

My surgeon, Dr. Paul Gray, came to my bedside once I was awake. His face was grim. "We have never seen radiation damage as bad as what we saw when we opened you up." His voice was somber as he described that my insides had been burned by the therapy that was meant to save me. The treatment was too intense for my organs and tissues to handle. "There has been a *lot* of damage. But now, through the nef tubes and loop ileostomy, we have found a way to help your body start to function again. This will be a long road, and you will need more surgeries to get through it, but for now, let's focus on getting you stable enough and strong enough to survive before we think about that."

I tried to comprehend everything he was saying and what it meant. I could feel pain in other places too. I'd learned that I also had several drains in various other locations, placed to help drain the fluid from all the radiation and any potential infection out of my body.

I winced in pain as I tried to see all the medical equipment attached to me.

Was *this* my new normal? I started to panic at the thought but couldn't speak.

A nurse that I knew as "Nurse Jodie" circled around me, taking vitals and waiting for me to ask questions. I took the bait.

"I have four bags," I said, looking down at my body in despair. The nurse took my hand and patted it. I continued, "How am I going to go home with these? How am I going to do this? How am I going to live life with these bags?"

Jodie looked at me and in a soothing voice, said, "CoCo you are going to be able to get through this. You have no idea how strong you are. Your bags do not determine who you are."

I didn't believe her at the time but her voice and smile made me feel better.

She grew to become one of my favorite nurses because she was always so supportive and positive. Most of all, I loved her because she had faith in me. She saw my strength despite it all.

Unfortunately, not everyone looked past my bags and tubes.

When anyone came to visit, I could feel their eyes settle on those areas of my body, trying to hide their horror. I wished I could disappear, but honestly, I was in so much pain, I had very little energy left for worrying about what I looked like. My body had been a source of pain my whole life. This was just a different kind of pain. My appearance wasn't on my radar.

My hospital stay was much longer than I expected. I was in for about three months, and through that time, could only see Ellie twice. Although my mom was still coming and going, my sister was the one who took most of her life off to be next to me. She was the perfect person to take care of me. Her strong spirituality helped me start my own path to keeping my promises to God—and to be able to start my healing journey. Linda was patient, positive, and the only person who never doubted that I was going to get out of there.

Eventually, we figured out a schedule of care, recognizing that my mom couldn't be there all the time. With Ellie taken care of by Sheri and J, it became a rotation between Kelly (Zach's mom) and Linda. They would be the main people to take care of me at the hospital (and, later, at the house).

My medical care team kept me focused on learning how to

function. Recovery was difficult and full of pain. Always pain. At one point, our dog died and I don't even remember anyone telling me that she did. I was on a lot of medication.

I had to learn how to eat, sleep, and even walk again. I had to learn how to handle my new mobility aids—which is exactly what ostomy and nephrostomy bags are! They're no different than needing a wheelchair to move or an oxygen tank to breathe. They're nothing to be ashamed of.

Yet at that time, I saw myself through strangers' eyes. And through loved ones' eyes as well.

I'll never forget the look on J's face when he first walked into my hospital room. His eyes went directly to my bags and then darted away. His face was filled with sadness and disgust. Or maybe it was fear? I'm not sure. He was the person who was supposed to love me in sickness and in health, and he couldn't even look at me—bags, tubes, and all.

Despite our constant fighting and near-divorce, I do have a grasp of how scary it all must have looked. I was terrified too. J admitted he would rather die than go through a cancer battle like the one I was going through. It was an awful thing to say, but if someone had told me a couple of years beforehand that this would be my journey, there's no way I could've imagined getting through it either.

I confided in my mom. "He can't even look at me, Mami," I said. "How can I live with a man who can't even look at me?" I explained that his face had made me sad, angry, and feel rejected.

"Nicole, J is a good dad. Give him a chance. It is very hard and impactful for a man to see a body so different from what they're used to. Men are very visual, and J sees a lot because you share a lot with him. I can see in his face how uncomfortable he feels. Both of you have been through a lot, and it takes time to process all of the changes you have been through. You need to understand that you're not the only one undergoing this change."

"Mom, I understand J is a good dad, but 'husband' and 'father' are two completely separate things. And you're basically telling me that it's okay for him not to accept my body because of my disabilities. That's not okay. I've been given the opportunity to be alive. And part of that, to me, means not only having peace in my life but being loved by the people around me. I don't want to have to hide certain parts of me, especially from my husband."

She thought any value I had as a wife or a girlfriend was gone, along with most of my kidneys and intestines. After all, my mother, like my sister and me, had been judged based on her appearance for most of her life. She wasn't trying to be hurtful. But her words made me hate myself just a little bit more nonetheless.

I had come to realize maybe J would never come to terms with my new body. If he had a hard time loving me before, how the hell must he feel now?

"I guess I don't just come with baggage," I tried to joke. "I come with actual bags." Neither of us laughed then.

While in the hospital, connected to I.V. medications and monitors, tubes, and bags, I was alone most of the time. J tried to visit as much as he could, but they were often awkward, sometimes angry visits. The longer my cancer journey was drawn out, the more I sensed resentment building within him. I felt bad because I could see that my cancer was slowly saving me and slowly killing him.

I had made it my sole focus to work on myself and my healing—both physical and emotional—every single day at the hospital. I wanted to make sure that when I went home, I was a different person. I started creating healthy habits in and out of the hospital. I worked hard on processing the drastic life changes that I was facing by writing pages upon pages of lessons, thoughts, prayers, and bible studies. I studied and certified myself as a life coach. I started to find out who CoCo really was in this new life. What did I like? What didn't I? What television shows did I like? What books did I find interesting? What were my favorite movies? I was sober, fighting for my life, and yet it was a whole new world.

Eventually, as time passed and the COVID rules weren't as strict anymore, J and Sheri started bringing Ellie to see me more often. In fact, Sheri became an even bigger part of our lives at that time. She came to my bedside many times when my health took a turn for the worse. She was there when I needed help and a hand to hold at the hospital. J obviously had to stay home with Ellie.

Visits with my little girl were my everything. I used them as fuel for motivation to keep going and to fight. She was my inspiration for not giving up. She was my reason for focusing on staying alive. The moment she would leave me I would break down and start hysterically crying and so would she. I can't explain the heartbreak that comes from seeing your baby girl scream, "I don't want to leave you, Mommy!" and always wondering if it would be the last time I'd see her. I teetered between recovering and getting sicker. Each day was different, a new medical milestone or challenge.

I also could never have a shower or a bath again. I couldn't even wet my whole back. There was just too much risk of infection. So I had to learn new ways to clean myself.

Here's the thing: you have no idea what you're capable of doing until you're forced to do it. At first, I couldn't look in the mirror. I had to fight not to be horrified by the look of my bags.

But then, I started thanking God for them. They saved my life. I made it my mission to make sure everyone close to me knew that too. I started adding them to my journal entries and devotionals. I made it a daily practice to be grateful for the medical aids that allowed me to be alive to hug my daughter.

* * *

I was released on a Monday, so J took Ellie to school, went to work, and left me in bed at home alone. I remember laying there, panicking. It was the first time in a long time I didn't have someone to help me move, eat, drink, and medicate myself.

I had no food. I wasn't strong enough to get up, and when I got behind on my medication, I was paralyzed with pain. I drank all the water I could reach early on in the day. I was leaking so badly out of my ileostomy; it was disgusting but I couldn't get up to empty it. I was ashamed, helpless, and angry—angry at my situation, at the outcome of the surgery, at being left alone, at me for being incapable of doing things on my own ...

How would I get out of bed without pain meds?
Who would pick up my medication?
How would I get up the little stairs with my walker?
How was I supposed to get up and cook?
Who will hold my bags when I try to clean myself?

I was a mess. *I guess that's nothing new*, I thought. *Same as always. Just a different kind of mess.*

When Sheri realized how much help I needed, she came and cared for me, helping in any way that she could. I don't know what I would've done if she hadn't. I was so grateful. We didn't have a perfect relationship but her offer of care meant a lot to me. And she is, to this day, a wonderful gramma to Ellie.

Eventually, I had a lady coming in to help me a few days a week. I also took advantage of any chance I had to have Kelly and Linda take care of me. I would have loved to have full-time care, but Emily moved to New York with her fiance, and my mom had to return to Miami to manage teenage twins and her new marriage. Linda had a job and a life she needed to get back to, even though I am sure she would've stayed by my bedside if she could. Kelly came every couple of months and stayed for weeks. I was grateful for every minute of help I received.

I will forever be thankful for all the trips and time people invested in coming to my side. I can't comprehend how hard it must have been for everyone to stop their lives to come visit me. The worst part was that because I was so sick, I couldn't even spend real time with them. The medications that were saving my life and taking my pain away were also preventing me from staying awake to create more memories with loved ones. This would have been a perfect opportunity to start rebuilding and nurturing my relationships with my family, but as much as I tried to stay awake and communicate clearly, I just couldn't. I would be so embarrassed when I realized that I had fallen asleep mid sentence or that I would lose my train of thought as I was speaking. I would end up crying out of frustration, laying my head back, and just stop talking.

LET'S DO THIS

It was now my job to figure out how to function in my new normal. I have always turned to makeup and fashion to make me feel better. But after the surgery, beauty took a backseat. At one point I even donated all of my pre-cancer clothing, thinking I would never be able to wear something that looked good again. I pretty much lived in J's XL clothes. For the first time in my life, I didn't do my makeup or hair. I just focused on recovering and surrendered to my healthcare team.

I was in and out of the hospital with infections and procedures. My kidneys would get infections, caused by the nephrostomy tubes, and so literally half my life was in the hospital on the verge of sepsis. Nephrostomy tubes are only meant to be used for weeks or months. In rare cases, eight to ten years maximum. I couldn't live without mine, and they were already needing to be changed roughly every four to eight weeks due to infection.

It was a delicate dance between embracing and experiencing life but also keeping on top of my symptoms so that I'd know to get admitted to hospital before something went too far. There were many times when I put off calling my doctor because I wanted to be part of an event or milestone, and each time, taking that risk took a toll on my health.

Tolls came in the form of increased pain, increased hospital stays, decreased time between tube changes or other procedures, and significant risk to my life. But what is the point of being alive if you can't enjoy it at least half the time?

Hospitals became my second home, but also one of the largest sources of anxiety.

I worried that I would die, or not get my medication in time, or that a nurse would make me feel like I was a bother or abusing the high dosages of medication I needed to get through the day, or that I would go days without eating because I had a unique meal plan (thanks to my ileostomy). All of these fears were rooted in things that had happened over and over again. If I felt my heart race from an oncoming panic attack, I would move as close to my little hospital room window as I could. If that didn't work, I would try to walk the halls or go outside, depending on how mobile I was at the time. Alone time at the hospital became my new normal.

I reminded myself that when I was working for other people, problems would be given to me to be solved: "If you have a problem, give it to CoCo. She'll figure it out," they would say. And I did. So what I realized was that I needed to put that energy and those skills to work for me. I had to turn them inward and work on adapting better to my body and my life, now that it had changed so drastically.

One of the healthy habits I implemented was to write down a list of all the things I couldn't do and, one by one, find solutions for them. That meant that inside the hospital I had to figure out how to make it a home, make it comfortable. I started packing all my favorite things, adult coloring books, and books to read to Ellie through video chat. I ordered all of my favorite snacks. My nail guy started coming to the hospital to do my nails. I packed my favorite pajamas, refusing to wear hospital gowns any longer. Most of all, I started advocating for myself. I stayed on top of my medication schedules, I learned how to take care of myself without help. I didn't want to have to rely on anyone to function in my daily life. Outside of the hospital, I learned that even if I didn't have people around me to help, I was thankfully living in 2021, when you could order anything and everything to wherever you were. I got an app for cleaning services, an app for grocery delivery, and an app for medication delivery. I would find an app for any task that needed to be done, but that I couldn't do. This kept life, my family, and myself moving forward, despite my medication situation.

The hardest part of it all was learning how to change my tubes and bags by myself. These were things that patients would usually never dare to try to do themselves, but I didn't want to sit and wait for Home Health all day. I wanted to live my life. I wanted to be able to travel to Miami with my daughter.

I wanted to live more while I was alive.

I overcame my fears and I truly embodied the definition of #cocostrong.

CHAPTER NINE

NO FILTER

It took a long time for me to really get to know my body in its new form again. I talk a lot about that on my social media now, but when this all started, I felt lost. After a lifetime of feeling used, abused, too fat, too thin, judged, ridiculed, embarrassed, ashamed, broken, and now sick, my body and I have been at war for a very long time.

Self-love had never been on the table for me. Not until this.

I began doing my makeup again. I don't care if some people think it's crazy to do a full face when you may not even leave your room that day; for me, it made me feel better. I spent many days doing my makeup, wearing my CoCo-style headband, and talking to my online community as I worked on making myself feel better. If I fell asleep, it was fine. I embodied the definition of "Sleeping Beauty."

New CoCo. New normal. Let's do this.

I found black stretchy shorts, safety pins, and snaps that were the perfect fabric and fit to allow me to tuck away most of my tubes and cover my nef bags. It worked so well that I could even wear my super cute ripped jean shorts without having everything hanging out below their hemlines.

I started to understand that clothing was made to fit me and not the other way around. I learned what would work with my body and make me feel comfortable with my bags full or empty. This was a necessity because of the high output that my ileostomy produced. I grew to be okay with the top of my ostomy bag, ostomy belt, and gauze showing. All the things I was so obsessed with covering in the beginning no longer mattered. I wasn't worried about people seeing the medical devices it took to keep me alive.

RAMONA IS A BITCH

Daily life with my bags and tubes wasn't easy but I was making it work. On one sunny afternoon, I was craving Starbucks and had to get Ellie from school. I got dressed in black leggings and a black and blue gingham bodysuit and slipped my feet into white Steve Madden rhinestone tennis shoes. With my hair swept back by my headband, my face freshly made up, and all my bags emptied, I scooped up Bruno (being a Boston Terrier breed, he was maybe fifteen or twenty pounds) and headed out in the direction of a big delicious coffee and my sweet girl.

In the Starbucks drive-through, I ordered a grande white chocolate mocha, iced, with two caramel pumps and a slice of banana bread. I got Bruno a pup cup and ordered Ellie a chocolate croissant, cake pop, and milk.

I tried to resist drinking mine before getting to Ellie's school but I caved. By the time Ellie jumped into the passenger side of the car, I had polished off most of my drink, *which meant we were on a deadline.*

"Starbucks!!" Ellie exclaimed and immediately took a bite of her cake pop.

"Just for you, baby!" I smiled, happy that my surprise got the reaction I'd hoped for.

We threw on the radio and sang, making up words when we didn't know them, dancing in our seats, and bursting into laughter whenever we hit bad notes. I wished we could have hit the highway and just kept on driving, staying in this moment forever.

We were about halfway home when I realized shit was about to get real.

As we sat at a red light, I reached down and felt my ostomy bag. It was full. Like *really* full. That was not good. Just like any food or drink, it never took long to go through my body. Because I had a one-of-a-kind ileostomy, it meant my digestive system was extremely small. The moment I took in anything sugary or liquid, I would end up with it in my bag in liquid form. I had to be very careful where I ate, what I ate, and how I ate. Not to mention, how I was dressed. Eating or drinking multiple times a day and the lack of nutrients being absorbed into my body is why I was often dehydrated and weak. It wasn't unusual to give myself I.V. fluids every other day.

"Fuck, that was fast," I muttered and tried calculating how much time I might have left to get home to empty Ramona (my bag) before it burst.

"Oh, baby," I felt tears threaten to fill my eyes. "Mommy might have a problem."

Ellie paused midway through a crumbly bite of her croissant. "Is your bag leaking?"

"Not yet …" I could feel pressure against the ostomy opening, a sure sign that it was about to pop. My heart sank and I looked around my pristine car. I dreaded the thought of it being covered with the contents of my ileostomy bag.

"I've gotta empty this *now*," I said, mostly to myself, trying not to panic.

I pulled onto the shoulder of the road, slammed on the brakes, threw the driver's side open, and hiked my sweater up and under my chin as cars zoomed past. The second I released the bottom of the ostomy bag, the contents burst out and down into the ditch. I kept my feet and legs as far away from the splash zone as I could.

"Do you need any help, Mommy?" Ellie asks from behind me. She wasn't afraid of anything. She just wanted to support me.

"No, baby girl. You're so sweet, but thank you."

Just as I felt myself begin to relax, I watched some of the dark liquid splash back, directly onto my shoes. "Shit," I said. But luckily, I had my ostomy clean-up emergency kit. This wasn't my first rodeo. I cleaned that up as best as I could, re-fastened the ostomy, and let my sweater back down.

"Mommy, those were your favorite shoes!" Ellie peers over at my feet from inside the car.

"That's okay, I can always get new shoes."

"Of course you can get more shoes, Mom," she said. "Because you already have so many!" Ellie smacked her little hand to her forehead for dramatic effect.

Even though my shoes were now ruined, I was relieved to have avoided total destruction of my car and wardrobe. "Close call, baby, but no leaks!" I sighed and shot her a weak smile over my shoulder, hoping this wouldn't ruin her day.

"Woo hoo! No leaks!" she whooped in celebration before scrunching up her nose. She was doing a little celebratory dance move involving fist pumps and waving arms. She knew I was upset and was trying to make me feel better. She was wise beyond her years.

"Ellie, can you imagine if we hadn't pulled over in time?! Now *that* would have been awful!" I said as I climbed back in beside her and breathed for what felt like the first time in ten minutes. "But you know what, Ellie?" I said, in my most serious tone of voice.

Ellie froze and her eyes grew wide.

"You are the sweetest, smartest, coolest kid I've ever met." I kissed her on the nose. It was the truth. I flopped back in my seat and looked at her, giving her the biggest smile I could muster.

Ellie smiled back mischievously and asked, " So does this mean I can be DJ?"

I had taught Ellie how to use my phone and master the Spotify app so that she could put all the songs she wanted. This was something I remember doing when I was a little girl.

"Yes! Ellie, you can be DJ!!" She stares at me expectantly. And then says "Mom ... do the thing.."

I winked at her "I got you, E!" I proceeded to do her official DJ introduction: "And nowwww we have D-D-D-D-D–J-J-J-J-J BELLIE ON THE BEAT!"

She beamed from ear to ear. We drove home singing all our favorite Taylor Swift songs at the very top of our lungs.

#COCOSTRONG

That night, I shared my roadside bag emergency story with my growing online community. Until #cocostrong, it felt to me as if social media was entirely about unrealistic perfection and obsessing over the way we look. But then, here I was, pulling up my shirt, showing my bags, showing my tubes—and of course, my scars—and people were still cheering for me.

I had spent most of my life feeling like my value was measured by how beautiful I was, and now I had this vibrant community showing me more love on videos when I was breaking down and being real, than on the ones in which I was posting in a beautiful outfit or doing a makeup tutorial.

My community wasn't just any online community. These were people who had heard my story, seen my fight, and eventually developed an unbreakable bond with me. We bonded through shared trauma and authentic moments of truth and self-acceptance. I spent more and more time on Instagram Lives with them, drawn to the beautiful power of their love and our inexplicable connection that transcended thousands of miles. For the first time in my life, people found not only value in my story and my words but in my body—as it was, scars and all. These beautiful humans saw beauty in me too, beauty in the ashes. I wanted to pave the way for everyone to be able to show and embrace disability aids without shame.

I went from feeling like it was Ellie and me against the world to being Ellie, me, and 170,000+ best friends against the world.

Not everyone was happy with me posting about my life online. When my mom heard about #cocostrong, she called me: "Nicole, I've had a lot of people reaching out about you sharing things on Instagram. I saw your video. What is the need and purpose of you showing your ostomy and tube cleanings and all that?"

"What do you mean, why?" I knew where this conversation was heading, but I wanted to hear it from her.

"No one wants to see that. Just because you are used to your body the way it is now, doesn't mean other people are. People may find it disgusting or have a hard time looking at it. Besides, it makes it look like you're victimizing yourself!"

I knew it.

I knew she was going to have a problem with me being so open about everything. I knew she wasn't the only one who would see my content this way, but I knew my purpose. I didn't want other people who were going through the same things as me to feel judged, alone, or lost. So, although I knew there would be criticism, I went with my own brave choice.

"Are you kidding me? Mom, you have no idea how much my story and my content has helped people, has helped me. I'm not victimizing myself, I'm telling my truth."

"Nicole, you don't see how this is affecting me. People are sending me DMs and criticizing me as a mother non-stop. They think I should always be with you when you get your tubes changed and have infections. You know I can't be there all the time. I do my best to be there as often as I can, but the twins need me, Gary needs me, Linda needs me, and my husband needs me. I can't be in six places at the same time."

"Mom, I don't think it's fair for you to say I'm victimizing myself or that I have to be careful about sharing my truth. I'm sorry it has affected you negatively. I didn't want that. I will ask them to stop saying negative things to you."

Afterward, I followed through on that promise. I explained, in a "Live" on Instagram that being negative to my mother wasn't acceptable and that it made our lives and our relationship more difficult. They couldn't see everything my mom had done for me since I became sick. With a now-healed heart, I wanted nothing more than to heal my relationship with my mom. But the hate that she was getting from social media was making it impossible for us.

I embraced my #cocostrong community. We started doing bible studies and praying together, and people who were going through similar problems started reaching out for help from me. *Me.* CoCo the screw-up. CoCo who had hurt everything and everyone she loved up to now was inspiring others to shine in the midst of their own darkness.

I soon learned that some social media platforms didn't like certain videos. I once posted a video after I had surgery—it revealed scars, scabs, surgical incisions, and of course there were some bloodstains. My account was suspended for thirty days! I was livid.

It was such bullshit.

Women can be online wearing nothing more than a thong with their nipples showing but it's not okay for me to show my ileostomy bleeding. How is that right? What I am going through is rare, but it's not just mine alone. There are hundreds of thousands of people around the world dealing with the same thing. Yet I can't show the reality of the second leading cause of death worldwide.

Doesn't social media understand that *this* is real life? Not just for me, but for many people going through medical challenges.

So now I'm better at playing by the rules. When I break them, I make sure it's worth it.

I started Coffee with CoCo, an online Instagram series, where we talked about tough subjects with extreme honesty. It became something everyone seemed to love, bringing us all together, and opening the door to talk about things beyond my sickness—sexual abuse, self-love, forgiveness, spirituality.

And I began writing this book.

Watching the numbers rise, and reading the comments of support and love, I realized that I had the power to reach and help people who needed to see someone else going through what they were going through.

My sister, the brilliant fashionista that she is, designed CoCo-style ileostomy bag covers. You can see them on my Insta.

I momentarily mourned the fact that I had gotten rid of so many of my previous clothes, now that I knew I could have worn them, but then I realized that allowed me to refresh my wardrobe.

I have a few favorite sweaters that hide pretty much everything, and then I have tank tops and crop tops that only show hints of tubes here and there. And I love how I look in all of them.

WORKING FOR MY DREAM

I logged into Zoom to try to fit in another session while I was still upright. The fear of not getting my book done was palpable. It felt like my clock had sped up, even though none of the doctors had officially said so.

"Hi, Jenn." I tried to smile but I was gritting my teeth from the pain. "Um, we're going to go to the hospital." I had been dealing with symptoms of infection or something else. Lots of pain, and not necessarily in the usual areas. But I knew what an infection felt like, and that was definitely happening as well. I had to get it under control to avoid septicemia.

She nodded. "Okay, good. It'll be good to get you on some antibiotics and have full-time care around you. What have the docs been saying today?"

"My urologist is at the other hospital. I have no urologist here …" I cringe and hold my breath for a moment until the wave of pain passes. When it passes, I continue, "So we've put a call in. I really like my urologist but I don't like the colorectal surgeon that he uses." Even though it's often my kidneys that are acting up, everything inside is so complicated in my case, I need a colorectal surgeon too. Besides which, this pain was in more areas and felt different than the last time.

"I was hoping to be able to go to this Christmas thing with Ellie tonight. That's what I've been holding off for," I said, wondering if I could manage the pain just one more night.

"I know. But maybe this way, you'll be home for Christmas with Ellie, which is even better," Jenn reminded me.

I couldn't even imagine missing Christmas with my little girl. I didn't want to do that to Ellie.

"Well, I'm here for whatever you want to do. We can work as much or as little as you want to today," Jenn offered.

I kept getting rushes of panic off and on for most of the last couple of days. And it was about the book. I wanted to make up for lost time before it ran out. I wanted to make a big push for as long as possible to record as much as possible before I ended up in the hospital or couldn't do it anymore. I took the computer to my bedroom and tried to find a position to sit that was bearable. I don't know how, but I was actually able to work for hours, as long as I stood up and leaned over the chair at times, or the bed. Working was a welcome distraction.

I talked about my family, my daily life, the fact that I have to wear diapers now, how I fucked up so much over the years, and how I got a call to turn myself in for theft while shopping for baby clothes; I talked about my childhood sexual abuse, the neglect, my constant search for home, for love and acceptance; and I talked about how I've always felt like people thought I was disgusting, and that I've wasted so much of my time trying to convince them I'm worth looking at, seeing. We talked about everything.

All. Of. It.

The session began to be interrupted by more and more text messages and calls from my palliative care team, and I knew it was time.

Before signing off, I promised, "I'll make a post about the book once I'm in a room. I always get significantly higher numbers of my CoCo Strong community logging into my Instagram Lives when I'm at the hospital." I know that my community is worried about what's going on and that they appreciate being shown the real stuff, even when I'm not looking perfect or smiling. They like to see the reality of all of this. I have the feeling that it helps them face their realities too.

"Okay babe, I've gotta go. I'll call you when I'm settled in the hospital."

And then I signed off.

THE SPRING SURGERY

As the infections continued to get worse and come more often, my oncologist referred me to the best reconstructive urologist in Dallas. I was in and out of the hospital every four weeks, a sure sign that something had to change. The team at Dallas had the knowledge to complete the complicated ileal conduit surgery that I needed.

Most of my intestines and anatomy in my pelvic area, having been so burned by radiation, had become solidified and it had almost formed cement-like clumps within me. This made simple bodily functions like passing urine through my ureter almost impossible for me.

Doing the surgery was a decision I made myself. I didn't want other people's opinions to factor into my final call of a life-or-death situation. I would have to live with the consequences so I wanted to decide on my own with my care team. My doctors seemed optimistic and I trusted their judgment and expertise. It took eight full months just to prepare for the surgery—getting my body strong enough and gaining enough weight to be able to endure the operation. Plus they had to schedule three separate surgeons to work on me in the same OR.

There was a risk I wouldn't wake up from it, but there was also a chance that it would be a game changer. No bags. No tubes. New life. I would be able to shower again and go swimming with Ellie. You don't realize how much you will miss those basic daily life freedoms and tasks until you can't do them anymore. I would hear J or other moms complain about the endless list of parenting tasks they were faced with on a daily basis, and all I could think of was how grateful I would be if I could do those same tasks.

Besides, what other choice did I have? If I didn't do something, I was surely going to die from one of my infections.

I rewrote my will so my sister would be in charge of making sure my decisions were honored if something were to go wrong. I had prayed for this for so long and truly felt that in my heart, this was going to be it. I thought of the things I'd get back—less pain, more independence, more health. I also hoped it would open the possibility of being intimate with someone in the future, whether it be my husband, or if we split up, someone else.

Because it was a different hospital from what I was used to, I had to figure out a whole new system and medical team.

On the day of surgery, I packed my stuff and checked in. J was with me. They got me into a beautiful room and some of my friends who I'd made through my community, came and helped me decorate the space so that I felt loved and at ease. I created a private channel for the people who wanted to keep up with the surgery. This allowed the people who wanted to stay up to date with my progress, to easily do so. I had over 70,000 people rooting for the surgery to be successful. Not only did I have my own prayers to give me courage, but I had their prayers, wishes, and love as well.

I can't fully describe how that felt.

Later that day, once I was settled into my room, my mom came to visit, booking a hotel near the hospital so she could be at my side.

The morning of my surgery, J and my mom arrived at 5 a.m. as I was being prepped. I've never been so nervous in my whole life.

I was taken down to the operating suites, and before I knew it, I dozed off to sleep.

HEARTBREAK

When I woke up from surgery, I could immediately tell that it hadn't gone well. Every time I thought there couldn't possibly be more pain, I was surprised.

J and a doctor were both in the room and they gave me the news that the surgery had failed. I thought I knew heartbreak before that day, but I had no idea.

I couldn't believe it. I had been so hopeful, so certain. I was so sure this was where God was leading me. The words being spoken to me were incomprehensible. I couldn't wrap my mind around the gravity of it all.

I still had my ostomy, tubes, all of it. And I felt worse than I did before I'd gone in.

A surgeon on the team solemnly explained that things were so burned inside me, that they couldn't complete the surgery. I didn't have enough healthy intestines. Every time they tried to break through the over-radiated cement-like tissue, I would just start bleeding out. After seven hours of trying, the doctors had gone out and explained the situation to my mom and J. They told them if they kept on trying, there was a high chance I would die.

"Please stop," my mom said and J agreed.

The doctors closed me up and sent me back to my room.

The community that I had was heartbroken right along with me, but the person who had to carry this pain and prevail was me.

Why did I want more?

Should I have been happy with what I had?

God had given me my goodbye with Ellie two years before. Every moment I had after saying goodbye was a bonus—a gift to be cherished.

Should I have just been happy with that? Was I being greedy?

I had an epidural for the pain for a full week. Even so, I found myself hoping to pass out so that I could get some relief from the agony. Within four days, I began coming to the realization that my sixteen-staple wound was getting infected. A mass was forming right in the middle. It felt and looked like I had a ball of something—an infection—beneath my skin at the site.

I kept pushing for answers about this ball of obvious infection. I didn't understand how the best hospital in the area, the one everyone raves about, could look at that and think it was nothing. How could they make such a huge mistake?

No one was listening, no one was taking care of me.

After weeks of being at that hospital, suffering and not feeling I was getting the medical attention I desperately needed. The doctors there wanted to discharge me and I let them. As soon as I got out of there, I texted Dr. Mathe of my Fort Worth medical team to tell him what had happened.

"I'm scared your surgeons won't want to work on me after I was operated on by another hospital," I panicked. Doctors didn't like to contradict or step on each other's toes if they could help it.

I sent him pictures of my wound to show him what I was worried about.

"Come into the hospital right away. We need to look at that," Dr. Mathe texted back after seeing the images of the large, ball-like bump on my stomach.

In three days, Dr. Mathe's team did what the Dallas team couldn't (or wouldn't) do in three weeks. I had a gigantic infection and it needed to be drained immediately. When they were done, I was left with a four-inch wide, five-inch deep hole in the middle of my stomach where the gigantic abscess had been. The "hole" that remained was just inches from my stoma. This increased the risk of output leaks traveling into the area they'd just drained—a sure way to die from septicemia.

I spent months recovering from the surgery, the abscess, and the heartbreak.

It was the first time since my diagnosis that I was without direction and without hope. My community started seeing a completely different side of me. They must have thought, *Where is our CoCoStrong that we know?*

I looked inward and continued my conversation with God. As I was healing, looking for answers, I received more bad news.

After they removed the abscess, my entire care team walked into my hospital room at the same time. Having them all come in together signaled this was not going to be a good conversation.

"You've been asking what your options are from here," Dr. Gray started. "We spoke to the doctors at UT and reviewed the post-op reports. I hate to say this to you, but there's nothing to do at this point, CoCo."

I tilted my head and stared at him, trying to understand what he was saying. I'll never forget the look on his face or the sound of his voice when he said those words.

Dr. Gray continued, "I personally won't go back in unless it is absolutely a sudden life or death emergency. At this point, we're just causing more damage and more scar tissue."

The more scar tissue I had, the less my organs could do what they were supposed to do.

Dr. McDonald, whose job it was to keep me from dying from an infection, painted a picture of the future. "The infections are going to continue to get out of hand. And with the surgery failing, there's no way to prevent them."

I knew that as long as I had nef tubes, my body would continue to reject them, continually expose my kidneys to bacteria, and result in a revolving door of infection. Worse, the more times we switch my nef tubes, the more scar tissue I develop. Eventually, we would run out of places in my kidney to insert them.

Whenever I had tough conversations with the team, I looked over at Dr. Mathe, trying to guess what he was thinking. He was the one I relied on for honest, considerate feedback and that day was no different.

He caught my glance, and softly said, "CoCo, we're out of ideas. We don't know what else we can do." All of my doctors were top in their field, but Dr. Mathe was known to be one of the top experts at my hospital and I trusted him. So, as he said those words, I could see the heartbreak went beyond my community, my family, and myself. I could see from looking at my medical team they were heartbroken too.

Dr. McDonald said, "Let's continue to give you all of our support and help you through whatever you need."

Dr. Mathe nodded. "You call the shots, CoCo, and we will make it happen. This is your fight. And you're the one who gets to decide when you're done fighting."

I NEED YOU

I was sent home a few days later with I.V. antibiotics, which I was used to administering at home. An intravenous pole lived beside the head of my bed at all times and even Ellie knew how to get the fluid packs for me so that I could hang them.

I got into my bed, pulled up my fluffiest blanket, invited Ellie to cuddle, flipped on my camera, and turned to my community. They knew Ellie well. We all danced, talked, and sang together during countless Instagram and TikTok live sessions.

I looked into my camera and confessed: "*Chicos*, I need you."

Ellie leaned in and looked at the camera too as people logged on.

Within seconds, several hundred were online with us. "It's been so hard lately. I've been thinking about everything that has happened. I felt my eyes fill with tears and shook them off. "I just wish so much that I could just get away and take a breather from everything."

More people joined the session and my phone dinged as comments started popping up on the screen.

> *maurensegurabonilla*: CoCo! How are you doing?
> *wen_2903*: We haven't seen you in a while!
> *nikky1309*: We miss you!

"*Ay Chicos*, I miss you guys so much, too. I feel like I have so much to catch you guys up on. Unfortunately, the news from my doctors has not been so good. They've basically told me that I have got to a point where I have no options."

As I spoke, I noticed my viewer count was reaching 700 already.

> *ilanith_mg*: CoCo, we love you!
> *lazu1921*: Oh my god, what did they say????
> *nikky1309*: You're a fighter, don't you give up!
> *ankehaberland*: CoCo, we're always here to listen. We love you. Don't give up!

"Guys, I will never give up. You know me. But it gets so frustrating. You know I feel very alone here sometimes and you know I wish I was closer to all of you. As I was saying at this point, the doctors have told me we don't have any more viable options. They are not willing to go back in and do more surgeries that could end up potentially harming me more. I have suffered so much these past couple of months. And I am really trying to work on understanding what the purpose was for this huge, failed surgery being on my path."

> *anamargaritavillalobos*: CoCo, if your health permits it, come to Costa Rica!!
> *moricejimenez*: OMG, yes please, come to CR!
> *anamargaritavillalobos*: Better yet, do an in-person Coffee With CoCo.
> *alealvarado9*: YES, YES, YES, YES! I vote for that!
> *j3nnif3r3103*: I vote for Coffee With CoCo! I'm in!

"Guys, you guys are crazy!" I stopped to think about it for a moment. It seemed far-fetched at first, but was it really so crazy? After all, I had been doing Coffee With CoCo live online for months. I was getting better at managing my health and illness. This could be a great opportunity to take a breather and do what I do best—connect with people who need hope, love, and acceptance.

"Okay. If we're going to do this, I need volunteers. I'm not going to go batshit crazy over planning this event because it'll get me sick. So, if you really want me to come to Costa Rica, DM me and we'll start planning it!"

> *lazu1921*: Wait, I just got on. Is CoCo coming to CR? OMG!!
> *johavillab*: Context pls!
> *gabytasolano*: No way!
> *natti_nana*: Where do I get tickets?!
> *j3nnif3r3103*: OMG, it's my lifelong dream to meet you. I'll see you at the airport.

navasadrianacalvo: I volunteer! Whatever you need. I'm at your service.

"Okay, guys. I guess this means we have an event to plan. So I'm gonna go, but be on the lookout because I guess we're going to be announcing more details soon. You guys are fucking crazy but that's why I love you. Only you could make this happen."

Before I even ended the live session, I looked at the viewer count, and we had 1300 people on it. I then opened my DMs and saw over fifty messages asking about the event and volunteering their time, services, and products to make this possible.

Before I knew it, I had two sold-out events (totaling 300 attendees) and I was booking a flight to go and finally meet and hug these wonderful people in person.

When the events drew closer, I felt my nerves increase. I hadn't been in Costa Rica since the trial with Carlos. The last time people knew I was in my country, I was a completely different person.

Would people from my past welcome me?

I reminded myself I was a new CoCo now. The people who were attending these events did not care about my past. They saw me for *me*.

The newspapers and television networks swung into action, requesting interviews while I was in the country and wanting to get an exclusive on my story and my visit. Ever since I got sick, people have been reaching out for my story. But this would be the first time they wanted to bring me in for on-camera, live interviews.

TOGETHER AT LAST

The #cocostrong community made it happen. Thank the Lord I had volunteers to essentially plan every aspect of the Coffee with CoCo events. It would have caused me too much anxiety if I had to do it myself.

When the plane landed, I was greeted by excited people from the #cocostrong community. Some held signs, one of them almost passed out when she met me, and some even asked for autographs (my first time ever signing autographs!). Even though we'd all been talking online for a long time, this was our first in-person meetup. We hugged, laughed, and felt the whirlwind of emotions that surrounded us. This was the opposite of how I had felt when I was last in my country.

The volunteers retrieved my suitcases—my extremely heavy suitcases. The airline, when you had a doctor's note, allowed people with illness to package medical devices and equipment up to 100 pounds. *See? Being sick ain't all bad!*

I packed for both fashion and survival. I brought bags of I.V. fluids, ostomy supplies, wound care supplies, medications, diapers, a port kit, needles, flushes, lots of clothes, and *lots* of shoes.

We planned the events around my medication schedule. At the time, I took 90 mg of oxycodone and 20 mg of methadone, three times a day just to be able to function while in pain. Then in the evenings, I was taking 2 mg of lorazepam to help calm my anxiety enough to sleep. As much as I hated taking all the medication, it was the only way I could have achieved any of these incredible moments.

My event team rented a car for me. They were prepared to drive me, but I quickly took the driver's seat for myself. I wanted to drive through the streets I grew up in, taking me back to the things I loved most about my home country.

After a couple of days of running around like crazy, the day was finally here—my first big in-person "Coffee with CoCo." I was freaking out at the idea of possibly disappointing the 175 people that were coming to the first event. I wondered if they would still love me when they saw me in person. I tried to put my doubts away and focus on the tasks in front of me.

To calm my nerves, I asked the whole team to pray with me. The ten of us gathered in a circle, held hands, and I led the prayer.

God, there is so much to be thankful for at this moment. Thank you for allowing me to travel safely to Costa Rica. Thank you for putting kindhearted, genuine people in my path who see value in my story and who want to see me accomplish my purpose. Thank you for allowing these ten amazing souls to put their hard work, time, and effort into this event. And thank you Lord for the 175 attendees of this event (the first of three events that weekend). May you speak through me, Lord, and ensure every single word that comes out of my mouth is impactful and changes lives. I am filled with gratitude, peace, and purpose as I go into this, and it is because You are right here with all of us. I pray this community family keeps expanding and becomes more cocostrong as time passes by. Lastly, I pray that Ramona behaves and I don't have to run out of the stage with a leak. I love you.

In Jesus's name, I pray. Amen.

We entered the event space and my jaw dropped. I was in shock. I had never seen a more beautiful sight. They designed everything in shades of pink (my favorite color) with butterfly features in the countless design details. I love butterflies.

Oversized balloons were filled with glitter and had #cocostrong written across them. Tables were covered in gift bags for the attendees. Everyone received a signature CoCo-style pink makeup headband.

The element that took my breath away when I saw it was the stage. The team positioned an oversized chair in front of giant pink metallic butterfly wings so that when I sat down and took the microphone, I would have butterfly wings. Tears filled my eyes. It was incredible. A butterfly is a symbol of transformation, hope, and beauty. It represents the journey of overcoming challenges, undergoing change, and emerging stronger and more beautiful than before. Just as a butterfly undergoes a metamorphosis, I have also gone through my own transformation, evolving in ways that are empowering and inspiring. The butterfly's ability to soar despite its previous limitations symbolizes, for me, the strength and resilience of women as they navigate life's challenges and embrace their own evolution.

I told my story which included raw truths, lessons I'd learned throughout my life, trauma, and medical journey. People asked questions and I answered every one of them.

As I grew weak, I slipped out of my heels and into pink, fluffy slippers. I was afraid to make that switch at first, but when I did, I was welcomed with loud cheering and clapping. They appreciated that I was there with my pain.

I stood when I could and sat when I had to. We also talked about body positivity, and embracing disability aids. In one very powerful moment sparked by the topic of accepting myself—bags, tubes, and all—I pulled up my pink Revolve dress to show everything that was underneath. People stood, some crying, some clapping. They were applauding not just for me, but for the beauty we were finding amongst the ashes, and the empowerment we all felt in that space together.

After each event, I went back to the hotel to hang I.V. fluids, get my next round of oxycodone and methadone, and try not to move for fear of making the pain worse. Whitney (my Godsend and the best stylist ever), somehow managed to refresh my hair and makeup while I fell asleep. She knew how much energy I needed before I could get back up and head out to the next event.

I knew my community had been waiting for months for this to happen. Nothing, short of an ambulance, could have stopped me from showing up for them. For as much pain as I was in, it all felt inconsequential in comparison to the exhilaration of having a whole room of people *look at me*, shocking scars and all, and love me for who I was.

Everyone left that event a different person with a new perspective. I was no exception.

As I flew back, my phone blew up. I was flooded with messages from attendees saying the event had empowered them to accept their body, feel new hope to keep going (some had confessed to being suicidal in the past), feel strong enough to go down a new path, and many other messages that filled my heart with joy. Somehow, taking off any filter and just being real was creating this huge impact in other people's lives.

That was the purpose behind everything I'd been through. Changing other people's lives—that was my purpose.

I got to Fort Worth, to the life I was used to, and noticed that everything felt and looked different. Ellie was as beautiful as before. J was still J. The streets were filled with the same traffic. But everything had changed. Because *I* was different now.

It's like I was seeing and experiencing everything from a new perspective, without the demons, self-doubt, or the feeling of drowning that I'd been battling since childhood.

I felt as if I had transcended. I still do.

For example, now when someone frowns or says something insensitive to me, I no longer flinch in shame or anger. Instead, I feel sorry for them. They must be miserable inside if making other people feel bad makes them feel better. Sure, when the moment calls for it, I am happy to set someone straight, but overall, I look forward to waking up in the morning just focused on how I make myself feel. No one else.

I now sponge up every ounce of love that comes my way, either from Ellie, my family, my sweet puppy Bruno, or my community. I even find recovery from procedures and infections to be easier emotionally to handle. I am now standing straighter, smiling bigger, and breathing deeper.

CHAPTER TEN

A STORY WORTH TELLING

I have been searching for "home" my entire life. I'm not talking about big square footage or a driveway filled with expensive cars. My idea of home is wherever the love is. It's a life where that love is shared unconditionally.

It took me a long time, but I found it. It's right here in my room (my sanctuary), with Ellie on one side of me, Bruno on the other, my sister texting me on my phone, and all of the wolves (self-doubt, critics, people who don't care enough to understand) at bay.

As I dissolve into a wall of pink fluffy pillows on my bed, I read the last pages of this final draft with my editor and my heart is full. I can't stop smiling as I think about how, in the end, cancer wasn't the biggest obstacle after all. It was what cured me of self-destruction and the non-stop spiral that surely would have ended my life much sooner than any diagnosis ever could.

I know there are still people who wish I wasn't telling my story for fear that it sheds light on things they'd rather keep hidden. They don't want me to be so brutally authentic in case it risks reflecting on them in ways they'd rather avoid.

But this is about me now. I've earned this moment.

My wish is to leave this earth an open book, my eyes closed, and my heart open.

I plan to leave a legacy of love, transcendence, and self-acceptance in my wake. I have created space for forgiveness—for me and for others who weren't able to be there for me the way I needed them.

I am proud of myself. I have overcome challenges no one ever should have to, and in the process, given my daughter an example of resilience against all odds.

I have created a legacy that is already changing lives around the world, proving that this is not the end for me. I am determined never to stop fighting until or unless the choice is taken away from me.

Now that's a story worth writing.

FROM THE #COCOSTRONG COMMUNITY

cynvillacam
I am truly amazed by your strength, you are one of those people who have their own light my coco. Attitude is what you have shown us day to day, faith and most of all self-love. SOS a fighter.

sha24913
Your a warrior.. I suffer from anxiety, and when I feel bad, I remember that there are people who are worse and move on just like you

patri_esquivel_
You are an example for all of us. Thank you Coco for teaching us to move forward in spite of everything. I love seeing you happy

taylorpachecolina
My love so far I see your story, you are an Inspirational woman, you have a clear mission through your testimony, I don't know why but I do know God speaks through you. My girl the designs of God no one understands them but have faith and confidence that he will always be at your side and you have the best of my best for you, I do not know you but you marked my life and that of my daughter who has your age, Blessings my love

maurensegurabonilla
I love you, it's what comes out of my heart every time I see you, because you radiate love, light and a lot of hope to every person around you

adriianacespedes
Beautiful you are so great you have such a beautiful legacy I admire you greatly God gave you a purpose and you have made a legend

tatyana_calcas
God bless you, You are a woman worthy of admiration, your fight, perse-

verance and above all your faith placed in God is what has made you come forward, You can follow that little one who still needs you

rosy.jimenez.g
Thankful to God for putting a young warrior in my path, full of love and courage. Day by day you leave us great lessons. I admire you a lot and best wishes for success with your book. Blessings TQM.

degava_26.02
Coco you are a wonderful woman. You are a blessing in our lives and you always leave us great lessons. May you be very successful with your book and be very happy with a heart full of peace. I love you so much

ttelcas25
Congratulations beautiful, God made you an instrument of love

marilu.munoz.92
Me in the midst of turbulence, I see you my girl and you fill me with hope, faith and strength to fight, even though sometimes I feel exhausted from the damage I feel above. Blessings my beautiful warrior, Strong and Brave always.

sandralilianadiazvillareal
A woman chosen by God, with processes so but so strong and continues and will continue standing, she holds a power that surpasses all understanding, second has a big engine at her side Princess Eli, strong girl and chosen by God to make coconut days the best are unique and this life story is so but so special,, I can only say that God continues to bless greatly that preservation and love see in years to come coco see eli dance his 15 years

milasfer63
Virtuous woman, God on your side worthy of admiration

sanmarmia
I've always said your way of handling situations is admirable. You have touched many hearts and lives through your testimony. And in a very special way. Make a lot of women and men have Faith in God again. Sending my love and prayers to you

lmlcastroabarca
Hermosa q diosito de conceda muchas paz y fortaleza para q continúe así dando su mejor pelea y mostrando día día su mejor versión de mujer valiente que no se rinde y apesar de la tormenta nos muestra esa carita feliz ..Yo la necesito su testimonio es mi inspiración

zamc.me
So much respect for a woman, a human being! Thank you for being you, thank you for teaching me, thank you for your example, thanks for teaching me to value what I have which is health, and thanks to God I have enough! And if I could share my health with you!

ilianacalvoalvarado
Many congratulations for the book and my admiration for your life's work, your courage and teaching. By sharing your experience, you are an example to so many people who go through difficult situations in their lives. Life is beautiful despite pain and strong experiences, sister sickness, faith makes you see it like this.. take on that challenge positively, makes you stronger and lighter. Thank you very much for opening that door to learn from your experience, for opening your heart, your personal life, for that wonderful person you become from the conversion and the example for your little girl. A big hug Coco, you're already a winner!

dimaroto
Coco a great example for all women

astridmorenogescritora
Congratulations on the launch of your book, I admire you so much for having so much strength and definitely is because God gives you, a strong hug and many blessings

jjoha_villarreal
How cute
You always give us life lessons.
With love everything is possible

gabrielac8711
Coco sos simply extraordinary! God made you unique with a unique purpose!

cindyjohanna.vega
An example of a great mother who always puts her children before herself

shir1781
You are an exemplary mother, blessings to you and Ellie

marilulucam
How divine they are Ellie always full of details to carry in her heart forever. It's admirable the mom you are, nothing stops you to fill her with love and magical memories

lilimorau
You are an amazing mom and God bless you every day and see your daughter happy that is priceless and believe that your daughter will treasure all those moments so beautiful that you have given her you know I admire you so much and always ask God for your health My little girl you are a great human being

dianavarb_
Nikki from my heart, I send you lots of strength, comfort, love, company and literally everything you need in all areas of your being. May the holy spirit be with you, manifest and watch over you always. I am praying for you beautiful, you got this!

sha24913
Coquito is hard. But you're not alone.. God. and we are with you always

mayela_s_a
Beautiful Coquito. I admire you a lot for being such a champion, so positive and for trusting God that everything can. A sincere hug!

degesepaty2011
I cried watching this video the truth you have given me a lot of strength to move on have made me be a stronger woman loving more my life my body self love going through a process I do not just give thanks and gracuas to God for giving me this life opportunity, and my motor is my 12 year old son because he says I'm his hero, but you are who has taught me this in all your stories you are always in my prayers @iamcocostrong I embrace you from Canada I know God has a purpose in our I love you so much

rodriguezsolanoanapatricia
You were chosen to draw many at the feet of our Savior your testimony and transformation is evident not made by the hands of men but FATHER I ADMIRE YOU

marleneruizzamb
You are simply beautiful, brave, warm, sincere and thank you for sharing the whole process without caps the things as they are. You have formed a community of followers that with all your process of ups and downs we have learned to love you forever my flirty girl.

kattiushkaro
You are a strong and very brave woman @Coco I admire you so much and I ask God to continue to watch over your life and that of your precious daughter a hug and many blessings

FROM THE #COCOSTRONG COMMUNITY

patricia.alvaradogonzalez.5
Thank you for those words that always value you, those moments with our loved ones, you are super Coco I love you a lot and I will always be watching your teaching messages. Take it one day at a time. My heart

jes_carv
And so many complaining, you are definitely a warrior God watch over you @iamcocostrong

cynthia.umana
Hello Coco!! A hug from Costa Rica. From the bottom of my heart.. My respects, you are too brave, no words!! I pray God gives you the miracle of total healing. Seriously my respects and admiration for such a brave woman!!!. A hug

clinacr
Super admirable Coco, it doesn't disgust me at all rather than important to normalize your physique regarding colostomy with other people who are still in denial for also having a similar problem.

degesepaty2011
You are a woman with many forces because it is the same God that holds you go forward he has a great purpose in your life, believe it do not stop and every day there is a big light on you because it is the power of the Holy Spirit helping you in every battle that you have overcome I applaud you I admire you and I have you in my prayers from Canada TQM

delaonan
You are a very special little person, with a great testimony of your life and struggle. You have so much strength! Live each day like it's your last. I admire you so much, you're beautiful.. and already leaves us a great legacy! One doesn't give up ai we have God on our side, He gives us that light of struggle and hope, the one you have beautiful.

yi_rois
COCONUT . In my 72 years I've never met anyone as warrior as you. You are an example for my life, I had many tests in my life and by the Mercy of God, I made it through. Your strength and Faith, it's awesome. That energy you pull from within is definitely from God. This your life lesson is for everyone. We will continue to cry out for you. Words Have Power.

kattiagmr
You have the right attitude in the face of adversity. Women like you just like my beautiful mother have taught me more about life than any University.

That's why women like you and my mother I love them, I love them with all my strength because they have taught me to love every moment and to live it intensely. It's these brave women the warriors the role models the best of the best there can be and there's nothing or the strong winds that can stop them. I love you even though I don't know you as a humble woman who admires another. I pray for you if you cry I cry and if you laugh I celebrate. Dedicated to the women who inspire me.

vickyvarb
Ay can't be sad that you have to go through all this for pure negligence, but you're going to overcome you're too strong and you're gonna come out victorious of all this my brave girl I send you a strong hug

milaz30
I value seeing you everyday on social networks, hoping to one day meet you in person. I value hearing your testimonies full of strength and courage, I value and thank God for your existence, I value how much I learn from you. Great my @iamcocostrong

jessieaguero
In our body the ileostomy is part of the miracle that we are.. and only God knows what we live and He gives us strength every day.. Because it's not easy.

jimena.guerrerorealpe
Beautiful you are a great example of Valentina and strength for me even with these we are beautiful I love you very much thank you for appearing in this medium to give me encouragement and example of overcoming

achavesv
Super incredible! the truth is that not everyone has the strength and courage to face something so hard, but I don't see it as a cause for shame, but a reminder that you are alive thank God and you can testify to love and resilience.

ceciling20
Coco you are a brave fighter woman, with a great internal strength that knows that your journey is hard, that you overcome day to day your physical pain, your fears. You teach us to value the day to day and you are a guide to many people who are on a similar path.
Not a step back! With your courage Your great Faith, God has taken you into His hands to guide you and HE is going to heal you. Two beacons of light and support for a great community. We love you and admire you!!! A warm greeting, familiar, strong, optimistic full of positive and multicolored vibes!!

Move on! Cocostrong multiply for the good of our society and you are part of this community we follow you!!! Go ahead!! We are with you!!!

ivecorea
Coco I admire you so much for your strength and faith...! Don't turn away from God, he is the one who has given you all these years your strength and courage. I will pray for you to recover from that infection and pain.

liz.blanco.1318
What a great message, my admiration to a woman too brave and beautiful everywhere she looks. You have impacted the lives of many women. Thank you for bringing so much courage. God bless you today and always.

LETTERS

GOD,

Thank you. Thank you for saving me. Thank you for making me the strong, resilient, faith-filled woman I am today. If there is anyone who knows just how much I've gone through, it is you. You've seen me at my worst. You've seen me be brought to my knees desperately wanting to finally heal, wanting to stop the pain. I've stopped asking myself and you questions that I don't really need the answers to. I've focused and leaned on the answers you have given me, on the paths you have shown me, the doors you have opened. I started trusting YOU.

When I look myself in the mirror, I know I still have difficult battles, but you know how hard I am working to continue growing, to continue fighting, to fulfill my purpose everyday. It is an honor to have the opportunity to help so many other people. As you healed my broken heart, you've helped me have another perspective in life and I can now see how many people need help, motivation, courage, and support. I see their pain, and I want to help others feel the healing just like I did. And now people see me. I see me. After so many years of silently begging for someone to look at me. I pray for Your continued leadership and protection. I'm determined to honor You and make You proud.

Please, ensure Ellie is always safeguarded, and remind her that just as You are forever in her heart, so am I.

I love You

In Jesus's name I pray,

Amen.

DEAR ELLIE,

Princesa you are my everything. I know you won't read this until you are older, I'm not sure what age you will be but I hope this letter to you transcends time and can help you no matter where you are in life or what you are going through.

Ellie, thank you. Thank you for saving my life. Thank you for coming into my life to change my world. Thank you for giving me the strength to overcome more than I could've ever imagined.

I'm sorry for how I failed you when you were a little girl. E, I know that growing up with mommy being sick is hard, I know it's unfair, and I know it's lonely at times. I want you to know that I have fought every single day so that I can be here with you and for you. I know it seems like I'm not with you a lot of the time, but don't ever doubt that the moments I have spent at the hospital away from you, the moments I have missed special occasions with you, those moments have broken me. They are so hard, I miss you every single second that I am away from you. But just like I have always said, we need to focus on the positive. And there is so much positive.

When you read this book you will understand how you were my biggest motivation, my rock. Every single time I was away from you I was fighting to get back to your side as soon as possible. I know we have talked about this a lot, but mommy's sickness has opened up the door for you to become an incredibly special, unique, resilient, empathetic, knowledgeable girl. When I think back on all of you have learned from accessing my port, changing my bags and cleaning my tubes to helping me shower, I'm at a loss of words. YOU ARE INCREDIBLE.

Thank you for all the times you've held my hand when I've been in pain. Thank you for being my biggest companion and my best friend. I hope that this book reminds you that you are seen and you are loved. I pray your future is incredible, and that you get everything you could ever wish for. Always remember to treat others the way you want to be treated and to never judge others based on appearance. Remember you will get 1 million NO's in this world but God will lead you to your YES's.

If I'm gone by the time you are able to read this, know that I'm watching over you and I am always in your heart. Know you have a great Daddy that loves you and has done so much for you. Know you have so many family members that will always be there for you. Thank you for brightening my life, my days, and filling my heart with so much joy. I hope this book makes you proud of your mommy. I will always be in your heart and watching over you, love.

Te amo, my beautiful princess.

With so much love,

Your Mommy.

J,

Writing this letter was more difficult than I thought. I hope that you get to read it and I really hope that you take the time to process my words with the peaceful intention I'm writing them. I know that we have different perspectives of what our story has been, but I hope you can understand that I am telling my story from how I have lived it.

First I will start with an apology. I regret the pain that I have caused you. I'm sorry for the times I have failed you. I'm sorry for all the bad decisions I made that impacted our marriage in such a negative way. Sometimes, when I think about all that we have gone through and see where we are today, despite the sadness that brings me, if I try to focus on the positive, I can see resilience, I can see that despite all the very hard things we have gone through we have found the best way we can to move forward. I can see that both of us have sacrificed so many things on our path, and many of those sacrifices have been for the purpose of giving Ellie her happiness and stability. I can see that we have felt hurt because both of us reacted differently to the last four years, and both have had very distinct experiences.

I don't know what the future holds, but I do pray that it will be more peaceful, that it will be better, that there will be more empathy and understanding from both sides. You have had the opportunity to leave so many times since the beginning, and yet, we have fought against so many obstacles and for that I thank you.

Sometimes I wonder why life has brought us here, and I believe we have had many lessons and experiences that have forced us to grow and heal. I thank you for working so hard, for being such an excellent father, for being there for Ellie. You have put her first in your life in a way that is very admirable and I feel so blessed to have you as Ellie's father.

I know that there is no instruction manual for the path we are on. We are both just trying to do the best we can. I am going to pray that we continue always putting Ellie first.

I know that when the future arrives, you will continue taking care of Ellie as you have done.

With love forever,
CoCo

LINDA,

I'm not even sure where to begin to thank you for the person you are in my life. First off, I want to start this letter by saying you have absolutely nothing to blame yourself for; we both tried to do the best we could given the situation we were facing. I know you never imagined that I had been suffering in a very similar way to you when we were kids. I'm so proud of you for finding your healing, your peace, and your path.

Thank you for being my protector for so long, for taking on an indispensable role during my battle with cancer, for being my strength throughout all those moments and months when I couldn't find it myself. You never gave up; from day one, you knew I was going to beat this cancer and you put your life on hold to give me all the strength I needed, and finally, I came out victorious. Thank you for showing me how amazing God is and for guiding me towards Him persistently, no matter how many times I said no, and for ultimately helping me develop the most important relationship in my life.

Thank you for being the aunt you are to Ellie, a second mom. You know I've entrusted you with my greatest treasure and I have no doubt that when the time comes for me to not be in this world, Ellie will have the best second mom anyone could ask for. I'm so thrilled about all the incredible things that are coming your way; if there's anyone who deserves that fairy-tale ending, it's you. You are an extremely talented woman and I hope all your dreams, both personal and as an entrepreneur, come true.

Ellie and I love you to infinity and beyond.

Xoxo,

CoCo

MOM,

I really hope you've read this book from start to finish. I know there are things in it you might wish I hadn't mentioned, but I honestly hope you can understand why I needed to share my story the way I experienced it. We've been through a lot of ups and downs over the years and made our share of mistakes. There are a few things I want to get across to you, and I hope you not only read them but also truly believe them in your heart.

I love you. We might not have always seen eye to eye on everything, and you probably feel the same about some choices I've made, but you're my mom, and I wouldn't trade you for any other.

I forgive you because I know you probably didn't realize how much some of the little things that were done and said hurt me, and I'm sorry for breaking your trust with my actions when I was younger. It made you question what you did wrong to deserve that, and no mother should have to feel that way. I'm not trying to downplay my past actions and decisions, but I'm not that person anymore. I hope that this book has helped you to understand why I did some of the things I did, so that we might be able to begin rebuilding our relationship and trust.

I would love to truly leave the past behind us and move forward, focusing on the love we do have, the time we have left, and the kind of mother-daughter relationship we want Ellie to see. At the end of the day, all I ever wanted was your approval, to have you look at me proudly and admire the strength I've had to summon every day to get to where I am now, despite all the obstacles I've overcome. I took a lot of strength, resilience, and God's help to make it here. You've done an incredible job with Linda, Tiffany, Gary, and me, despite all the trials and turbulence we've faced, both as a family and as individuals.

Thank you for everything you've done for Ellie and what you'll keep doing in the future when she needs you and Titi even more. Today, I'm letting go of all the anger and resentment I might have held onto over certain things; I don't want to carry them with me anymore. Thank you for never giving up, for always fighting for us, and for showing us what it means to be a strong mom.

I love you.

CoCo

DEAR GARY,

I can't express my gratitude enough - truly, you have been my knight in shining armor. It's rare to come across someone with such a genuine heart, a person who seeks nothing more than to spread peace and happiness to those around him. For all the incredible memories you've gifted me, for an enchantingly beautiful childhood filled with moments both grand and beautifully simple, I thank you deeply. I cherish the memory of those times when you supported me in my quest to conquer the 1000-page club competition, and the moments when you were the only one who saw my potential for positive leadership, affirming that my good qualities could shape a future so bright, if only I made the right choices. For all of this, I thank you.

I must admit, it's been painfully hard watching the space grow between us, feeling how life has, in ways, pulled us apart. Yet, through all of this, I want you to know, from the bottom of my heart, that you are the best dad I could have ever asked for – not just for me, but for all of us. The impact you have made on my life since the day we met is immeasurable, and I hope, as you turn the pages of this book, you'll see not just the journey I've been on but also the profound influence you've had on every aspect of my existence.

My love for you doesn't wane with distance. Instead, it grows stronger, bridging the gap between us, carried in the words of this letter and the pages of the book I'm sharing with you. I hope it brings you closer to my world, to my experiences, and above all, lets you see just how much you mean to me.

Gary, you are and always will be, the best dad. I hope this book resonates with you, bringing back memories, sharing my gratitude, and reaffirming our bond that time and distance can never erode.

I love you, unconditionally and forever, no matter the miles between us.

With all my love,

Xoxo

CoCo

ACKNOWLEDGMENTS

To my editor and publisher, Jenn, thank you, thank you, thank you for believing in my story, for seeing how impactful it could be to other people, for saving my story from the ashes, and for working so hard to make my dreams come true. You are an incredible woman, and I hope that when you look at yourself in the mirror, you see just how amazing you are. You are a fucking badass, and I truly can't wait to see everything that Entourage does in the future because I have no doubt that amazing things are waiting for you.

My community, thank you for being my biggest companionship. Thank you for being with me in my hardest of times, for leading me into my purpose, for seeing me, and accepting me—the real CoCo. May this book give you guys courage, strength, and hope. You are enough, no matter what you've gone through. Remember just because you've had some challenging chapters doesn't mean your story can't end well. Every story has bad chapters. It's about finding the strength to turn the page. Hold onto that in your struggle, in your journey, in your pain, and then turn your pain from your worst enemy to your best friend. Please remember, you were never too broken to be healed, too damaged to be cherished, or too lost to be found. I love you guys, can't wait to meet you. I can't wait for the years to come, and I will forever be thankful for all that you guys have given me. Love you, coquettes!

To the friends that have been there since the beginning, thank you. Thank you for your support, your love, for believing in my story, for accepting the good and the bad, and thank you for all the crazy fucking memories. I know that we look back on this book, on all the partying, and mainly focus on the bad experiences, but I want to thank you for all the amazing nights. The ones where we danced a little too long & drank a little too much—the ones that truly marked unforgettable memories for us. And thank you for being there for me in the hard times, through the hardships, flying to come visit me, staying with me on my phone for endless hours. I love you.

Nikky, you came into my life at the moment I least expected it. We are so alike in so many ways, and I see so much of myself in you. You are such a hard worker and so ambitious, and I truly cannot wait to see what the future has for you. You can accomplish whatever you set your mind to. I hope this book is a testament to that. Thank You for helping me in my journey, for finding my purpose, for working tirelessly to make my dreams come true. I love you, and I am so thankful that you are part of what CoCo represents but also a part of my life and a friend I will cherish forever. Don't ever forget how amazing and valuable you are. Te amo.

Ana M. Villalobos, thank you for being such a faithful follower, for always being there to listen to me when I unravel my life, and for jumping in to help with this book with open arms.

Christina, thank you for believing in my dreams and for being my only friend who has been through every single phase of my life. We can be apart for months and still catch up right where we left off. Thank you for believing tirelessly in my purpose, in my dreams. I'm so happy to call you my best friend, but calling you a sister in Christ is a true honor and a blessing. I'm proud of what we've gone through together, to see where God has led us, and I'm so proud to call you my friend.

Kelly and Scott, I have no words to explain how thankful I am for everything you've done for me, for coming to take care of me so many times, even while mourning. You both are beautiful souls, and I am so grateful to have you in my life. Despite the pain, I know that He's always with us. This book would never have been possible without you

ACKNOWLEDGMENTS

pushing me forward into finding my purpose and starting my journey as a life coach. Thank you for never doubting me. I love you both.

Bibi, thank you for being the friend you are, for being so supportive throughout the years, and for valuing my loyalty. You're my only high school friend with whom I still talk, the one who has always seen my pure heart.

Sheri & PawPaw, thank you for everything you have done for Ellie and me. I am truly blessed that Ellie has such fantastic grandparents. Thank you for all the support you have given me since the moment I became a Roper. The path hasn't been easy, but we have come out stronger on the other side. Thank you both for your support and love. Love you so much!

Gaby, thank you for being one of my few friends in Texas, for running to take care of me at every chance you get, and for visiting me at the hospital when I am there. You've been an amazing support when I need you the most. I love you so much, and I am so thankful to call you my friend.

Whitney, who knew that the day I met you, you were going to be such an impactful person on my path to self-love. Thank you for always being a voice of confidence to me, for taking care of my beautiful hair, for coming to the hospital when I need help, and helping me feel beautiful despite my disabilities and sickness. Thank you, love.

To my doctors and nurses, thank you. Your care and support have been beyond what I could have ever imagined and have become crucial in my life. Thank you for never giving up on me, for always advocating for me, and doing your utmost to comfort me in my illness. I truly don't know what I would have done without all of you. Thank you, and I love you.

Chris, thank you for always making me laugh and for being such an amazing example of a supportive partner to Jenn. Thank you for working tirelessly on my book and for being such a significant part of making this possible. I appreciate you.

Bruno, my love, finding you was like finding the best friend and perfect companionship I had been searching for. Thank you for being there for me through the tears, happiness, or loneliness. I'm so incredibly happy to have you in my life.

Steve, thank you for being the best babysitter in the world. Knowing that my dog is well taken care of with his family gives me peace of mind every single time I am in the hospital. Finding you was a blessing, and I am so glad to know that Bruno has a loving home whenever I'm not around. Thank you for understanding how my sickness can require last-minute changes and for always saying yes to me. I appreciate you more than you will ever know.

Emily, thank you for being such an amazing friend when I first arrived in Texas. Your support in helping me make many life decisions has been invaluable. Thank you for visiting me every week on your day off, spending hours with me even when I was simply asleep. I am so happy that you have built such an amazing life for yourself. I pray that Matt, Levi, Seth, and you are always blessed with health, love, and peace.

Zach, thank you for all the amazing memories. You are missed every single day. I take comfort in knowing you are in heaven, watching over me, and finally experiencing the peace you deserve. Love you.

Tiffy & Gary, I'm so proud of the people you have both grown up to be. I love you and I hope that you are both finding your happiness and your own path at college. I hope this book teaches you how important healing is, how it is necessary to let go of the past, and become the best version of ourselves for the future. Los amo.

My family, thank you for your love. For the good memories. For the support you have given me, and for believing in me. Thank you Mamita, Tio, Mario & TiTi. Love You.

RESOURCES

- Substance Abuse and Mental Health Services Administration National Helpline
  (800) 662-4357
- Eating Disorders Awareness and Prevention
  (800)-931-2237
- National Sexual Assault Hotline
  (800) 656-4673
- Childhelp National Child Abuse Hotline
  (800) 422-4453
- National Domestic Violence Hotline
  (800) 799-7233
- S.A.F.E. (Self Abuse Finally Ends)
  (800)-DONT-CUT
- National Suicide and Crisis Lifeline
  988

ABOUT THE AUTHOR

Nicole "CoCo" Roper is a motivational speaker, life coach, cancer hero, and disability advocate. By being painfully transparent about her journey with cancer, CoCo draws people into her world, online and in person. She shares everything, good or bad, with a community of over 170,000 followers on Instagram and TikTok.

CoCo also speaks at sold-out events such as "Coffee with CoCo" and motivational workshops designed to inspire people to happiness.

CoCo built six- and seven-figure fashion brands before her cancer diagnosis. Despite a traumatic personal life, CoCo has proven to be a brilliant entrepreneur whose CoCoStrong brand stands for resilience against all odds, both in the USA and Costa Rica.

Follow her on social media for more of CoCo's story.
Instagram & TikTok: @IAMCOCOSTRONG
Web: www.entouragemedia.ca/lookatme

www.ingramcontent.com/pod-product-compliance
Lightning Source LLC
Chambersburg PA
CBHW072151070526
44585CB00015B/1088